DEMOCRATIC CHALLENGES,
DEMOCRATIC CHOICES

COMPARATIVE POLITICS

Comparative Politics is a series for students and teachers of political science that deals with contemporary issues in comparative government and politics. As Comparative European Politics it has produced a series of high quality books since its foundation in 1990, but now takes on a new form and a new title for the new millennium—Comparative Politics. As the process of globalization proceeds, and as Europe becomes ever more enmeshed in world trends and events, so it is necessary to broaden the scope of the series.

The General Editors are Max Kaase, Vice President and Dean of Humanities and Social Sciences, International University, Bremen; and Kenneth Newton, Professor of Comparative Politics, University of Southampton. The series is published in association with the European Consortium for Political Research.

OTHER TITLES IN THE SERIES

Mixed-Member Electoral Systems: The Best of Both Worlds
Edited by Matthew Shugart and Martin P. Wattenberg

Coalition Governments in Western Europe
Edited by Wolfgang C. Müller and Kaare Strøm

Political Institutions: Democracy and Social Choice
Josep M. Colomer

Parties Without Partisans: Political Change in
Advanced Industrial Democracies
Edited by Russell J. Dalton and Martin P. Wattenberg

Extreme Right Parties in Western Europe
Piero Ignazi

Democracy Transformed?: Expanding Political Opportunities in
Advanced Industrial Democracies
Edited by Bruce E. Cain, Russell J. Dalton and Susan E. Scarrow

Delegation and Accountability in Parliamentary Democracies
Edited by Kaare Strøm, Wolfgang C. Müller, and Torbjörn Bergman

Democratic Challenges, Democratic Choices

The Erosion of Political Support in Advanced Industrial Democracies

RUSSELL J. DALTON

OXFORD
UNIVERSITY PRESS

9352446

OXFORD
UNIVERSITY PRESS

Great Clarendon Street, Oxford OX2 6DP

Oxford University Press is a department of the University of Oxford.
It furthers the University's objective of excellence in research, scholarship,
and education by publishing worldwide in

Oxford New York

Auckland Bangkok Buenos Aires Cape Town Chennai
Dar es Salaam Delhi Hong Kong Istanbul Karachi Kolkata
Kuala Lumpur Madrid Melbourne Mexico City Mumbai Nairobi
São Paulo Shanghai Taipei Tokyo Toronto

Oxford is a registered trade mark of Oxford University Press
in the UK and certain other countries

Published in the United States
by Oxford University Press Inc., New York

© Russell J. Dalton 2004

The moral rights of the author have been asserted
Database right Oxford University Press (maker)

First published 2004

British Library Cataloguing in Publication Data
Data available

Library of Congress Cataloging in Publication Data
Data available
ISBN 0–19–926843–6

1 3 5 7 9 10 8 6 4 2

Typeset by Newgen Imaging Systems (P) Ltd., Chennai, India
Printed in Great Britain
on acid-free paper by
Biddles Ltd., King's Lynn

Preface

My formative political experiences occurred during the Vietnam war period, when student protests often took over the campus at UCLA and debates about America's role in Vietnam and the actions of our government shaped the thinking of many college students. A few years earlier, I could see the smoke rising from the fires during the Watts riots from our house in West Los Angeles. These were times that taught one to be cynical about politics, to distrust politicians, and to worry about the future of democracy as well as one's own. These were experiences that were shared, to varying degrees, by those who lived through the period—whether it was in Los Angeles, or observing the May Revolts in Paris, the Provo demonstrations in Amsterdam, the anti-war demonstrations in Stockholm, or the student protests in Rome.

At the end of the twentieth century, the United States and most other advanced industrial democracies were enjoying an era of historically unprecedented affluence, peace and security. Yet over this 40-year time span we have systematically become more sceptical about government, more distrustful of politicians, and more cynical about the workings of the democratic process. This book's goal is to chronicle this shift, the suggest the reasons for it, and to discuss the implications for the political process in contemporary democracies.

This book developed with the help of many friends and colleagues. Part of the genesis was a collaborative project with Martin Wattenberg, which produced a book on the changes in political parties in Western democracies (*Parties without Partisans: Political Change in Advanced Industrial Democracies*, 2000). Marty also provided comments on the manuscript and a valuable stream of data on citizen attitudes towards politics.

A number of colleagues generously assisted in the collection of national data series and providing advice on this project: Atle Alvheim, Clive Bean, Harold Clarke, Cees van der Eijk, Olafur Th. Hardarsson, Soren Holmberg, Ken'ichi Ikeda, Jeffrey Karp, Michael Lewis-Beck, Ian McAllister, Anthony McGann, Nonna Mayer, Fritz Plasser, Helmut Prochart, Bradley Richardson, Risto Sänkiaho, Kaare Ström, Aiji Tanaka, Peter Ulram, and Bernard Wessels. The data for this study were provided by the Inter-university Consortium for Political and Social Research, the Zentralarchiv für empirische Sozialforschung, the UK Data Archive at Essex, the Norwegian Social Science Data Services, and the Swedish Social Sciences Data Services. Miki Caul Kittilson, Andrew Drummond, Mark Gray, Nhu-Ngoc Ong, and Bogdan Radu provided valuable research assistance at various stages of this project.

This project also benefited from my collaboration in two edited collections on citizens' changing views of government—*Critical Citizens: Global Support for Democratic Governance* (ed. Pippa Norris, 1999) and *Disaffected Democracies: What's Troubling the Trilateral Countries?* (ed. Susan Pharr and Robert Putnam, 2000)—and I would like to thank the editors of these books for their advice and input. Finally, my thanks to Bruce Cain and Susan Scarrow, with whom we developed a collaborative project on democratic institutional change that might result from public dissatisfaction and pressure (*Democracy Transformed?: The Expansion of Citizen Access in Advanced Industrial Democracies*, 2003). Our discussions about the transformation of contemporary democracy with Bruce, Susan and the other participants of this project stimulated my thinking on this topic.

The empirical base for much of the research presented here comes from the national election studies series collected by survey researchers in each nation. I am greatly indebted to all these scholars, even if the list is too large to include here. Without the decades of data these research teams have assembled, we could not track how citizens and democratic politics are changing—and these election studies are now vital national resources for their respective countries. But assembling comparable cross-national and cross-temporal data is also a challenging task, since national archives differ in the accessibility and formatting of their data and the information useful for tracking specific questions over time. I am sure that some of the trends reported here are incomplete, and I encourage sceptical researchers to add to the empirical evidence by locating additional time-points or additional data series. Not all the data I uncovered fit my general conclusions (though I report all I found); but my experience was that, the more data I acquired, the stronger the patterns appeared. So more data collection is welcomed and encouraged, since it will improve our understanding of how citizens are changing.

It should also be noted that the core of the analyses and a nearly complete draft of the manuscript were finished before the horrific events of September 11, 2001. Certainly, these events reshaped, at least temporarily, how Americans think about politics and the world. I considered adding a separate chapter on these post-9/11 shifts in public opinion, but then decided against it, for several reasons. As time has progressed, it appears that many of the post-9/11 shifts in political support were temporary and narrowly focused on government responses to these events. These reactions were essentially limited to the American public, and were not apparent in other nations. In addition, the central theme of this book is to understand the long-term shift in public orientations towards government—and I do not believe this development was fundamentally changed by September 11. Thus, we include some post-9/11 American data in the epilogue to Chapter 2, but the book focuses on the longer term transformation of advanced industrial democracies.

My great thanks to the fine people at Oxford University Press in the United Kingdom, who moved this project to publication with ease and grace. This completes a series of three interrelated books on democratic change I have recently published with Oxford; and the Press's support has made this an enjoyable and successful enterprise. I especially want to thank Dominic Byatt for his invaluable support and guidance on this series, and Michael James for his care in copy-editing this manuscript.

I also want to acknowledge the financial support for this project from several sources. This research began with a generous Research Fellowship from the German Marshall Fund of the United States, which led to some additional data collection and several of the papers that developed into chapters of this book. Subsequent work was supported by research grants from the Center for the Study of Democracy at the University of California Irvine, the Institute for European Studies, the University of California Berkeley, and the Rockefeller Foundation. A portion of the work was completed while I was a POSCO Fellow at the East–West Center in Hawaii. The support of all these institutions is greatly appreciated.

I began this work generally subscribing to the position that the decline in trust in government represented a negative challenge to contemporary democracies—and this study does document negative consequences of these trends. But along the way I became convinced that these trends also represent the driving force of democratic development—the expectation that democracies can improve, can give greater access to their citizens, become more transparent in their processes and more accountable for their actions. Similar dissatisfactions in earlier periods, on the part of either the public or contending elites, is what has moved democracy forward in its development. Thus, these trends are also as an opportunity to rethink and reshape the democratic process. How we respond to these opportunities will determine whether this is beneficial for the process and its citizens.

Russell J. Dalton
Irvine, California
August 2003

Contents

List of Figures

List of Tables

1

The Challenge to Democracy

CONTEMPORARY democracies are facing a challenge today. This challenge does not come from enemies within or outside the nation. Instead, the challenge comes from democracy's own citizens, who have grown distrustful of politicians, sceptical about democratic institutions, and disillusioned about how the democratic process functions.

As citizens in advanced industrial democracies enjoy an improved quality of life and benefit from the post-cold war peace, there are signs of growing public doubts about the political process. These sentiments are perhaps most visible in the United States. Beginning with the crises and political scandals of the 1960s and 1970s—Vietnam, urban unrest, and Watergate—Americans' trust in their politicians sank steadily lower. President Jimmy Carter returned from Camp David in 1979 and warned that declining public confidence 'was a fundamental threat to American democracy'. Trust in government partially rebounded during the first Reagan administration, as the president tried to revive a sense of political purpose and renew the political spirit with uplifting references to a 'new morning in America' and to America as the 'shining city on the hill'. By the end of the Reagan and Bush administrations, however, public scepticism had reasserted itself, fuelled by new crises and new scandals. Even after a partial revival of political support following the dramatic economic gains of the late 1990s, few Americans agreed with President Bill Clinton's claim in the 2000 State of the Union address: 'My fellow Americans, the state of our union is the strongest it has ever been.' Americans' sentiments towards government spiked upward after September 11, 2001, but these feelings also eroded rapidly as politics returned to 'normal'.[1]

---

[1] In the wake of the horrific acts of September 11, 2001 there was a dramatic increase in political support among Americans. Trust in politicians and confidence in political institutions sky-rocketed, and public demonstrations of political support—flying the flag, contributing to 9/11 charities, and other patriotic actions—became commonplace. Some analysts claimed that this re-engaged Americans in their society and politics. The core analyses for this book were essentially completed before September 11, 2001. In the epilogue to Chapter 2 we consider the new data on American images of government, and whether this alters the conclusions generated from our time series analyses (see also Mackenzie and Labiner 2002; Morin 2002).

Knowledgeable political analysts and observers see implications in these trends for the democratic process. In his farewell address to Congress, Senator Bill Bradley gave an alarming description of American democracy:

Democracy is paralyzed not just because politicians are needlessly partisan, although we are. The process is broken at a deeper level, and it won't be fixed by replacing one set of elected officials with another... Citizens believe that politicians are controlled: by special interests who give them money, by parties which crush their independence, by ambition for higher office that makes them hedge their position rather than call it like they really see it, and by pollsters who convince them that only focus-group phrases can guarantee them victory. Citizens affected by the choices we have to make about spending and regulation simply don't trust that the choice was made fairly or independently, or, in some cases, even democratically. They doubt that the facts will determine the result, much less the honest convictions of the politicians. Voters distrust government so deeply and so consistently that they are not willing to accept the results of virtually any decision made by this political process. (Bradley 1997: 5–6)

On Bradley's account, American democracy is losing legitimacy among its citizens, who are the foundation of the democratic system. A recent bipartisan report on the state of American politics echoed these sentiments: 'Too many of us lack confidence in our capacity to make basic moral and civic judgments, to join with our neighbors to do the work of community, to make a difference. Never have we had so many opportunities for participation, yet rarely have we felt so powerless' (Bennett and Nunn 1997: 6). These themes are echoed in many other recent observations by political scientists and practising politicians.

The broad trends of decreasing political support in the United States are now well-known, documented by a host of academic and popular publications. Invariably, political analysts point to some of the unique and specific characteristics of American politics as reasons for these trends. The presidency suffers from the accumulation of negative events that range from Watergate to the Lewinsky affair. These analysts suggest that restoring the dignity of the office will restore public trust. The Congress suffers from its own set of scandals and various factors that have altered the legislative process (Hibbing and Theiss-Morse 1995; Cooper 1999*a*). Reform Congress, they say, and trust will improve. Politicians have become more concerned about pleasing special interests (Craig 1993): thus, change the structure of campaigns and enact finance reform so that political support will rebound. Other analysts suggest that the media are to blame, and the growth of investigative and attack journalism have demoralized the American public—so the media should be reformed (Patterson 1993; 2001; Sabato 1991). Perhaps the most perverse view is that America suffers from too much democracy, and restricting the democratization process will improve public images of government (Huntington 1981; Hibbing and Theiss-Morse 2002). Our study maintains that such 'simple' explanations are insufficient, and the suggested reforms will not restore Americans' trust in their government.

The first theme of this book is that each of these explanations may be partially correct, but misses a larger reality. The erosion of political support is not explicable by the unique political experiences of recent American political history or the unique problems of specific American political institutions. Public doubts about politicians, political parties, and political institutions are spreading across almost all advanced industrial democracies—in nations that have not experienced Vietnam, Watergate, Abscam, Iran–Contra, or the Woodward–Bernstein media effect (or the Lewinsky affair). For instance, Sweden created the post-war model of social democracy that many other European states sought to emulate, but the Swedish public also became more sceptical about their political process. In the Swedish case, nearly all of the specific factors cited in the American literature on political support are absent: Sweden did not face Vietnam, Watergate, Richard Nixon, racial conflict, or even hostile television journalists (since the state-owned television was deferential towards government). This should give us pause before we focus on specific explanations of two such widely different cases.

This pattern is repeated across the advanced industrial democracies. As scandals strained the faith of the British in their political institutions in the mid-1990s, Parliament set up the Nolan Committee to inquire into 'standards in public life'. In testifying during the committee's initial hearings on ethics in government, Ivor Crewe (1995) stated: 'There is no doubt that distrust and alienation has risen to a higher level than ever before. It was always fairly prevalent; it is now in many regards almost universal.' Even on the other side of the world, New Zealanders have become less trustful of their governments, which led to a fundamental electoral reform in the early 1990s. During the 1990s the Federal Republic of Germany achieved a historic ambition: to unify Germany as a free and democratic nation. And yet support for the political process sank among the German public over roughly the same period. Indeed, as Germany accomplished this national goal, the President of the Federal Republic chastised German political parties in terms fairly similar to Senator Bradley's. President Richard von Weizsäcker (1992: 164) said politicians and political parties were 'power-crazed for electoral victory and powerless when it comes to understanding the content and ideas required of political leadership'. Recall, for a moment, that this is what democracy's avid supporters are saying about the democratic process. This should make us realize that contemporary democracies are facing a real challenge—and that this is a challenge we share.

Admittedly, anxiety about the health of democracy is a regular feature of political science and political punditry. Analysts early in the twentieth century worried about the ability of democracy to endure, especially when faced by non-democratic challenges (Lippmann 1922; Laski 1931). There was an important national debate about our political goals during the Eisenhower administration, and John F. Kennedy consequently asked Americans to renew their commitment to state and nation (see Mueller 1999: ch. 7). A host of new studies and critiques of democracy have been published over the past quarter century. Perhaps the most prominent academic study from this era is *The Crisis of Democracy*, in which Michel Crozier, Samuel Huntington, and Joji Watanuki (1975) nearly forecast democracy's imminent demise.[2] The introduction to their book, for example, includes an ominous quotation from Willy Brandt, who supposedly predicted: 'Western Europe has only 20 or 30 more years of democracy left in it; after that it will slide, engineless and rudderless, under the surrounding sea of dictatorship' (quoted in Crozier, Huntington, and Watanuki 1975: 2).[3]

Fortunately, the passage of time has shown that these predictions were wrong. But it appears that there are new, and real, causes for concern among those who value the democratic process. In the past, the lack of support for the democratic process contributed to the collapse of Germany's Weimar Republic in 1933 and other democratic failures. In other cases, the rejection of democratic norms and procedures by political extremists has led to violent attacks on the political system. Even though we see a fundamentally different pattern in the present political malaise, the potential implications of changing public sentiments are still very significant.

By assembling the most comprehensive ever cross-national body of evidence, this book describes the changes in citizen trust in politicians, political institutions, and the democratic process that have affected nearly all advanced industrial democracies. Citizen orientations towards the democratic state are changing in fundamental ways that are likely to have equally important implications for policy-making, and democracy's future.

The causes of such trends are complex. In each nation there are specific events or series of events that national experts generally link to public opinion trends; for instance, the problems of civil unrest, Vietnam, Watergate, and subsequent political scandals in the United States. Austrian political scientists point to the change in post-war party alignments and the breakdown of a corporatist consensus; experts on Canada point to the struggle over Quebec and national identity issues; and so forth. These events probably are an important part of the explanation, but the parallel nature of the trends in advanced industrial democracies forces us to look for broader sources of change. Coincidental unique political crises across a large and diverse set of nations is an improbable explanation of general patterns; it is more likely that some systematic forces are changing the relationship between citizens and the state in advanced industrial democracies. Thus we will downplay explanations based on proper nouns—such as Watergate, Japan's 1990s

---

[2] Another group of European scholars cautioned about the weakness of Western democracy, albeit from a different theoretical perspective that was intertwined with criticism of capitalism (for example, Offe 1972; 1984; Bobbio 1987; Habermas 1975).

[3] There has been some debate over the accuracy of this quotation, since Crozier et al. do not identify a source. Moreover, the statement is in sharp contrast to Brandt's well-known admonition that Germany actually needed to 'risk more democracy'. Even if Brandt did not make this statement, other prominent Europeans certainly echoed the sentiments. For instance, the French political observer Jean-François Revel declared that 'democracy may, after all, turn out to have been a historical accident, a brief parenthesis that is closing before our eyes' (1983: 3).

recession, or a specific policy failure—and search for broader factors that are affecting advanced industrial democracies and that may give rise to more critical sentiments towards government.

Several observers of these trends have also questioned their implications for contemporary democracies. I believe that changes in citizen orientations towards government are having real and significant consequences for the political process. Some of these effects are detrimental to the short-term or long-term development of democracy. Other effects offer the potential for reform and renewal that is the very strength of the democratic process. The final accounting is not clear, and it depends on how citizens, elites, and institutions respond to these trends.

In summary, our goal is to determine whether feelings of political support are changing among contemporary publics. This first involves the conceptual question of defining the important elements to study. Second, we need to assemble the appropriate cross-national and cross-temporal evidence to evaluate claims about the sources of these changes in public opinion. Finally, if political orientations are changing, what are the implications for the democratic process? This study addresses all three questions.

THE MEANING OF POLITICAL SUPPORT

Before we begin, some theoretical clarification is needed. Discussions of popular orientations toward politics often intermix different aspects of citizen evaluations, such as feelings of political alienation, cynicism, or distrust. Sometimes the evidence of public discontent is no more than dissatisfaction with the incumbents of office, even though this might be considered a normal and healthy aspect of the democratic process. The theoretical distinctions between different levels of support and different objects of political support are often blurred (or ignored) in the debate over public trust and confidence in democracy. In other instances, the theoretical significance of public opinion findings is uncertain because the wording of the survey questions is ambiguous. Thus, a simple but necessary starting point is to explicate a conceptual framework for studying political support.

We begin with David Easton's description (1965; 1975) of the various elements of political support as a framework for our research.[4] Easton distinguished between support for three levels of political objects: *the political community*, the *regime*, and *political authorities*. The political community stands for the nation or the political system in broad terms. Easton (1965: 178) defined a political community as

a group of people who come together to draw up some kind of constitution to regulate their political relationship . . . The particular structure of the relationship may change, the members of the system may be ranked, subdivided and rearranged politically so that

---

[4] Almond and Verba's (1963) distinction between different elements of a political culture is also useful, but because it does not distinguish between the relative importance of different elements we have found Easton's framework more useful.

the structural patterns are fundamentally altered. But as long as the members continue to evince an attachment to the overall group in which the changing interrelationships prevail ... they will be supporting the existence of the same and continuing community.

Regime support refers to public attitudes toward the constitutional order of a nation. Easton (1965: ch. 12) distinguished between different elements of the regime. Regime principles define the broad parameters within which the political system should function. At the broadest level, this involves choices about whether political relationships should be organized as a democratic, authoritarian, or other political form. A shared consensus on such values would seem to be a prerequisite for a stable political order, and history has sadly shown what can occur when the democratic consensus fails (Linz and Stepan 1978). A second major component of the regime consists of the norms of behaviour, which Easton called the operating rules or the rules of the game. These involve the specific rules or norms governing political action. For instance, communism as a principle varied in its application from its Marxist roots, to democratic centralism, to Stalinist authoritarianism, to Gorbachev's glasnost and perestroika. Similarly, democracy can take multiple forms that involve different assumptions about the role of the citizen, the political rights of individuals, the acceptance of dissent and political conflict, and other features of the political process. Finally, the category of regime support also includes orientations towards political institutions, such as evaluations of parliament, political parties, the courts, and other institutional actors.[5] The public must accept the institutions of governance as legitimate, and accept the decisions made by those who control these institutions.

We distinguish between these different aspects of regime support for several reasons, both theoretical and empirical. Theoretically, 'regime support' is a broad term that includes different elements. For instance, there are important distinctions between support for the norms of a regime and support for the specific institutions of a regime. Indeed, one can observe how public demands for institutional changes, such as the recent electoral reforms in Italy, Japan, and New Zealand, represent the public's desire to better realise the norms of the democratic system. Acceptance of democracy as a principle is more central to defining the political community, while acceptance of the specific institutions of democracy are more instrumental judgements. In addition, empirical research has shown that longitudinal trends differ across these three areas, so it is important to treat them separately (for example, Dalton 1999).

Easton defined a third level as including the political authorities: those individuals who currently hold positions of political authority, such as prime ministers or legislators, or in a broader sense the pool of political elites from which government leaders are drawn. For instance, how do citizens evaluate the present incumbents of office rather than the office itself? Evaluation of political authorities is an important element of the political process. As Easton (1965: 215) stated,

---

[5] Easton tends to include institutional support within the categories of authorities. However, I reserve the category of authorities to represent distinct and individual actors to separate these evaluations from those generalized beyond a single candidate or government official.

if a system is to be able to deal with its daily affairs of converting demands into binding decisions, it is not enough for the members to support the political community and the regime. It is true, support for the structure of authority . . . would assure the perpetuation of the basic rules and structures through which demands might be processed.

In short, in a well-functioning political system the citizens support the incumbents of government who make authoritative political decisions, as well as endorsing the general principles of the political system.

Easton's distinctions between levels of support guide the analyses presented here. For both theoretical and empirical reasons that we discuss in Chapter 2, we include the subcategories of regime support to consider five levels of political support:

• Political community
• Regime: Principles • Regime: Norms and procedures • Regime: Institutions
• Political authorities

It is often difficult to draw such fine theoretical distinction in public opinion surveys. Empirical research finds that support for the political authorities frequently carries over to support for political institutions and the political system (Muller and Jukam 1977; Fuchs 1989; Canache, Mondak, and Seligson 2001). Public opinion survey questions measuring political support also frequently overlap between levels. Does a general 'trust in government' question, for example, measure support for the incumbents or for the regime (Miller 1974a; Citrin 1974)? Despite these empirical problems, it is important to begin with this theoretical distinction.

This framework is also important because public orientations towards different objects of support carry different political implications. For instance, discontent with political authorities normally has limited systemic implications. Citizens often become dissatisfied with political office-holders and act on these feelings to select new leaders at the next election. Dissatisfaction with authorities, within a democratic system, is not usually a signal for basic political change. Negative attitudes towards political officials can exist with little loss in support for the office itself or the institutional structure encompassing this office. As the object of dissatisfaction becomes more general—the regime or the political community—the political implications broaden. A decline in support for the political process might provoke a basic challenge to constitutional structures or calls for reform of the procedures of government. Weakening ties to the political community in a democratic system might foretell eventual revolution, civil war, or the loss of democracy. Thus, Easton (1975: 437) observed, 'not all expressions of unfavorable orientations have the same degree of gravity for a political system. Some may be consistent with its maintenance; others may lead to fundamental change.'

Another conceptual question involves the nature of political orientations towards these various levels of politics. One can imagine a wide range of feelings, attitudes, or orientations that citizens might hold at each of these levels of political support. What does it mean to trust the government or to have confidence in political institutions?

One approach stresses the evaluative aspect of political support. Russell Hardin (1998; 2002), for example, maintains that trust can exist only when one knows about an individual and how his or her interests relate to our own. To Hardin, trust represents 'encapsulated interests' whereby one expresses confidence that another's interests will lead him or her to behave as expected.[6] Certainly, such cognitive and evaluative elements should be an important element of political support. If individuals see corruption in government, they should use this information to adjust their orientations towards political figures. To some extent, political support must be based on such judgements if it is to have meaning.

At the same time, political support can also involve affective feelings. Almond and Verba (1963), for instance, maintained that attachments to the political community were often socialized early in life as political identities were first formed (see also Easton and Dennis 1969). More recently, Jane Mansbridge (1999) discussed political trust as based upon moral or altruistic values, and Claus Offe (1999) described trust as a categorical trait that develops separately from evaluative judgements. In short, these scholars maintain that orientations towards political objects— what we are calling political support—can tap affective feelings as well as the evaluative calculations that Hardin and others emphasize.

This dichotomy between evaluative and affective feelings runs through the literature on political support. David Easton (1975), for instance, contrasted specific support, which is more directly tied to evaluations of a political object, and diffuse support, which reflects more generalized and affective orientations. While the former might reflect the immediate performance of government, the latter represents deeper political feelings that might provide a potential reservoir of support in times of political stress. Dieter Fuchs (1989) similarly distinguished between affective, cognitive, and evaluative elements of political support—each with its own implications. Thus, it is important to recognize the distinction between the evaluative and affective elements of political support as we analyse public opinion.

In summary, as Senator Bradley noted in the quotation cited above, one can and should distinguish between support for the present incumbents of office and broader support for the regime or political community. Democracy provides

---

[6] One byproduct to Hardin's rational choice approach is the claim one cannot trust an institution or organization (1998; 2002a). After reviewing Hardin's arguments, my conclusion is that he is discussing something different from what we generally mean by feelings of trust or political support. Perhaps it would be better to describe Hardin's analyses as describing verbal or non-verbal contracts, which are different from what most people mean by political support or trust. Indeed, what is missing is the affective component that keeps all human interactions from becoming the rationally calculated actions that rational choice theories presume.

a vehicle for removing incumbents when the public is dissatisfied with their performance, thus renewing the democratic process. The ominous sign, however, is that most political observers believe that public dissatisfaction now reaches beyond the political authorities to the institutions and norms of the democratic process. This is the nature of the current challenge to democracy.

THE IMPLICATIONS OF DECREASING SUPPORT

During a recent election in Germany, I was talking to a party representative at an election information booth, and he gave me a souvenir pen from the party. As I left, a German friend advised me to 'use the pen now, because after the election it will stop working...just like the party'.

If such feelings of political cynicism are increasing in advanced industrial democracies, what are the implications of these trends? In many ways, decreasing support for democratic politics seems to conflict with the performance of government. The end of the cold war created a new euphoria about democracy and the democratic process among many politicians and political analysts.[7] One can arguably claim that democracy has become the dominant form of political system in the world, with most nations functioning as democracies or trying to achieve this status.

Several analysts also note that advanced industrial democracies have a very positive record of policy performance (for example, Bok 1998; Barnes and Gill 2000). Living standards have risen to levels that would have been unimaginable at the mid-point of the twentieth century. Democratic guarantees of political and civil rights have generally grown over recent decades. As President Clinton claimed in his 2000 State of the Union address, there is a great deal to admire in the experience of contemporary democracies. Even in new policy areas, such as the environment or women's rights, democracies have made significant policy advances in the past few decades. In many ways, the millennium seemed to represent the best of times.

This record of positive policy performance led some sceptics to question whether declining support has meaningful political implications. The first analyses of the empirical trends in the United States debated the significance of these trends. Arthur Miller (1974a: 951) concluded that the data showed 'hostility toward political and social leaders, the institutions of government, and the regime as a whole', thus implying fundamental implications for American politics. Jack Citrin (1974) was more sanguine, claiming that measures of distrust were essentially tapping orientations towards the incumbents, and thus the system

---

[7] The most prominent examples of this genre are Huntington (1991) and Fukuyama (1992), but many other examples can be found in the academic and the popular press. Having cited Huntington, I should also note that he was a long-term sceptic of the democratization potential in established democracies and developing nations (Huntington 1981; 1984) and remains very pessimistic in his more recent writings about human interactions (Huntington 1996).

implications were limited. Using a baseball analogy, he offered hope that a new manager, a new set of players, or a winning season would change these sentiments.[8] But many, many seasons have passed since then, and the managers and players have changed several times, yet distrust persists.

More recently, John Mueller (1999) questioned whether a dissatisfied or at least somewhat cynical public is not the 'normal' pattern to expect for democracies. Mueller joined Samuel Huntington (1981) in attributing at least a portion of the decline to intellectuals, academics, and political figures, who clamour about how democratic reality falls short of democratic ideals: 'the cynicism about the [political] form so commonly found in democracies, and so often lamented by democratic idealists, is partly—may be even substantially—caused by them' (Mueller 1999: ch. 7).

Another explanation is that people have simply become more realistic about politics, shedding the naive idealism of an earlier period (for example, Citrin 1974). From this perspective, the realism that people now hold may lead to a more reasoned and reasonable politics. Dissatisfaction can be the stimulus for political reform to address some of the shortfalls of contemporary democracies. To a large extent, I agree with the reforming potential of a public that expects more of the democratic process. But even reform requires a degree of trust that may be lacking in the public's present disaffection with government. Dissatisfaction is real and significant; the issue raised by these scholars is what will come of these feelings.

To be blunt: I disagree that current feelings of dissatisfaction and distrust are either a normal or an insignificant political development. The political culture literature argues that citizens must be supportive of the political system if it is to endure—and this seems especially relevant to democratic polities. In addition, democracy is at least partially based on public endorsement of the political decision-making process; it is not and should not be measured primarily by the efficiency of its policy outputs. Democracy is a process and a set of political expectations that elevate democracy above other political forms. Otherwise, we should praise authoritarian regimes that increase living standards or improve the performance of their economies; but we do not, and the citizens of these nations often do not, because free individuals expect more of their political system.[9] We return to this theme in the conclusion, once the evidence has been presented and analysed.

---

[8] 'Political systems, like baseball teams, have slumps and winning streaks. Having recently endured a succession of losing seasons, Americans boo the home team when it takes the field. But fans are often fickle; victories quickly elicit cheers. And to most fans what matters is whether the home team wins or loses, not how it plays the game. According to this analysis, a modest "winning streak" and, perhaps, some new names in the lineup may be sufficient to raise the level of trust in government' (Citrin 1974: 987).

[9] Miller (1974*b*: 1001) also responds to Citrin's baseball analogy to address this point: 'Analogies between baseball and politics are weak and rarely help us understand either, although I would remind Professor Citrin that the endless changes of baseball managers and players in which many teams engage have not brought back the fans who became disinterested

Equally important, public opinion has a practical impact on politics. Even if some analysts argue that people are wrong to distrust their government, the reality is that these feelings of distrust do exist in the minds of many citizens. If people distrust the government, then this becomes a reality that shapes individual behaviour and ultimately the workings of the political process. More generally, if democracy relies on the participation of its citizens as a basis of legitimacy and to produce representative decisions, then decreasing involvement as a consequence of distrust can harm the democratic process.

As citizens become sceptical about political parties and fail to develop affective ties to political parties, this can change the nature of electoral politics (Dalton and Wattenberg 2000). An electorate that is not emotionally bound to political parties should display greater volatility in its voting choices and a greater willingness to respond to short-term electoral factors. Scepticism about the existing parties may also facilitate the emergence of new parties or the fragmenting of the existing parties. Moreover, if voting shifts and new parties do not regenerate political support—as is expected in democratic theory—this may stimulate a new spiral of political distrust (Miller 1974*b*).

The electoral example illustrates how decreasing political support has ambiguous implications for the evolution of democracy. Changing orientations towards political parties and different processes of vote choice have the potential to move electoral politics towards its democratic ideal—encouraging voters to choose the government on the basis of policy goals rather than hereditary party affiliations or group loyalties. At the same time, these trends could also allow voters to be more easily manipulated by political elites and the rhetoric of campaigns, without sufficient means to enforce democratic responsibility between elections. Both outcomes represent real and significant changes in the nature of democratic electoral politics—but it is not yet clear which pattern will predominate.

There is also evidence that feelings of political distrust stimulate the rise of unconventional, elite-challenging actions such as protests, demonstrations, and political violence. Muller and Jukam (1977), for instance, found that support for the political regime was strongly related to unconventional political action in Germany (see also Barnes et al. 1979). Studies of American protestors have similarly demonstrated that distrust stimulates political violence (Aberbach and Walker 1970; Craig and Wald 1985). It is natural to expect that, as citizens become disenchanted with electoral methods of political input, they turn to other channels of interests articulation—especially if some of the social forces producing this distrust also encourage new orientations towards political participation (Inglehart 1990).

in the game because of its inherent structural flaws—for example, its lack of speed. Furthermore, the visible actors in baseball have little if any impact on the rules of the game; in politics, they make the rules. A change in the political leadership, therefore, holds the potential for profound systemic political change ... On the other hand, a replacement of political leaders with no subsequent improvement in the performance of the government may generate a new spiral of political distrust.'

Again, this development can have mixed implications for contemporary democracies. Excessive protest and political violence may threaten the principles of democratic discourse and collective decision-making. Intolerance and violence are not fertile grounds for democracy. But it is also possible that this expansion of direct action provides new groups with access to the democratic process, and allows new views to be heard. Indeed, the free speech movement, the environmental movement, the women's movement, and other contemporary social movements have clearly strengthened the democratic process, while simultaneously making it more contentious (Meyer and Tarrow 1998; McAdam, Tarrow, and Tilly 2001).

If citizens become more distrustful of politicians and the political process, this may alter other relationships between citizens and the state. Democratic polities are based on the presumption that citizens will voluntarily comply with the laws. If political distrust increases, this may lower voluntary compliance in areas such as tax laws and acceptance of government regulation (Schloz 1998; Schloz and Lubell 1998; Uslaner 1999). Between 1958 and 1998, the percentage of Americans who thought that people in government waste a lot of tax money increased by almost half. It should not be surprising that compliance with income tax laws has decreased over this same period in the United States, or that attacks on the Internal Revenue Service (IRS) have become an appealing political issue for some political figures. If minorities distrust police, if conservatives distrust the IRS, if people are generally sceptical about government, this has real consequences for policy. These examples highlight a general feature of democracy: democracy functions with minimal coercive force because of the legitimacy of the system and the voluntary compliance of the public. Declining feelings of political trust and political support can undermine this relationship, and thus the workings of democratic governments.

More generally, the economics literature argues that trust facilitates transactions—so the decline of political support should have equivalent affects on political relations (Arrow 1972; Putnam 2000). The concern with declining support expressed by Bradley, Bennett, Nunn, and other political experts undoubtedly reflects their awareness that elected officials are now confronted by a public that treats them with scepticism and distrust. Thus elites lose the efficiencies that trust produces; they must spend more time assuring and informing voters that their interests are being represented—even if such efforts appear ineffectual. For the public, decreased support also creates new costs because a distrustful citizen should feel the need to invest more time monitoring government (although this has not restored confidence). Thus, the transaction costs of democratic politics increase as political support wanes.

There are also institutional correlates of this declining political support. If citizens lose faith in political parties and other institutions of representative democracy, they may shift their allegiance to alternative political channels, such as citizen action groups, issue-based movements, and anti-system institutions. If citizens lose faith in the government-managed media in Europe or the major commercial broadcasters in the US, they may turn to alternative information sources, such as cable television or talk radio. In sufficient degree, such changes can alter the very workings of the democratic process by eroding the role of political parties and changing the patterns of political information and interest articulation in advanced industrial democracies.

A dissatisfied public also has the potential to create even more fundamental changes in the structure of democratic politics (Cain, Dalton, and Scarrow 2003). For example, John Curtice and Roger Jowell (1997) show that political dissatisfaction within the British public generated support for institutional reforms— restricting the House of Lords, limiting the Official Secrets Act, and judicial review of legislation—that became part of the political programme of New Labour. Political dissatisfaction is also fuelling calls for participatory reforms of the process of representative democracy more generally (Dalton, Buerklin, and Drummond 2001). Popular dissatisfaction is cited as a prime factor in recent restructuring of the electoral systems in New Zealand, Japan, and Italy (Shugart and Wattenberg 2001). Frequent calls for campaign finance reform and term limits in the United States undoubtedly spring from a dissatisfied public. A lack of public support for government can generate, and is generating, constitutional change in contemporary democracies.

Institutional reform again illustrates the varied political consequences that might flow from public doubts about government. Institutional reform of an electoral system can lead to a better electoral system, or at least address real problems that had emerged in recent elections. The pressure for democratic constitutional change in Britain demonstrates how discontent with present democratic procedures can lead to processes that are more democratic. Indeed, several democratic theorists argue that dissatisfaction with present institutional structures and processes may lead to an expansion of the democratic process. Benjamin Barber (1984), for example, believes that dissatisfaction may fuel calls for institutional reforms that develop new forms of 'strong democracy', and Robert Dahl (1989) has discussed the potential for a third democratic transition that extends the possibilities of the democratic process. Thus, current public dissatisfaction with the functioning of the democratic process may generate the reformist pressures to expand and strengthen the process.

Political scientists are debating these potential consequences of declining support, and we discuss these issues in the chapters that follow. The range of potential effects is substantial—and the extent of political distrust suggests that real changes will occur. But it is still unclear which aspects of politics will be more strongly affected by changing citizen orientations towards politics. In addition, many of these aspects of politics involve a range of outcomes that will have different implications for the functioning of the democratic process. Whether these developments strengthen or erode the democratic process depends, in large part, on the choices that citizens and elites make. Thus, these challenges to democracy also represent choices about democracy's future.

THE EMPIRICAL BASE OF THIS STUDY

This project begins by tracking different elements of political support over time for the advanced industrial democracies. This requires broad cross-national evidence; we want to examine the general experience of advanced industrial democracies as a group. Equally important, the cross-national variation in public attitudes may provide a method to explore rival theories about political support.

Our research thus focuses on the long-term member states of the Organization of Economic Cooperation and Development (OECD). Because we are interested in the politics of advanced industrial democracies, we do not include OECD nations that have had relatively recent democratic transitions (Greece, Spain, and Portugal) or the micro states (Luxembourg and Iceland). The remaining OECD nations provide the most reasonable approximation of advanced industrial democracies: Australia, Austria, Belgium, Britain, Canada, Denmark, Finland, France, Germany, Ireland, Italy, Japan, The Netherlands, New Zealand, Norway, Sweden, Switzerland, and the United States. In addition, these nations offer substantial variation in party systems, electoral experiences, and other political factors that are embedded in our two theoretical models. Furthermore, we are more likely to identify existing empirical data sources for these nations.

In addition, we need to track public opinion over time because our research questions are intrinsically dynamic. Have public evaluations of politics and government changed since the apparently more halcyon days of the 1960s? What are the correlates of these patterns, both in terms of the causal theories and in terms of the putative effects?

The changing nature of politics in advanced industrial societies first became apparent during the late 1960s and the 1970s. Trends for the last decade or two are relevant to our inquiry, but we want to consider the broader question of whether the relationship between citizens and the state changed in fundamental ways during the second half of the twentieth century. To the extent possible, we track political change since the 1960s across the advanced industrial democracies. The planned end-point for the project was the last election in 2000 or earlier. I felt the temptation to add new data as an additional election survey became available, but this could be an unending process of revision with so many nations included in this study. With but few exceptions I resisted this temptation to go beyond 2000, and thus most survey series end in the late 1990s.

Until recently it would have been impossible to carry out this research project with sufficient cross-national and cross-temporal breadth because the empirical resources were simply not available. This project is possible only because we can draw upon existing research programmes on public opinion in advanced industrial societies. The strongest empirical evidence in this book comes from the national election studies that now are independently conducted in most of these nations.[10] The willingness of colleagues to share their data and provide supplementary information on national opinion data provides the foundation for this research. It is a credit to the public opinion research community that such data-sharing norms have developed.

In addition, this research draws upon a variety of cross-national studies, many of which also have a longitudinal component.[11] There are now four waves of the World Value Surveys/European Value Surveys: 1981–3, 1990–4, 1995–8, and 1999–2002. Another valuable resource is the Eurobarometer series that surveys citizens of the member states of the European Union, beginning in the early 1970s and continuing to the present.

By bringing together the empirical evidence for a larger number of democracies, and by tracking opinions over a relatively long period, we will map the broad contours of public orientations towards the democratic process, and determine whether these orientations are systematically changing in advanced industrial democracies. We seek to answer the fundamental question of whether citizen orientations towards political systems are changing in these nations, and what the implications of these changes are for the democratic process.

PLAN OF THE BOOK

The research of this book proceeds in three stages. Part I of the book, Chapter 2, presents the empirical evidence to track the changes in political support within advanced industrial democracies. Because we are interested in long-term changes in citizen attitudes, we assembled public opinion trends that cover as long a time span as possible, ideally beginning in the 1960s or 1970s. In most nations, we thus rely on national public opinion series, often the national election study. The advantage of these series is that they normally replicate the same survey questions over time and

[10] Most of the data in this volume were obtained through the Inter-university Consortium for Political and Social Research (ICPSR) at the University of Michigan. Information about these data is available on the ICPSR web site www.icpsr.umich.edu. In addition, the American National Election Study (ANES) maintains a website with many of the time trends presented here, www.umich.edu/~nes. We also received national data series from several other data archives, including the Zentralarchiv für empirische Sozialforschung at the University of Cologne, the Norwegian Social Science Data Services, the Swedish Social Science Data Service, the United Kingdom Data Archive at the University of Essex, and the Social Science Data Archive in Canberra.

[11] Several large international data collections are used in various chapters of this work. The World Values Survey (WVS) is a coordinated series of surveys, now in its fourth wave, http://wvs.isr.umich.edu; the Eurobarometer conducts regular surveys of the member states of the European Union, http://europa.eu.int/comm/public_opinion; the International Social Survey Program (ISSP) is a coordinated series of surveys conducted by sociological institutes in several nations, www.issp.org; and the Comparative Study of Electoral Systems is a coordinate set of post-election surveys conducted by national teams in the late 1990s. Most of these data were acquired from the ICPSR or the other archives described in n. 10.

are high-quality surveys. In addition, we analyse several large cross-national surveys, such as the World Values Surveys or the Eurobarometer surveys, that enable us to compare identically asked questions of political support across nations.

We assembled a mass of data, and the reader will see many different perspectives on what we believe is a general pattern of decreasing public confidence in politicians, political parties, and political institutions. Certainly, any single questionnaire item is fallible, but attention to the wording of one question becomes less relevant when a general pattern occurs across a range of different indicators—and this is what we found. In addition, we attempted to assemble all the national public opinion series that are accessible for analysis; our goal is to provide a census of data sources, and not selectively report public opinion findings. I know that additional data series must exist, and I hope that this book will encourage others to find additional evidence so that we can better understand how and why contemporary public opinion is changing.[12] I believe that this book presents the most comprehensive empirical evidence now available on the topic.

Part II of the book examines rival theories to explain changing orientations toward government. Kornberg and Clarke (1992: 21) suggest that there are two principal sources of political support. One consists of socialization experiences that create values and orientations influencing specific political evaluations. We examine such factors in Chapters 4 and 5. The second source involves cost-benefit calculations concerning the way that political actors perform or processes function. Such factors are examined in Chapters 6 and 7.

As an introduction to these analyses, Chapter 3 summarizes the major theories in the literature and provides an initial empirical test of rival hypotheses. These analyses document the broad contours of political support, and how the correlates of support differ depending on whether we are talking about political authorities, the regime, or the political system.

Chapter 4 provides a more detailed tracking of the social correlates of decreasing trust in government. Many of the hypothesized causes for decreasing support have implications for the pattern of political trust across social groups. For instance, some researchers suggest that the development of advanced industrial economies has marginalized the less affluent and less educated, and these groups have become more critical of government. Chapter 4 examines such possible explanations for the decline of political support by tracking the opinions of social groups across time.

---

[12] It is inevitable that some data will temper or even contradict the general patterns described in this volume, because political phenomena are complex and seldom uniformly fit a model. But my experience has been that the accumulation of additional data has generally reinforced the patterns presented here. The first presentation of some of the national election studies trends was at the 1997 annual meetings of the American Political Science Association; as additional data were added for the eventual book chapter (Dalton 1999), the patterns became more distinctive. An expanded data set for a second publication (Putnam, Pharr, and Dalton 2000) yielded even stronger trends of declining political support. We add substantially to these data in Chapter 2.

A related theory stresses the changing values and political norms of contemporary publics as an explanation for decreasing political support. The decline in respect for authority and changing norms of political engagement are sometimes cited as explanations for why the citizenry is more sceptical of the traditional processes and institutions of representative democracy. Chapter 5 thus examines the relationship between postmaterial values and the various levels of political support.

Analysts often cite poor policy performance as another source of declining political support. Chapter 6 focuses on economic evaluations as a potential predictor of support, marshalling both cross-sectional and cross-temporal evidence. Most cross-sectional opinion surveys demonstrate a strong relationship between images of governments' economic performance and political support. This chapter asks whether this is sufficient evidence of a causal relationship.

Beyond their role in the performance of the economy, governments also are responsible for ensuring the general well-being of their citizens, which involves them in issues ranging from the provision of social services to the guarantee of human rights and the protection of the environment. Chapter 7 considers how performance on these multiple dimensions may influence citizen evaluations of government.

Part III of this book examines the potential consequences of support. As we have argued above, if declining feelings of support are politically significant, they should have real and demonstrable effects on the attitudes and behaviours of contemporary publics. Chapter 8 assembles a diverse array of survey evidence to assess the likely consequences of changing levels of political support on contemporary publics. It is claimed that feelings of political support are amorphous orientations that lack real political consequences. We demonstrate a range of significant effects in this chapter.

CONCLUSION

In various nations, at various times, over the past generation, noted political analysts and observers have claimed that the relationship between citizens and their government is changing in fundamental ways. The following quotation illustrates these sentiments:

The general temper of the world is one of profound and widespread disillusionment. Our generation seems to have lost its scheme of values. Certainty has been replaced by cynicism; hope has given room to despair. The movements of art, literature and music seem to deny the tradition that created the great achievements of the past and to seek their inspiration in forms which are a denial of its whole meaning . . . The war dealt a mortal blow at religious belief as a body of permanent sanctions for behavior; and the churches seem to have become rather a way of performing a time-honored ritual than a method of influencing the convictions of men. The institutions which, a generation ago, were hardly challenged—the public schools in England, the right of American business men to shape the ethos of their civilization—are now criticized with an angry hostility which assumes that they are permanently on the defensive. About the whole character of our desires there is a temper of feverish haste, a recklessness, a want of calm, which suggests an ignorance of the things to be sought in life. The spirit which denies has triumphed over the spirit which affirms.

These words seem to capture the spirit of the age, and they could have been written by Ronald Inglehart, Michel Crozier, or several other analysts of advanced industrial democracies. But these words were written in 1931 as Harold Laski described Western democracies beset by the Great Depression (Laski 1931: 13–14).

I cite Laski at this point for several reasons. We should remember that there have been earlier periods of democratic challenge. Indeed, the tensions and internal contradictions of the democratic process are a source of its vitality. A sense of history will enrich our understanding of contemporary politics. In addition, even though Laski's words seem a prophetic description of our age, I believe our current situation differs from earlier periods of democratic challenge. Laski, for example, described the crisis of democracy which arose from anti-democratic sentiments and which gave rise to communist and fascist attacks on democratic principles and processes. Today, democracies face a challenge that may appear similar to previous periods of political malaise, but I maintain that this challenge primarily springs not from democracy's failure but from its success. The current challenge is one of democratic choices: not choices between democracy and its alternative, but between choices that may move democracies closer to their theoretical ideal. While Laski and others worried about the possible non-democratic choices faced in earlier eras, I will argue that we should be optimistic because there are democratic choices before us.

PART I

The Evidence of Change

2

Changing Citizen Orientations

DISCUSSIONS about the looming crisis of democracy have become commonplace in political research for at least the past quarter-century. For example, in *The Crisis of Democracy*, Crozier, Huntington, and Watanuki (1975) worried about the fragility of democracy in Europe, North America, and Japan. These authors saw the public as disengaging from politics and disenchanted with the democratic process. As I noted in Chapter 1, many other scholars shared these concerns as the advanced industrial democracies struggled through the tumultuous 1960s and early 1970s.

These accounts, however, often lacked substantive evidence to support their negative evaluations about the state of democracy or their even more dire predictions about democracy's future. Certainly, the evidence of decreasing trust and disengagement was well-documented for the United States (Miller 1974*a*; Lipset and Schneider 1983), but it was not clear that this pattern held for other advanced industrial democracies. The student protests that spread across Europe in the 1960s, and the citizen mobilization that followed in their wake, were taken as evidence that the public at large was becoming critical of the democratic process. The empirical evidence was very mixed, however, despite the strong pronouncements of some political commentators.

The first broad compilation of empirical data on citizen orientations towards their governments actually discounted claims that the political attitudes of contemporary publics had fundamentally changed (Fuchs and Klingemann 1995). These authors summarized the findings of *Citizens and the State* in fairly sanguine terms: 'The hypotheses we tested are based on the premise that a fundamental change had taken place in the relationship between citizens and the state, provoking a challenge to representative democracy . . . the postulated fundamental change in the citizens' relationship with the state largely did *not* occur' (Fuchs and Klingemann 1995: 429).

A subsequent round of comparative opinion research called this conclusion into question (for example, Dalton 1999; Norris 1999*a*; Pharr and Putnam 2000). This chapter goes beyond these previous analyses to compile a larger and more systematic assessment of how people view political actors and the political system in advanced industrial democracies. We determine whether citizen orientations towards politicians, political parties, political institutions, and the principles of democracy are changing in systematic ways. In short, has a malaise finally touched the democratic spirit?

ASSEMBLING THE EMPIRICAL EVIDENCE

Several theories link the decrease in political support to broad, ongoing changes in the nature of advanced industrial societies (see reviews in Norris 1999*a*; Pharr and Putnam 2000; and Chapter 3 below). If there is an extensive and long-term shift in public attitudes towards government, then it presumably results from common processes of social and political change, not from unique political scandals or separate policy problems that coincidentally and simultaneously occur in many nations. For instance, some scholars claim that increasing economic strains in contemporary democracies, often linked to the impact of global economic interdependence, are the root cause of the public's disenchantment with politics (for example, Alesina and Wacziarg 2000). Alternatively, others claim that the processes of social and political modernization, especially changing public values and expectations about politics, are increasing public scepticism towards politics (Inglehart 1990; 1997*a*).

Such broad explanations differ in their theoretical premises and the causal processes they emphasize, but they generally suggest that long-term changes in the social and political conditions of advanced industrial societies may be eroding public support for the political process. If we accept this statement, *it suggests the type of empirical evidence we should collect.* Ideally, we should assess these theories with long-term trend data, especially series that begin in the more halcyon period of the late 1950s and early 1960s. Fortunately, many OECD democracies have national series of public opinion polls, some beginning in the 1950s and 1960s, others with more recent origins.[1] In many instances, the independent national series use similar survey questions (or their functional equivalents). This overlap arose from the social networks of the initial generation of academic public opinion researchers.[2] Together, these existing survey series, and more recent cross-national studies from the 1980s and 1990s, provide a rich and valuable resource for our research.

In examining public opinion, we also must be sensitive to the different levels of political support as outlined in Chapter 1. This book adopts the basic Eastonian framework, distinguishing between orientations toward the *authorities*, the *regime*, and the *political community*. Public orientations toward political authorities arise from different sources and have different implications from orientations towards the political system or the general community. A political system may endure when

---

[1] This work focuses on the OECD nations that are long-established advanced industrial democracies. I exclude Greece, Spain, and Portugal because they are relatively new democracies and without the affluence and long histories of the other established democracies in our study.

[2] Researchers from the early American election studies at the University of Michigan, primarily Philip Converse, Warren Miller, and Donald Stokes, assisted researchers from several nations in the development of national election surveys. Philip Converse collaborated on French and Canadian election studies. Warren Miller established collaborative ties with the Dutch and Swedish election teams. Donald Stokes participated in electoral research in Britain and Australia. This collaboration led to the replication of many items from the Michigan election surveys.

citizens become dissatisfied with its officials; indeed, elections are designed to translate such dissatisfactions into a new group of political elites. However, the lack of support for the political community suggests the political system may be at risk.

In addition, it is important to differentiate between types of citizen orientations. Almond and Verba (1963), for example, differentiated between affective and evaluative beliefs. Affective beliefs involve an acceptance or identification with an object; evaluative beliefs involve a judgement about the performance or appropriateness of the object. Similarly, Easton (1965) distinguished between diffuse and specific support (see also Muller and Jukam 1977). According to Easton, diffuse support is a deep-seated set of attitudes towards politics and the operation of the political system that is relatively impervious to change. Diffuse support has also been interpreted as measuring the legitimacy of a political system or political institutions. In contrast, specific support is more closely related to the actions and performance of the government or political elites. As noted in Chapter 1, this dichotomy also taps an enduring distinction between evaluative and affective interpretations of political support (Warren 1999).[3]

Combining these two dimensions—political level and the type of belief—gives us a familiar map of public orientations towards politics and the political system (Table 2.1).[4] The rows of the table define five different levels of popular orientations that expand upon Easton's tripartite framework (see Chapter 1). The columns of the table distinguish between *evaluations* that reflect judgements about political phenomena (what Easton labels specific support) and general *affective orientations* that represent adherence to a set of values (diffuse support).

Previous empirical research demonstrates that it is difficult to isolate each type of orientation because public sentiments can blend adjacent orientations (Muller and Jukam 1977; Fuchs 1989; also see Chapter 3). Indeed, much of the initial debate on survey-based analyses of political support centred on whether questions on political trust measured orientations towards the incumbents, or broader evaluations of general political elites and the government (Miller 1974*a*; Citrin 1974). This theoretical distinction is important to maintain if the public does distinguish between incumbent, regime, and community evaluations.

---

[3] There is an extensive discussion of the meaning of various terms used to describe political support: what do we mean by trust, what is the nature of confidence, can we trust institutions or is trust limited only to other individuals (for example, Warren 1999; Hardin 2002). This debate often occurs among theorists who do not actually study public opinion. Thus, distinctions about theoretically conceived notions about political support have limited relevance unless they can be translated from pages of prose to measurable traits in public opinion. In reality, the difficulty lies in making distinctions between such finely differentiated orientations towards government, which makes refined philosophical theorizing largely irrelevant.

[4] This 5×2 table was first presented in a 1997 paper at the American Political Science Association that provided an initial analysis of support trends in advanced industrial democracies. This paper was subsequently revised and published as Dalton (1999) and a version of this framework was adopted by the editor of the collection in which it appeared to describe the patterns in the entire volume.

Changing Citizen Orientations

TABLE 2.1   *The types of political support*

Level of analysis	Evaluations	Affective orientations
Community	Best nation to live	National pride
		Sense of national identity
Regime: Principles	Democracy best form of government	Democratic values
Regime: Norms and procedures	Evaluations of rights	Political rights
	Satisfaction with democratic process	System norms
		Participatory norms
Regime: Political institutions	Performance judgements	Trust institutions
	Output expectations	Support party government
Authorities	Candidate evaluations	Trust politicians in general
	Voting support	Identify with party

To illustrate this framework in more detail, the cells of the table contain typical public opinion questions that might measure each type of belief. Affective orientations towards the political community might be tapped by questions such as feelings of national pride or a sense of national identity. Evaluations of the nation and political community might be measured by questions that ask which is the best nation in which to live. At the other end of the continuum, affective feelings towards political incumbents might be measured by a sense of party identification, which assesses long-term affective ties to the political parties. By comparison, questions on candidate support or voting intentions tap short-term and evaluative feelings towards the parties and the candidates.

This is not an original framework—but it is essential to emphasize the distinction between various measures of political support. These differences are sometimes blurred in research on political support, and these differences are politically significant in interpreting our findings.[5] Democratic political systems must keep the support of their citizens if they are to remain viable. Yet, since all governments occasionally fail to meet public expectations, short-term failures to satisfy public demands must not directly erode diffuse support for the regime or political community. In other words, a democratic political system requires a reservoir of diffuse support independent of immediate policy outputs (specific support) if it is to weather periods of public dissatisfaction.

It is difficult to assemble all the data necessary to fill in this matrix. A long series of election studies and other opinion surveys for the United States provides a rich, though not complete, database for studying political support; and there is extensive commercial polling on these topics. In other nations, however, the data series are normally thinner and begin more recently. The most extensive data are

[5] Two good examples of close attention to the theoretical and empirical differences between these various aspects of political support are Muller and Jukam (1977) and Fuchs (1989).

available for the last decade, but the baseline measures from earlier periods are less common. Within these constraints, I have assembled long-term trends in political support from the national election study series, or a comparable data series, for as many advanced industrial democracies as possible. The results, I believe, provide a definitive assessment of the trends in political support in advanced industrial democracies.

SUPPORT FOR POLITICAL AUTHORITIES

Public concerns about the democratic process normally begin with questions about the holders of power. Americans might not doubt the institutions of governance, but they might criticize Richard Nixon's actions during Watergate, George Bush's involvement in the Iran–Contra negotiations, or Bill Clinton's multiple indiscretions. There is some evidence that the American public has become more focused on candidates and more demanding in judging them (Wattenberg 1991: ch. 4). Greater scepticism and doubts about political elites seem to be a common development in other advanced industrial democracies.[6] However, evaluations of specific incumbents tend to be cyclical in a stable democracy. When governments and office-holders lose favour, they are replaced by new political figures at the next election, who may restore public confidence at least temporarily: this is the nature of democratic politics. Moreover, specific evaluations of the incumbents are the least significant aspect of political support, since this focus is on individuals rather than the institutions and processes of the political system. Therefore, I will not dwell on evaluations of individual candidates or individual political parties because this is the most limited measure of political support.

It is more important to determine whether dissatisfaction with specific politicians has generalized to broader, more diffuse orientations towards political authorities (the lower right cell in Table 2.1). I approach this topic with data from two sources: general trust in politicians as a collective, and affective attachment to political parties.

The most extensive evidence on public evaluations of political authorities as a group comes from the United States with its long series of the American National Election Studies. Various pieces of evidence point to growing American scepticism of their politicians (Figure 2.1). The early readings show that there was a time when most Americans believed that one could trust the government to do what was right, that there were few dishonest people in government, and that most officials knew what they were doing. These positive feelings remained relatively unchanged until the mid-1960s and then declined precipitously.

---

[6] For instance, Falter and Rattinger (1997) show that public evaluations of all three 'established' German political parties decreased during 1977–94; there has also been a trend of decreasing trust in Canadian politicians (Kornberg and Clarke 1992) and declining sympathy for the American parties (Wattenberg 1996).

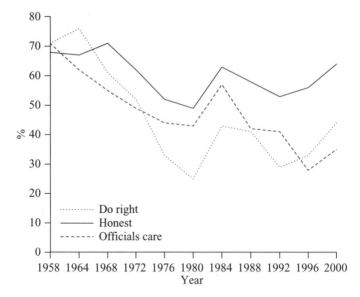

FIG. 2.1. American trust in government officials, 1958–2000
Source: American National Election Studies.

Conflict over civil rights and Vietnam paralleled Americans' eroding public confidence in their leaders; in concert with Watergate and a seemingly endless stream of political scandals, support declined even further over the next decade.

Trust of government officials reached a low point in 1980, and then the trend temporarily reversed during the upbeat presidency of Ronald Reagan. The symbolism of the Reagan administration and the allegories of the Great Communicator Reagan stressed the positive aspects of American society and politics. Opinions rebounded in 1984, but the decline continued in later elections. By the end of the Bush administration the indicators were near their historic lows. In 1996 only 33 per cent of the American public felt they could trust the government to do the right thing most of the time, only 28 per cent believed the politicians care what people think, and only 47 per cent thought most government officials were honest. There is evidence of some rebound by the 2000 election, but levels of support remain far below the levels of the 1950 and 1960s (see epilogue to this chapter).[7]

[7] Although the American National Election Studies shows a rebound in political support between 1994 and 2000, commercial polls do not display the same trend. The epilogue to this chapter focuses on public reactions to 11 September, but these data also document the lack of a clear rebound in political trust in the 1990s in the *New York Times* poll. Only 22% trust the government at least some of the time in November 1994, and the October 1998 reading is 26%. See Figure 2.6 in the epilogue to this chapter.

Virtually all other long-term public opinion series replicate these downward trends (Nye, Zelikow, and King 1997; Lipset and Schneider 1983; 1987). For instance, another series from the General Social Survey asked Americans if they agreed with the statement 'most public officials are not really interested in the problems of the average man'. The number of cynical Americans increases from 60 per cent in 1973 to 76 per cent in 1993. The Pew Research Center for the People and the Press (1998*a*) extended an earlier trend on evaluations of the ethical and moral practices of federal government officials; 34 per cent of Americans were critical in 1964, rising to 68 per cent in 1997. The Gallup Poll asked Americans about whether they saw big business, big labour, or big government as the biggest threat to the country; the percentage citing government as the biggest threat increased from 35 per cent in 1965 to 64 per cent in 1995. Similarly, since 1966 the Harris poll has tracked sentiments on two measures of political alienation, both of which display growing public cynicism over time (Harris Poll 1994).[8] The mass of evidence thus demonstrates that the American public has become increasing sceptical and distrustful of the politicians who lead them.

These trends have been an ongoing concern of US policy-makers for the past quarter-century; something real is changing in the climate of American politics. Viewing these trends in the late 1970s, President Jimmy Carter opined about the malaise of the political spirit and what was needed to restore public confidence in the political process. The Reagan presidency sought to reverse this trend. But political events seemed to justify the public's scepticism: Koreagate, Iran–Contra, and other scandals. At the end of the Bush presidency, the public's disenchantment had reached new lows. The depth of these trends in the 1990s led to the cynicism that surrounded Clinton's impeachment, and public calls for the renewal of American politics and political norms (for example, Bennett and Nunn 1998).

Cross-national evidence similar to these US time series was initially quite rare. Crozier, Huntington, and Watakuki (1975) claimed that political support was generally declining in the Trilateral democracies, but their actual empirical evidence was limited to American public opinion. Other semi-popular publications proclaimed the crisis of democracy in advanced industrial democracies, but often these presentations lacked empirical evidence to substantiate their claims. Ola Listhaug's (1995) comparative analysis of trust in politicians in four nations (Denmark, the Netherlands, Norway, and Sweden) yielded mixed patterns (see also Miller and Listhaug 1990). Listaug (1995: 294) concluded that the data 'do not justify . . . a uniformly pessimistic—nor an excessively optimistic—picture of developments in political trust'.

It is possible to go beyond this earlier research by drawing upon the resources of national election studies and national public opinion polls. Following Listhaug's lead, I assembled data from a large set of advanced industrial democracies, and

---

[8] The questions were: 'the people running the country don't really care what happens to you' and 'most people with power try to take advantage of people like yourself.'

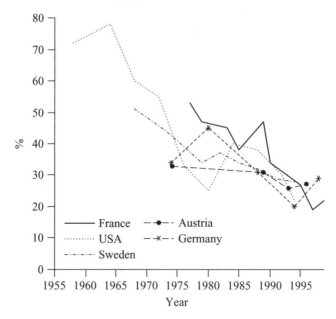

FIG. 2.2. Decline in feelings that politicians care what people think
Source: National election studies of the five nations.

with a longer data series that enables us to go substantially beyond prior research. As an introduction to these data, Figure 2.2 presents the trends from five election study series on the comparable question of whether politicians care what people think. The US data track the trend reported above, and these trends are now mirrored in the data from Austria, Canada, France, and Italy. For instance, between 1965 and 1997, the proportion of Canadians who felt that politicians cared about their views decreased from 52 per cent to 32 per cent. This figure graphically illustrates the decreasing trust in politicians among these nations.

   Table 2.2 broadens these analyses by presenting several different measures of confidence in politicians and government available from surveys in fifteen nations. The table presents the per annum change coefficient (regression coefficient) for each time trend. Many of these items use similar wording because they were influenced by the University of Michigan's pioneering studies in electoral research. Individual nations sometimes include a slight variation of these standard questions, and new items to measure political support.[9]

   By expanding the cross-national and cross-temporal breadth of the empirical data, there is clear evidence of a general erosion in support for politicians and

---

[9] The specific question wordings and data sources are available from the author.

TABLE 2.2   *Trends in confidence in politicians and government*

Nation	Per annum Δ	(St. error)	Period	(N of time-points)
Australia				
Trust government	−0.247	(0.333)	1969–98	(7) AES
Federal MPs honest	−0.491*	(0.073)	1976–98	(19) Gallup
Austria				
Only interested in votes	−0.385	(0.228)	1974–96	(4) AES
MPs lose touch	−0.577*	(0.101)	1974–96	(4)
Politicians don't care	−0.297	(0.114)	1974–96	(4)
Britain				
Only interested in votes	−0.331	(0.185)	1974–00	(8) BSA, other
MPs lose touch	−0.259	(0.176)	1974–00	(8)
Party over nation	−0.796*	(0.231)	1974–00	(8)
Improve government	−0.636*	(0.284)	1973–96	(6)
Canada				
Government doesn't care	−0.611*	(0.157)	1965–97	(8) CES
MPs lose touch	−0.599*	(0.149)	1965–97	(8)
Denmark				
Politicians don't care	−0.185	(0.194)	1971–94	(9) DES
Make right decisions	−0.169	(0.281)	1971–94	(11)
Finland				
Only interested in votes	−0.389	(0.261)	1978–91	(11) Gallup
MPs lose touch	−0.495*	(0.158)	1974–94	(11)
A party furthers interests	−0.891*	(0.421)	1974–91	(15)
France				
Government doesn't care	−1.685*	(0.280)	1977–97	(8) FES
Officials honest	−1.183*	(0.227)	1977–00	(5)
Germany				
Officials don't care (2)	−1.270*	(0.249)	1969–94	(5) GES
Officials don't care (4)	−0.524	(0.352)	1974–98	(5)
MPs lose touch	−0.525	(0.318)	1974–91	(3)
Iceland				
Politicians trustworthy	−0.850	(0.613)	1983–95	(4) IES
Italy				
Officials don't care	−0.451	(0.176)	1968–97	(5) Misc.
MPs lose touch	−1.353	(1.134)	1968–91	(3)
Trust government	−1.165	(0.615)	1968–91	(3)
Japan				
Trust national politicians	−0.572*	(0.158)	1976–96	(5) JES
Many dishonest politicians	−1.943	(0.942)	1976–92	(3)
Netherlands				
Only interested in votes	0.785*	(0.200)	1971–94	(8) DES
MPs don't care	0.903*	(0.189)	1971–94	(8)
Promise too much	−0.653*	(0.102)	1977–94	(5)
MP friends	−0.325	(0.151)	1977–94	(5)
Personal interest	0.150	(0.188)	1977–94	(5)
New Zealand				
MP out of touch	−4.500	(2.835)	1993–99	(4) NZES
Norway				
Only interested in votes	−0.029	(0.298)	1969–93	(4) NES
MPs don't care	−0.240	(0.402)	1969–93	(4)
Trust politicians	0.062	(0.166)	1973–97	(7)
Politicians knowledgeable	−0.348	(0.267)	1973–97	(7)

TABLE 2.2 (*Continued*)

Nation	Per annum Δ	(St. error)	Period	(N of time-points)
Sweden				
Only interested in votes	−1.215*	(0.141)	1968–98	(10) SES
Lose touch quickly	−0.625*	(0.132)	1968–98	(10)
Trust index	−1.370*	(0.099)	1968–98	(10)
United States				
Trust government	−0.957*	(0.282)	1958–00	(11) ANES
Politicians don't care	−0.787*	(0.122)	1952–00	(13)
Leaders crooked	−0.277	(0.153)	1958–00	(11)

Notes: The per annum change is the unstandardized regression coefficient of time on each variable; the associated standard errors are in parentheses (see chapter appendix on significance).The original variables are coded so that negative regression coefficients indicate a decrease in trust over time.
* Coefficients significant at the 0.05 level.

Sources: Most series are based on the national election study series for each nation. Australia: Gallup and AES, Australian Election Study. Austria: AES, Austrian Election Studies. Britain: BSA, British Social Attitudes. Canada: CES, Canadian Election Studies. Denmark: DES, Danish Election Studies. Finland: Gallup Polls. France: FES, French Election Studies. Germany: GES, German Election Studies. Iceland: IES, Icelandic Election Studies. Italy: multiple survey sources were used. Japan: JES, Japanese Election Studies. Netherlands: DES, Dutch Election Studies. New Zealand: NZES, New Zealand Election Studies. Norway: NES, Norwegian Election Studies. Sweden: SES, Swedish Election Studies. United States: ANES, American National Election Studies.

government in most advanced industrial democracies.[10] The patterns of decreasing political trust in the United States (Figure 2.1) produce the significant negative change coefficients apparent in the table.[11] This downward spiral is replicated in almost every other case, the major variation being in the timing and pace of decline.[12] This is striking. Regardless of recent trends in the economy, in large and small nations, in presidential and parliamentary systems, in countries with

[10] Listhaug (1995) studied trends in only four nations (Denmark, the Netherlands, Norway, and Sweden). In a broader cross-national context, we can now see that these four nations are not representative of advanced industrial democracies. Moreover, even in these nations the addition of later time-points shows decreasing trust in Denmark, Norway and Sweden (Borre and Andersen 1997; Holmberg 1999).

[11] To be consistent with the studies in Klingemann and Fuchs (1995), we measured the statistical significance of trends based only on the small number of election survey time-points in each nation. The appendix to this chapter presents a more extensive discussion of the alternative ways to measure statistical significance in opinion survey series. In the appendix it is argued that using time-points as a single value is an extremely conservative way to measure of the significance of these trends.

[12] One common limitation of these surveys is their short length for many nations. If the American series had only started in 1976, for example, the marked drop in political trust would be less evident (or even invisible). The respective 1976–96 coefficients would be: trust (0.057), crooked (0.114), and don't care (− 0.714).

few parties and many, in federal systems and unitary states, the direction of change is the same.

Especially noteworthy are the specific patterns in Germany, Italy, and Japan. Political support generally grew during the post-war decades in these nations, as part of their successful democratic development. But then something caused these trends to reverse and trust eroded from its 1970s high points. In West Germany, for instance, political support increased between the 1950s and 1970s as democracy took root in the new Federal Republic. Germans became more supportive of political elites, more allegiant to political parties, and more supportive of the democratic process (Baker, Dalton, and Hildebrandt 1981; Conradt 1980). Then, trust in politicians decreased in the 1980s and even more in the 1990s. Using polling data from the Allensbach Institut, Hans Mathias Kepplinger (1996; 1998) traced the gradual rise and then decline in political trust in Germany over the post-war period (also see Scarrow 1996). Political support grew in the post-war decades also in Italy and Japan as democracy established itself, then the trend shifted and citizens in those countries became more cynical of government (see also Tanaka 2001). The fact that support trends *reversed* in these three nations suggests that some new force entered into the public's political calculus to erode political support.

The sharpest deviation from the pattern of declining trust is the Netherlands. The two longest Dutch opinion series, 'MPs don't care' and 'political parties are only interested in votes', show statistically significant improvements between 1971 and 1994. These are the only two statistically significant positive coefficients in the table. However, two of the three additional measures that are available for the 1977–94 period display a decline. We can speculate on why the Netherlands differs from other nations, but without further empirical evidence this will remain mere speculation.[13] Norway and Denmark also display a mixed pattern, which justified Listhaug's early caution. However, when we examine support measures across this larger set of nations, there is an obvious pattern of spreading public negativity towards politicians and the government.

Partisanship

The erosion of political loyalties is seen even more clearly in another measure of support for political authorities: party identification. The concept of party identification has such a prominent position in electoral research because scholars see

---

[13] I suspect that the Dutch time series begins too late to capture the stable period of Dutch politics before the end of pillarization and the realignment of the party system in the late 1960s (what would be equivalent to US opinion levels post-1974 as described in the preceding footnote). Rudy Andeweg (1992: 183), for instance, maintains that the Provo violence of 1965–6 damaged the legitimacy of government and authority more generally, and that these changes of public orientation occurred before the first Dutch election studies in the 1970s. Also, it is possible that the first time-point in 1971 reflects a sharp drop linked to the events of the late 1960s, similar to the US drop-off immediately after Watergate. But, without more extensive Dutch time series data, we cannot decide between these alternative explanations.

these orientations as key determinants of many different aspects of political behaviour. In terms of our research interests, partisanship encompasses a mix of elements. On the one hand, partisanship represents an affective feeling towards a political party that is generalized beyond the evaluations of a specific candidate. Partisanship measures not just whether individuals like a specific Democratic or Republican candidate, but whether they identify themselves as a Democrat or Republican based their general support of the party and its candidates. On the other hand, partisanship also taps normative attitudes regarding the role that political parties should play in the democratic system. Herbert Weisberg (1981) maintains that, as well as support for a specific party, feelings of party identification tap support for the *institution* of the party system in general.

Given the importance of partisanship in the literature on electoral behaviour, the first signs of weakening partisan attachments among the American public surprised many electoral scholars (Nie, Verba, and Petrocik 1979; Converse 1976). In 1952 a full 77 per cent of Americans expressed a partisan attachment; this proportion spiralled down to 59 per cent in the 2000 election. A similar trend seemed to occur in Britain and other European party systems (Dalton, Flanagan, and Beck 1984). These findings raised the question of whether there was a general decrease in partisanship—partisan dealignment—in advanced industrial democracies.

Previous cross-national research doubted that partisan dealignment was generally affecting the advanced industrial democracies (Schmitt and Holmberg 1995; Holmberg 1994). To reassess the evidence, I extended the time span and the cross-national breadth of the data that Schmitt and Holmberg analysed to include nineteen nations (also see Dalton 2000*b*).[14]

Our broader base of empirical evidence now presents a clear picture of partisan dealignment (Table 2.3). The second data column shows the trend in the percentage of the public identifying with any party. In seventeen of the nineteen nations, the regression slopes for overall party identification are negative—a striking consistency for such a diverse array of nations. For instance, 65 per cent of the Swedish public expressed party ties in 1968, compared with only 42 per cent in 1998. Similarly, all of the coefficients for the percentage of strong partisans are negative, albeit of different strength and statistical significance. The United States, Britain, and Sweden display the decrease in partisanship that has long been observed in the literature, and these cases are now joined by most other advanced industrial democracies. If party attachments reflect citizen support for the system of party-based representative government, then the simultaneous decline in party attachments in nearly all advanced industrial democracies offers a strong sign of the public's affective disengagement from political authorities.

---

[14] One reason for the difference from Schmitt and Holmberg (1995) is the inclusion of eight additional nations (Australia, Austria, Canada, Finland, Iceland, Japan, New Zealand, and the United States); partisanship decreases in each of these nations. In addition, extending the time series in several other nations strengthened the evidence of dealignment.

TABLE 2.3   *Trends in party identification*

Nation	% with PID	% identifiers		% strong identifiers		Period	Time-points (N)
		Per annum Δ	signif.	Per annum Δ	signif.		
Australia	92	−0.179	0.19	−0.593	0.00	1967–98	(8)
Austria	67	−0.916	0.00	−0.663	0.00	1969–99	(7)
Belgium*	50	0.090	0.60	−0.285	0.03	1975–99	(22)
Britain	93	−0.202	0.00	−0.882	0.00	1964–01	(10)
Canada	90	−0.386	0.05	−0.150	0.17	1965–97	(9)
Denmark	52	0.001	0.95	−0.207	0.36	1971–98	(9)
Finland	57	−0.293	0.49	−0.147	0.61	1975–91	(4)
France*	59	−0.712	0.00	−0.329	0.02	1975–99	(22)
Germany	78	−0.572	0.00	−0.573	0.00	1972–98	(8)
Iceland	80	−0.675	0.02	−0.250	0.05	1983–99	(5)
Ireland*	61	−1.510	0.00	−0.767	0.00	1978–99	(19)
Italy*	78	−0.979	0.00	−0.770	0.00	1978–99	(19)
Luxembourg*	61	−0.317	0.12	−0.316	0.00	1975–99	(22)
Japan	70	−0.589	0.00	n/a	n/a	1962–00	(12)
Netherlands	38	−0.329	0.13	−0.129	0.36	1971–98	(9)
New Zealand	87	−1.530	0.00	−1.270	0.00	1975–99	(9)
Norway	66	−0.542	0.06	−0.450	0.05	1965–97	(9)
Sweden	64	−0.733	0.00	−0.543	0.00	1968–98	(11)
United States	77	−0.370	0.00	−0.154	0.06	1952–00	(12)

Note: The % with party identification in the first column is the average of the % expressing an identification in the first two surveys in each series. The per annum change is the unstandardized regression coefficient; the significant level of the time coefficient is given in the following column.

Sources: Nations marked with an asterisk (*) are based on the Eurobarometer surveys and 1999 European Election Study; other nations are based on their respective national election studies.

Again, the striking pattern is the uniformity of the decline, across systems with different electoral systems, different numbers of parties, and different systems of party cleavages. Seldom is the public opinion evidence from such a diverse group of nations so consistent in following a general trend. The major variation is in the timing of the decline rather than the direction of the trend. Dealignment in the United States, Britain, and Sweden was a long-term and relatively steady process that moved partisanship to a lower baseline, and this baseline has remained relatively steady for the 1990s. In other instances, the changes have been more recent. For instance, partisanship in France and Ireland has eroded over the past two decades. German partisanship, which had previously strengthened during the post-war period, dropped off markedly for the elections in the 1990s, although initial signs of dealignment existed in the late 1980s. The collapse of the Progressive Conservatives (PC) and New Democratic Party (NDP) in the 1993 Canadian elections similarly accentuated a dealignment trend in Canadian politics. The dealignment trend in Japan and Austria also accelerated in the 1990s in response to the breakdown of political consensus in both nations.

Questions about party identification are the most reliable and valid measure of party attachments, but a variety of other data reaffirm the patterns described here. The richest data source is the American National Election Studies. Responses from the open-ended 'likes and dislikes' questions suggest that Americans are less likely to focus on political parties in discussing contemporary politics, and when parties are mentioned the references are increasingly neutral toward *both* parties (Wattenberg 1996). Feeling thermometer ratings of the two parties have also declined over time, as have general beliefs that political parties are responsive to the public's interests. Furthermore, Wattenberg (1996: ch. 7) shows that there is a clear generational component to these changing orientations, so that these trends are likely to continue.

Greater scepticism and doubts about political parties seem to be a common development in other advanced industrial democracies.[15] A Gallup question found that only 30 per cent of Canadians expressed quite a lot of confidence in political parties in general in 1979—already a fairly low level of support—and this drops to only 11 per cent in 1996. Enmid surveys show that the proportion of Germans who express confidence in the political parties has decreased from 43 per cent in 1979 to only 26 per cent in 1993 (Rieger 1994: 462). Surveys in both Germany and Austria find that public confidence ratings of political parties are at the bottom of a list of diverse social and political institutions (IPOS 1995; Plasser and Ulram 1991: 35). The recent restructuring of the party and electoral systems in Italy, Japan, and New Zealand were accompanied by feelings of antipathy toward the political parties (Bardi 1996; Vowles and Aimer 1994). For example, in 1983 Japanese trust in parties reached a highpoint; 70 per cent felt that political parties help people's voice be heard—by 2001 this had decreased to 21 per cent (Tanaka 2001). Similarly, the British public has become significantly less trusting of political parties and politicians (Webb 1996; Curtice and Jowell 1995). There is similar evidence of extensive public dissatisfaction with Norwegian and Swedish political parties (Strøm and Svåsand 1997; Holmberg 1999). More generally, in autumn 2000 the Eurobarometer 54 study found that confidence in political parties averaged only 18 per cent across the European Union, far below the average confidence levels of sixteen social and political institutions examined in the survey.[16] Indeed, very few scholars today argue that public support for political parties and the structure of party government is increasing in their nation of specialization.

SUPPORT FOR THE REGIME

Increasing public scepticism about politicians and political authorities appears to be a common development in many advanced industrial democracies, but political

---

[15] In addition to the evidence cited below, the 'parties are only interested in my vote' question in Table 2.2 measures public orientations towards political parties (in Austria, Britain, France, the Netherlands, Norway, and Sweden).

[16] The autumn 1997 Eurobarometer yielded comparable results.

scientists disagree on whether these opinions reflect doubts about political authorities or more fundamental questions about the political institutions and the democratic process. For example, Arthur Miller (1974*a*; 1974*b*) and Jack Citrin (1974) debated the initial evidence of decreasing trust in government in the United States. To Miller, these data signalled the spread of political alienation and discontent with the institutions of government; Citrin argued that these trends primarily represented a disenchantment with the incumbents of government offices and recent governmental performance. Therefore, I sought data that clearly focused on trust in government and especially trust in the institutions of the democratic regime. One common measure assesses broad public images of government:

Would you say the government is pretty much run by a few big interests looking out for themselves or that it is run for the benefit of all the people?

This question is frequently asked in national election studies and in several recent large cross-national survey projects.

Figure 2.3 presents these images of government in the 1970s and 1990s for eight nations. The spread of negative sentiments is very apparent. For instance, in the mid-1970s (even after a decade of student protests and the onslaughts of the Red Army Faktion) only a third of the Germans thought that government was run by big interests; by the mid-1990s this proportion had doubled. The modest change in the US occurred only because these beliefs in government had already experienced their major decline before the 1975 survey used in the table.[17] With a single exception (Britain), over the past twenty years contemporary publics have become less likely to believe that the government is run for their interest.

We can be more precise in measuring images of governing institutions. A common series of questions asks about confidence in specific institutions of government. Some of the longest and most extensive time series are again found in the United States. One survey question asks respondents how much confidence they have in specific institutions, such as the courts, parliament, and major social groups (labour unions, business associations, and the press). In the mid-1960s a large proportion of Americans expressed a great deal of confidence in the Supreme Court, the executive branch, and Congress. Confidence dropped dramatically by the early 1970s, and slid further for the executive and Congress over the next two decades (Figure 2.4). (Interestingly, the least partisan and least political institution, the Supreme Court, has generally retained the public's confidence over this same period.) By 2000, barely a tenth of the American public had a great deal of confidence in the people running the White House or Congress—certainly a dramatic statement of Americans' dissatisfaction with government. Similarly, time series from the American National Election Studies

---

[17] The American National Election Study indicates that the proportion believing government was run by big interests increased from 29% in the 1964 election study to 66% in the 1974 survey.

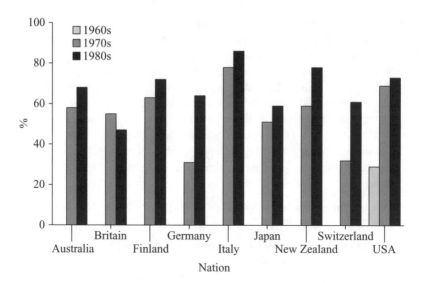

FIG. 2.3. Belief that government is run for the benefit of a few big interests

Source: For most nations, 1974–5 Political Action Survey and 1995–8 World Values Survey; Japan, Japanese National Election Studies; New Zealand, first time-point is from 1985 Study of Values; United States, 1964 American National Election Study.

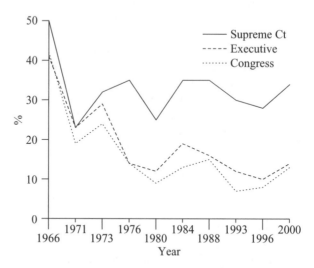

FIG. 2.4. Confidence in American political institutions, 1966–2000

Note: Figure entries are the % expressing a 'great deal' of confidence.

Source: Harris and General Social Survey Polls.

show a trend of decreasing belief that parties, elections, and the government are responsive to the public's interests (Dalton 2002: ch. 12). Americans' dissatisfaction with government now extends beyond just the incumbents in office to the institutions themselves.[18]

Comparable long-term cross-national data on trust in political institutions are less frequent and extensive than measures of trust in politicians or partisanship.[19] If we focus on a key institution of representative democracy—parliament—there are considerable data from multiple sources. Table 2.4 presents trends in confidence in parliament for seventeen advanced industrial democracies. Where possible, we use national opinion survey series because these tend to cover a longer time span with more frequent measurements; when such data are not available, I track confidence in parliament based on the four World Values Surveys. Each of the six long-term national series—Britain, Canada, Germany, New Zealand, Sweden, and the United States—displays a substantial drop in confidence in the national legislature.[20] For instance, 48 per cent of the British public expressed quite a lot of confidence in the House of Commons in 1985, compared with only 24 per cent in 1995. A majority (51 per cent) of Swedes expressed confidence in the Riksdag in 1986—even though this postdates Swedes' trend of decreasing political trust—and by 1996 only 19 per cent had confidence in parliament. There are four different data series available for the US Congress, and each depicts the same pattern of decline (also see Hibbing and Theiss-Morse 1995). The less frequent World Values Survey (WVS) time series that is available in most nations reflects this same pattern of decreasing confidence, even though this series begins in 1980 after political support had already dropped precipitously in several nations.

There is a contemporary malaise in the political spirit involving the three key elements of representative democracy (what I will refer to as the three Ps): politicians, political parties, and parliament. Moreover, this is not a temporary disenchantment with the present government or the present sets of political candidates.

---

[18] Confidence has not decreased in all political institutions: a point I will examine more closely in a subsequent chapter. For instance, data from Gallup and the Pew Research Center for the People and the Press (1998*a*) show that trust in state and local government increased between 1972 and 1987, suggesting a transfer of political support. In addition, 1987–97 comparisons from the Pew Center find that favourable attitudes towards most specific federal agencies also increased over time. The two noticeable exceptions to these trends were the FBI and Internal Revenue Service, which both suffered from critical external reviews in the later 1990s.

[19] Ola Listhaug and Matti Wiberg (1995) described the decline in confidence in government institutions in Europe using the 1980 and 1990 waves of the World Values Survey (WVS). This trend has continued in most cases where data from the World Values Survey in the mid-1990s are available (also Klingemann 1999). But since the fourth wave of the WVS did not include all these items, and the 1995–8 time-point is available for only a handful of nations, we do not present these data here.

[20] SOFRES, the French public opinion firm, asked a more dramatic question on parliamentary support. In 1988, a full 66% of the French public thought it would be a serious issue if the National Assembly were eliminated; by 1994 only 39% shared this opinion (SOFRES 1996: 182)!

TABLE 2.4   *Trends in confidence in Parliament*

Nation	Per annum change	Period	Source (N)
Australia			
Parliament	−1.667	1981–96	WVS (2)
Belgium			
Parliament	0.055	1981–99	WVS (3)
Britain			
Parliament	−2.399*	1981–96	Gallup (8)
Parliament	−0.222	1981–99	WVS (3)
Canada			
Parliament	−1.152*	1979–96	CIPO (8)
Parliament	−0.385	1981–96	WVS (3)
Denmark			
Parliament	0.722*	1981–99	WVS(3)
Finland			
Parliament	−1.476	1981–99	WVS (4)
France			
Parliament	−0.833*	1981–99	WVS (3)
Germany			
Parliament	−0.896*	1984–99	IPOS (12)
Parliament	−1.206	1981–99	WVS (4)
Iceland			
Parliament	1.026	1984–99	WVS (3)
Ireland			
Parliament	−1.056	1981–99	WVS (3)
Italy			
Parliament	0.222	1981–99	WVS (3)
Japan			
Parliament	−1.422	1976–2001	JES (6)
Parliament	−0.302	1981–2000	WVS (4)
Netherlands			
Parliament	0.500	1981–99	WVS (3)
New Zealand			
Parliament	−1.386*	1975–93	Heylen Polls (11)
Norway			
Parliament	−0.533	1982–96	WVS (3)
Sweden			
Parliament	−2.242*	1986–96	SOM (10)
Parliament	0.111	1981–99	WVS (4)
United States			
Congress	−0.507*	1966–2000	Harris/GSS (22)
Congress	−0.917*	1973–97	Gallup (19)
Congress	−0.942	1981–2000	WVS (4)
Congress	−0.499*	1966–98	Harris (27)

Note: Table entries are the per annum change in the % expressing a great deal or quite a lot of confidence in each institution. The per annum change is the unstandardized regression coefficient.
* Per annum changes significant at the 0.05 level.

Sources: The WVS data are from the 1981–3, 1990–4, 1995–8, and 1999–2001 World Values Survey. Other data are from individual national survey series: CIPO, Canadian Institution of Public Opinion. IPOS, Institut für praxisorientierte Sozialforschung. JES, Japanese Election Studies. SOM, SOM Institut.

In many instances these patterns have persisted over several decades and across changes in government administrations. Moreover, the cross-national breadth of this pattern suggests it is a general feature of contemporary politics in advanced industrial democracies, not the specific experience of only a few nations. Thus, these trends lead us to ask how far the public disenchantment reaches: does it touch core beliefs in democracy and commitments to the democratic process?

REGIME NORMS AND PROCEDURES

Broader and more fundamental measures of regime support include orientations towards the norms and procedures of the political regime. These orientations tap evaluations of system performance (the left cell in the third row of Table 2.1). We measured these feelings with a relatively long time series on satisfaction with the functioning of the democratic process.[21] Previous research is divided on whether this is a measure of specific or diffuse support (for example, Fuchs, Guidorossi, and Svensson 1995; Canache, Mondak, and Seligson 2001). I believe that the question's wording leads respondents to treat this as an evaluative measure, mixing regime judgements and evaluations of the political incumbents. In short, I interpret this item as measuring specific support because it emphasizes system performance.

Figure 2.5 presents the time trend for the member nations of the European Union. Averaged across these nations, it appears that satisfaction with the functioning of democracy was fairly stable from the early 1970s to the late 1980s. As Fuchs and Klingemann (1995) note, however, satisfaction drops off significantly in the early 1990s. Subsequent data show that these lower levels of political satisfaction continued to the end of the decade. In the 1998 Eurobarometer survey, a plurality of Europeans (48 per cent) said they were dissatisfied with the workings of the democratic process in their nation—not a result that should encourage pride and a sense of self-respect among politicians.

Frankly, it is difficult to interpret this satisfaction measure because so many factors are potentially involved in such systemic judgements. Individuals may be satisfied with democracy as a process despite their growing cynicism of politicians and the institutions of representative democracy. The substantial changes in the process of democratic politics over this period—expanding citizen involvement and new forms of public input—may counterbalance dissatisfaction with other elements of the process. Alternatively, dissatisfaction with the working of the democratic process may reflect some of the same dynamics as candidate evaluations: if individuals are dissatisfied with the incumbents, they vote them out at the next election, and this, it is hoped, renews satisfaction with the process.

Despite these caveats, regime evaluations have diminished in the past decade for European democracies, but the long-term trend in these opinions is

---

[21] The specific question asks: 'On the whole, are you very satisfied, fairly satisfied, not very satisfied, or not at all satisfied with the way democracy works (in R's country)?' Sometimes the question includes a prompt referring to the functioning of political parties.

Changing Citizen Orientations

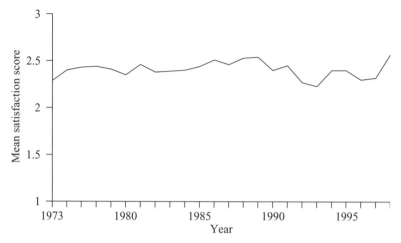

FIG. 2.5. Satisfaction with the working of the democratic process, 1973–1999

Note: Figure combines the Euro-six (Belgium, France, Germany, Italy, Luxembourg, and the Netherlands) weighted by population size. It represents the mean score of the satisfaction with democracy question, coded so that 1 = not at all satisfied, 4 = very satisfied.

Sources: European Community surveys and Eurobarometer surveys, 1973–99.

relatively flat. (It would be preferable to have a measure of democratic performance that began earlier in time to see whether other changes predate the Eurobarometer series.)

Even more important are public orientations towards the principles of the democratic process. In earlier periods, public dissatisfaction with politicians or the workings of the democratic process often led to (or arose from) disenchantment with democracy. This was the case with the democratic challenges of the inter-war period (Linz and Stepan 1978). Even during the immediate post-war period, dissatisfaction with democracy was often focused among anti-democratic extremists on the left or right (Powell 1982).

Unfortunately, diffuse or affective measures of support for democratic norms and procedures are relatively scarce, especially time series data. To the extent that such data are available, they suggest that support for political rights and participatory norms have actually grown over the past generation. For instance, the available long-term data suggest that contemporary publics have become more politically tolerant during the post-war period (Thomassen 1995; McCloskey and Brill 1983). The expansion of democratic rights to women, racial and ethnic minorities, and homosexuals has profoundly changed the politics of advanced industrial democracies within the span of a generation. At least in principle, there is widespread public endorsement of the political values and norms that underlie the democratic process.

In addition, there is at least indirect evidence that perceptions of the citizens' role now emphasize a more participatory style and a greater willingness to challenge authority. Inglehart's (1990; 1997*a*) research on postmaterial value change—with its emphasis on participatory values as a measure of postmaterialism—reinforces these points. Inglehart finds growing emphasis on political and social participation as core value priorities. Contemporary publics expect to participate in the democratic process, and political interest has increased over time (Dalton and Wattenberg 2000: ch. 3).

However, data on cross-national and cross-temporal public orientations towards the democratic process are limited. It would be extremely valuable to expand future data collections to focus on public norms regarding how the democratic process should function.

SUPPORT FOR DEMOCRACY

Many of the survey questions analysed so far have measured support for the incumbents or institutions of the democratic process, or could be interpreted in these terms. One might argue that dissatisfaction with politicians, parties, and even parliaments is a sign of the vitality of democracy (or an objective reading of politics by the public). If there is a crisis of democracy, this dissatisfaction must have been generalized to the political regime and its principles.

There is an abundance of empirical data on public attitudes toward democracy—the next level of political support. For example, a frequently used opinion survey asked whether democracy was considered the best form of government. Although there is no long cross-national time series for this question, the presently high degree of support suggests there has not been a major erosion in these sentiments (Table 2.5).[22] On average, more than three-quarters of the public feel that democracy is the best form of government even if it has its problems. Moreover, in comparison with a Eurobarometer survey of the late 1980s, support for democratic government has increased in most West European nations (also see Klingemann 1999; Fuchs, Guidorossi, and Svensson 1995). Another question in this survey was less evaluative and demonstrates that support for the idea of democracy is nearly universal within Western democracies.

---

[22] The two questions were as follows: 'I'm going to describe various types of political systems and ask what you think about each as a way of governing this country. For each one, would you say it is a very good, fairly good, fairly bad or very bad way of governing this country: Having a democratic system?' 'I'm going to read off some things that people sometimes say about a democratic political system. Could you please tell me if you agree strongly, agree, disagree or disagree strongly, after I read each one of them: Democracy may have problems but it's better than any other form of government?'

TABLE 2.5   *Support for democracy (per cent)*

Nation	Approve of idea of democracy	Democracy best form of government
Austria	96	97
Belgium	91	92
Britain	87	78
Canada	87	87
Denmark	98	99
Finland	88	90
France	89	93
Germany (West)	95	97
Iceland	98	97
Ireland	92	93
Italy	97	94
Japan	92	92
Luxembourg	92	95
Netherlands	97	86
Sweden	97	94
United States	89	87

Sources: 2000–2 World Values Survey; 1999 European Values Survey.

Another measure taps democratic principles by asking whether society should be changed by revolutionary action.[23] Table 2.6 provides time series data from eight nations. These data span the oil shocks and resulting economic crises of the mid-1970s and early 1980s, periods of political violence, challenges from new social movements, and the miscellaneous political scandals described in this chapter. Nevertheless, since the early 1970s, support for revolutionary social change represents a mere trace element in each nation. Indeed, support for improving society through gradual reforms is consistently the most preferred response in each nation.

If I shift our attention to affective orientations, there is limited cross-national evidence on the democratic values and norms of contemporary publics. A long series of German public opinion surveys, as one example, shows broad popular support for the principles of self-determination, participation, and free expression that underlie the democratic process (Dalton 1994; Kaase and Pfetsch 1992). Recent cross-national surveys of the advanced industrial democracies similarly display general consensus on most democratic principles, such as support for a free press or a multiparty system (for example, Pew Research Center 1991).

[23] The question wording is as follows: 'On this card are three basic kinds of attitudes concerning the society we live in. Please choose the one which best describes your own opinion: (1) The entire way our society is organized must be radically changed by revolutionary action, (2) Our society must be gradually improved by reforms, and (3) Our present society must be valiantly defended against all subversive forces.'

TABLE 2.6 *Attitudes toward social change*

	US			Germany			France		Belgium		Italy		Netherlands		Canada			Japan		
	1981	1990	1999	1970	1990	1995	1970	1990	1970	1990	1970	1990	1970	1990	1981	1990	1999	1981	1990	1999
Change society by revolutionary action	5	6	8	2	2	2	5	4	3	4	7	7	6	2	4	4	7	2	1	4
Improve society through reforms	66	67	71	70	59	84	78	70	69	65	73	79	74	70	67	74	69	42	48	65
Defend society against subversives	20	11	15	20	28	12	12	20	14	18	10	9	15	23	19	12	16	15	13	12
No opinion	9	11	6	8	11	2	5	7	13	14	9	5	5	6	10	9	8	41	22	20

Note: Table entries are the distribution of opinion on the attitudes towards social change question.

Sources: 1970 European Community Survey; 1981–3, 1990–1, 1995–8, 1999–2001 World Values Survey.

SUPPORT FOR THE POLITICAL COMMUNITY

This section examines feelings toward the political community. Identification with the political community is the most fundamental of political identities—to think of oneself as American or British predates specific political identities, such as party or ideological ties. Almond and Verba (1963) described these feelings as 'system affect', a strong emotional attachment to the nation that presumably provides a reservoir of diffuse support that can maintain a political system through temporary periods of political stress.

One can imagine that these sentiments have not been immune to the dissatisfactions that have affected other aspects of political support. Expressions of patriotism seem less common, and more anachronistic, than they did a generation ago. Growing emphasis on multiculturalism in many societies raises questions about the breadth and depth of a common national identity. In Europe, the development of European Union attachments may weaken national identities. A decline in national identities would spell a crisis for the nation state, and not just a crisis of the political system.

One measure of such feelings involves pride in one's nation.[24] Table 2.7 displays the percentage who feel proud of their nation for a set of advanced industrial democracies.[25] National pride is common in most nations, since such identities are essential to citizenship. The United States is often the apparent international leader in expressions of national pride at Olympic events and other settings, but these sentiments are shared by many other democracies. In contrast, the Germans and Japanese are somewhat hesitant in their statements of national pride, which I attribute to the lingering reaction to the nationalist extremism associated with the Second World War.

Beyond these cross-national variations, it is apparent that national pride has not eroded over the last two decades.[26] Indeed, the most recent World Values Survey/European Values Survey suggests that national pride is generally growing, which is surprising given the high baseline of opinions in the first survey in the series. When longer time series are available for specific nations, they too show a pattern of relative stability or growth in national pride over time (for example, Topf, Mohler, and Heath 1989). In fact, the post-war nation-building process in

---

[24] I want to thank David Easton for pointing out that what might be occurring is not the decline of national identities but the addition of new identities (to regions, Europe, or social collectives) or the nesting of multiple identities that may exist somewhat separately from national loyalties.

[25] The question asked: 'How proud are you to be (nationality)? 'The responses were:' (1) very proud, (2) quite proud, (3) not very proud, and (4) not at all proud.' The figure presents the 'proud' and 'very proud' responses.

[26] Inglehart (1990: 411) describes a very large drop in national pride between 1970 and 1980 for a subset of European nations. This trend is not mentioned in Inglehart's most recent analysis of national pride trends (1997a: 304–5). Because of the dramatic change across differences in survey organizations, I am cautious about the 1970–80 comparisons. In addition, trends by the same survey organization within some of these nations fail to show a similar trend (see for example Institut für Demoskopie 1993).

TABLE 2.7 *Feelings of national pride*

Nation	1981–4	1990–3	1995–8	1999–2001	Change
Australia	98	n/a	97	n/a	−1
Austria	n/a	83	n/a	92	+9
Belgium*	79	82	74	84	+5
Britain*	88	89	85	89	+1
Canada	95	94	n/a	95	0
Denmark*	75	87	87	93	+18
Finland	85	83	89	94	+9
France*	80	87	75	90	+10
Germany (West)	65	68	58	66	+1
Iceland	92	95	n/a	98	+6
Ireland	94	98	96	98	+4
Italy*	80	88	83	88	+8
Japan	64	66	62	59	−5
Netherlands*	64	77	73	80	+16
Norway	77	83	89	n/a	+15
Sweden	73	84	89	87	+14
Switzerland	n/a	82	78	n/a	−4
United States	97	98	98	96	−1

Notes: Table entries are the % who feel proud or very proud of their nation. Missing data are not included in the calculation of percentages. Nations marked by an asterisk (*) use Eurobarometer 42 (December 1994) for the 1995–8 time point.

Sources: 1981–4, 1990–3, 1995–8, and 1999–2001 World Values Surveys; 1999–2000 European Values Survey.

several Western democracies has led to increasing national attachments in nations such as Austria and Canada (Ulram 1994: 91; Kornberg and Clarke 1992: 107). As one would expect from affective feelings of community attachment, these sentiments generally have proved relatively impervious to the erosion in political support affecting other orientations in these nations.

DISSATISFIED DEMOCRATS

By some measures, this may be considered the golden age of democracy. At the beginning of the twenty-first century, more nations in the world have become, or strive to be, democracies than at any other point in human history. Furthermore, most of the political ideologies that once stood as major rivals to democracy, such as fascism and communism, have seemingly lost their legitimacy and general appeal. Democracy has brought peace, freedom, and prosperity to the peoples of the nations we are studying. Thus, many scholars, including some who have previously forecast the demise of democracy, now herald its accomplishments (Huntington 1991; Fukuyama 1992).

Why, then, have many citizens in advanced industrial societies become disenchanted with their democratic processes? We find that citizens have grown more distant from political parties, more critical of political elites and political institutions, and less positive toward government—this points to fundamental changes in the political orientations of democratic publics over the past generation. Our findings contrast with the sanguine conclusion of Fuchs and Klingemann (1995) summarized at the beginning of this chapter, who argued that public sentiments towards the state were not changing. Our empirical analyses yield very different results.[27] Today there is a scepticism of the political spirit affecting almost all advanced industrial democracies.

The general pattern of these trends varies across the objects of political support. The decline in political support is most dramatic for evaluations of politicians and political elites. The deference to authority that once was common in many Western democracies has partially been replaced by public scepticism towards elites. Ronald Inglehart (1999) argues, in a theory that will be tested in Chapter 5, that changing public values are generally reducing support for authority of all types, and politics is included in this process.

Feelings of mistrust have gradually broadened to include evaluations of political institutions. Political parties are considered the key institutions of democratic politics. So strong is this belief that E. E. Schattschneider (1942) coined the oft-repeated maxim: 'modern democracy is unthinkable save in terms of political parties'. Yet affective attachments to political parties are weakening in almost all contemporary democracies, and confidence in political parties as institutions is also declining. Moreover, these sentiments are carried over to parliaments and the institutions of representative government more generally. Taken together, contemporary publics are losing faith in the central agents of representative democracy: political elites, political parties, and parliaments.

Although virtually all of these time series show a downward trend, the specific trajectories differ. The decline came early in some nations, later in other. In some cases the trend emerged slowly but steadily, in others the change was more abrupt. There also is not a single inflection point in these trends, such as the turbulent period of the late 1960s and early 1970s. The national literatures often link the trends to the unique historical experiences of the nation.[28] In Britain, for

---

[27] The evidence available to Klingemann and Fuchs indicated declines in party identifications in only 8 of 14 nations (1995: 430); the updated and expanded data document declines in 17 of 19 nations. Similarly, while they found a 2–2 split in the trends for trust in politicians (1995: 430), I document declines in at least 13 of 15 nations.

[28] We have not cited the specific literature of each nation, but interested readers should consider these case studies: Australia (Bean 1999; McAllister 1992), Austria (Ulram 1994; 2000; Pelinka, Plasser, and Meizner 2000), Britain (Curtice and Jowell 1995; 1997; Webb 1996; Bromley, Curtice, and Seyd 2002), Canada (Kornberg and Clarke 1992; Clarke, Kornberg, and Wearing 2000), Denmark (Borre and Anderson 1997; Listhaug 1995), Finland (Borg and Sänkiaho 1995), France (Mayer 2000), Germany (Kepplinger 1996; 1998; Fuchs 1999), Iceland (Hardarson 1995), Italy (Della Porta 2000; Morlino and Tarchi 1996; Bardi 1996), Japan (Pharr 1997; 2000), New Zealand (Bean 1999; Vowles and Aimer 1994; Karp and Bowler 2001), Norway (Strøm and Svåsand 1997; Listaug 1995; Miller and Listaug 1990), and Sweden (Holmberg 1999).

example, the decline is linked to the economic struggles of the nation; in Canada it is linked to the fractious regional conflict; in Austria to the collapse of the Social-Liberal consensus. These characteristics might argue against a common cause, but I think this would be a mistake. The closest analogy might be water flowing off a mountain: a constant force is pulling it down, but the specific course depends on local context. The important factor is not that the downward course follows different routes, but that gravity is everywhere having an influence. Our question is what the political equivalent is of this gravitational force.

I also expect that in some nations these trends may be reversed in a recent election or public opinion poll. Indeed, it would be unwise for politicians to ignore these trends in public opinion, and at least some political figures will attempt to reverse them.[29] Moreover, although the statistics in this chapter often plot linear trends, I do not expect that these are linear and certain trends. The Reagan administration, for example, consciously (but temporarily) increased the political confidence of Americans, and there is evidence of such temporary trend reversals in other nations. Yet I suspect that such trend reversals may represent only short-term deviations from the general trend. Since political trust is decreasing in most advanced industrial societies, this is likely due to factors that go beyond a single political leader or a single administration. To really alter systemic trends, systemic changes may be required in the polity or the political system.

The clearest example of such a systemic change is Americans' reaction to the September 11, 2001, terrorist attacks. Although I had decided to end the analyses of this book with data from 2000, public reactions the terrorist attacks on the World Trade Center and the Pentagon merit consideration. In an epilogue to this chapter, I review the data on how these events affected political support. Briefly stated, there was a dramatic surge in support following the terrorist attacks as Americans rallied to their government in this time of crisis. But over time sentiments have begun regressing back to their pre-9/11 levels. Even the horrific assault by terrorists did not substantially change Americans' image of their politicians and political institutions. Thus it is unclear what would be required to return sentiments to the support levels of the 1960s. At the same time, our overall findings are significant in identifying attitudes that have *not* changed across the advanced industrial democracies. Even though contemporary publics express decreasing confidence in democratic politicians, parties, and parliaments, these sentiments have not carried over to the democratic principles and goals of these regimes. Most people remain committed to the democratic ideal; if anything, these sentiments have apparently strengthened as satisfaction with the actuality of democratic politics has decreased. Hans-Dieter Klingemann (1999) notes that

---

[29] It is also clear that some politicians and political groups recognize these trends and are acting in ways that contribute to growing public scepticism (Fried and Harris 2001). One example is the tendency for members of the US Congress to run against Congress at election time, criticizing the institution while asking the voters to return them to Washington to counter the sins of other members of Congress.

'dissatisfied democrats'—dissatisfied with political institutions but supportive of democratic principles—is now a common attitudinal pattern in advanced industrial democracies. Pippa Norris (1999*b*: 269) similarly concludes that recent data 'indicates the emergence of more "critical citizens, who value democracy as an ideal yet who remain dissatisfied with the performance of their political system, and particularly the core institutions of representative government"'. As citizens are criticizing the incumbents of government, they are simultaneously expressing support for the democratic creed. This makes the present situation distinct from earlier historical periods, such as the Weimar Republic or other fascist movements of the interwar period, when dissatisfaction with democratic politicians and political institutions signified a deeper dissatisfaction with democratic norms and procedures. In *The Crisis of Democracy*, Michel Crozier (1975: 47) offered an observation that also fits our empirical findings:

> What is at stake, therefore, is not the democratic creed and the Christian ethos, which are less directly threatened than they were for example in the thirties, but the contradiction between these core political beliefs and the principles of action that could make it possible to implement them.

Lipset and Schneider (1987: 22) stressed this same theme in their study of political support.

One of the main goals of this volume is to understand this new type of critical citizen, who is dissatisfied with the democratic process but who remains strongly committed to democratic values and ideals. What factors account for these changes in citizen orientations towards the state, and what are the consequences of these patterns of opinion? Much has been written on both points, but often without the empirical evidence to judge between rival theories.

In answering these questions, we must realize that this pattern is common across a wide range of advanced industrial societies. We can take perverse assurance in the finding that the negative trend in America (or most other OECD nations) is not a unique failing of our home nation. The problems of decreasing political support are shared by democracies in Europe, North America, and the Pacific. At the same time, this should be a cause of concern. The problems of decreasing support are not limited to the impact of Watergate or Vietnam (or the specific problems cited in the respective national literature), but seem to reflect general forces that are affecting most advanced industrial democracies. This suggests that the causes may reach deeper than, and go beyond the actions of, any one national government.

To understand the meanings of these trends, the subsequent chapters in this book will examine different theories to explain them, and thereby increase our understanding of their political implications. Thus, I will join the ongoing debate on the vitality of contemporary democracy. We know that citizen orientations towards the polity have changed; now we must seek the causes and consider the consequences of these trends.

EPILOGUE: AMERICAN REACTIONS TO
SEPTEMBER 11, 2001

Americans, and most of the world, watched their televisions with horror as the two jetliners crashed into the World Trade Center on the morning of September 11, 2001. The shock worsened as the reports came in that the Pentagon had also been hit. Then the first tower collapsed, and then the second. This was not reality, it must be a movie or a television special-effects spectacular—but it was real.

Thousands died that day, more than from the attack on Pearl Harbor that launched American involvement in the Second World War, and millions of Americans were touched directly by the events. In the face of the crisis, and the threat to America, the nation united in a way that had not been seen in decades. Robert Putnam (2002*b*) wrote that 'almost instantly, we rediscovered our friends, our neighbors, our public institutions, and our shared fate'. Americans sought out ways to help New Yorkers and others affected by the events. Donation bins appeared in stores and shops; the media ran advertisements for donations to the police and fire departments and other organizations; restaurants banded together to offer contributions from dinners purchased during 'help New York' nights; children and schools collected money and cards for those in need; and more. Thus, Putnam (2002*b*) concluded that Americans were starting to come together again, reversing the long trend of social isolation and disengagement that he had documented in his earlier research: 'As 2001 ended, Americans were more united, readier for collective sacrifice, and more attuned to public purpose than we have been for several decades.'

Public images of government also shifted abruptly. The sense of suffering that followed the terrorist attacks on New York and Washington was felt by nearly all Americans. In addition, the nation faced a foreign enemy, an experience that both drew us closer to one another and provided an obvious rationale for governmental action. And in the wake of September 11, the government acted and acted effectively. President Bush soothed the nation through his words and the memorial services for those who died in the attacks. His appearance at Ground Zero in New York City also captured the emotions of most Americans, in recognizing the victims and articulating America's self-confidence in this time of crisis. Debates about the need for government or the performance of government faded, since the need for governmental action was more obvious than perhaps at any time since the Second World War. And the successful campaign in Afghanistan demonstrated that the United States was a formidable power.

It also quickly became clear that these events were changing Americans' image of their government. The *Washington Post* conducted a public opinion survey in late September (the reporting date was 9/27) and found that, for the first time in three decades, a majority of Americans said they trusted the federal government to 'do what is right'. Several pundits immediately saw this as a fundamental change in public images of government. One claimed that 'this is a watershed event resulting in a true shift in public opinion. I think this is ... more likely to be a long-term change'; another opined 'these events should have a positive effect on attitudes toward government, a galvanizing effect, bringing people together and showing them the relevance of government' (cited in Morin and Deane 2001). Other analysts were more cautious.

If the world did change fundamentally after September 11—or at least Americans' images of government and the world—then this would alter the basic findings of this volume. Thus, in this epilogue we extend the analyses of the project to examine American opinions following September 11, and then draw out the implications for the themes of this project.

Public Reactions

The first evidence of change came from the *Washington Post*'s replication of the standard trust in government question (Morin and Deane 2001). This question was quickly replicated by the *New York Times*' poll, which has a denser data collection over the last two decades. As Figure 2.6 illustrates, there was a sudden and dramatic surge in political trust. Only 31 per cent of Americans trusted the government to do right in the *New York Times* poll of January 2001, and this jumped to 55 per cent in early October.

Other commercial and academic polls found the same pattern: Americans' trust in their government had soared to heights not seen in over a generation.

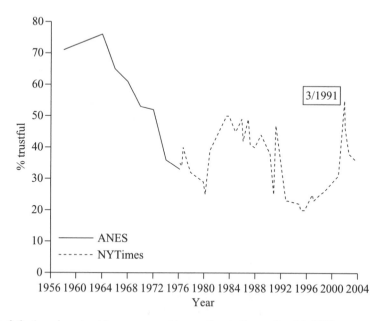

FIG. 2.6. American trust in government in reaction to September 11, 2001
Sources: American National Election Studies, 1958–76; *New York Times*, 1976–2003.

Moreover, these attitudes broadened to other objects of political support. The National Opinion Research Center (NORC) found that the percentage expressing great confidence in Congress and the Executive Branch increased more than four-fold (Smith, Rasinski, and Toce 2001).[30] Similarly, even though Americans already ranked high in national pride, all the NORC indicators of pride in nation increased after September 11.

Indeed, these were amazing times in America. Individuals who had never owned an American flag purchased one, and displayed it on their car or home in an act of national solidarity. By one account, Walmart stores sold 6,400 US flags on September 11, 2000—and 116,000 on September 11 a year later. Putnam (2002*b*) replicated measures of personal trust and social engagement from his 2000 survey, and found a growing sense of community among Americans. The outpouring of contributions to 9/11 charities was unprecedented, and the individual acts of courage—by New York firefighters and police, and average New Yorkers—became a balm in these times of national pain.

But, from the outset, other analysts cautioned that earlier bursts in political support following crisis events had been temporary—even if a truly comparable event did not exist. Perhaps the most insightful findings came from an ABC News poll, which asked Americans to distinguish between their images of government on national security issues an on social issues (G. Langer 2002*a*). In January 2002 the ABC poll found that 68 per cent of Americans trusted the government to deal with national security issues, but only 38 per cent trusted the government on social issues. Langer concludes that

people have not changed nearly as much as their frame of reference has changed. It seems likely that before September 11th people assessed the government chiefly in terms of social policy, an area in which trust was low, and still is. Today, however, more people are focused on national security, an area in which trust runs high.[31]

With the passage of time, and the return of politics to the 'normal' patterns of debate and competition, political support has regressed. By January 2002, trust in government dropped by 9 per cent in the *New York Times* poll, by mid-year it had fallen a further 8 per cent (Figure 2.6). The *Washington Post* poll, the Gallup Poll,

---

[30] The following comparisons are based on the 2000 General Social Survey, the NORC survey in October 2001, and spring 2002 GSS (see Smith, Rasinski, and Toce 2001).

Great confidence in:	2000	2001	2002
Congress	12.7%	43.4%	13.1%
Executive branch	13.5%	51.5%	27.4%
The military	39.7%	77.4%	54.8%

[31] In Chapter 7 we suggest that one factor eroding political support is the fragmentation of political interests, which makes it difficult for government to address public policy preferences in a manner that fulfils most people's policy preferences. The exceptional focus on national security issues after September 11, and the corresponding increase in political support, illustrate the workings of this process in reverse.

and other opinion series tracked a similar decrease in Americans' confidence in their government (Morin 2002; Hetherington and Nelson 2003; *The Economist* 2002).The General Social Survey also found a sharp drop in confidence in government institutions by the spring of 2002—evaluations of Congress were within a percentage point of their 2000 reading.[32] The most common reference standard is the time trend from the American National Election Study. In the post-election survey in 2002, trust in government was approximately 10 per cent higher than in 2000, which also suggests that the surge in trust after September 11, 2001 was ebbing.

Mackenzie and Labiner (2002: 1) examined the breadth of political support in 2002, and concluded that

The events of September 11th and the dynamic responses of federal officials provided one of those rare moments of danger when Americans are closely tuned to their government. Such moments are times of opportunity, times for government to convince its citizens that things are under control, that the people in charge are dedicated and competent, that government—in a word—can be trusted...They [Americans] expressed their admiration for what they saw in positive assessments of performance and higher levels of trust. But the moment passed, apparently without long-term effect.

Mackenzie and Labiner then demonstrate that, by May 2002, trust in government had fallen back almost to its pre-9/11 levels. Favourability towards the federal government and elected officials had similarly eroded. Citizens were favourable towards President Bush, but these positive sentiments no longer carried over to politicians or the institutions of the regime. The moment had passed.

Discussion

The events of September 11, 2001 demonstrate that orientations toward government can change—three decades of declining support were reversed in a few hours as Americans rallied around their government. A similar spike in support had accompanied the Gulf War conflict in 1991 (see Figure 2.6). But, like this earlier example, as politics generally returned to 'normal', Americans' support for politicians, political parties, and political institutions returned to the low levels described in this study. Moreover, the September 11 effect was essentially limited to the American public, and comparable (albeit temporary) upsurges in support did not occur in other Western democracies.

If even the horror and tragedy of the World Trade Center attacks did not fundamentally alter Americans' images of their political leaders and government, then one must assume that the patterns described in the rest of this volume are enduring features of contemporary democratic politics. September 11 may have changed Americans' images of the world, but it did not change their images of their government and their position within the democratic process.

[32] See n. 30.

Appendix

Measuring Significance

Although many of the analyses in this book describe trends in linear terms, we know that not all trends have followed a straight-line descent. In the United States, for example, early declines have lowered trust in politicians to a plateau and opinion trends have fluctuated around this new baseline for the last two decades. In some nations, there are obvious positive and negative deviations in the long-term trend for specific elections. Our general expectation is that over the last third of the twentieth century the general trend is downward, although there are variations in the patterns of decline. Thus, we use linear trends to measure whether the general pattern is one of decreasing support (albeit not necessarily linear).

This appendix discusses how to measure the significance of changes in public opinion over time. Two methodologies have been used in the public opinion literature. The *time series* approach uses each survey result as a single point in a time series, and assesses the statistical significance of the trend across surveys, with the N equal to the number of separate national samples. This methodology is used for many of the time trends in this study. It is equivalent to analyses of aggregate economic statistics or other national characteristics over time.

In contrast, the *survey* approach focuses on the raw survey data, measuring whether the differences in opinions over two or more surveys are statistically significant. Because these comparisons are based on large survey samples, the N for these comparisons is quite large—usually several thousand or more. Because the comparisons are based on these individual-level data, differences are much more likely to be statistically significant.

Employing these two techniques on the same cross-sectional data yields dramatically different estimates of statistical significance because of the large differences in the N used in calculating probability statistics. A brief example based on changes in American party identification illustrates the effects of the two approaches. Between 1964 and 1970 the percentage of Americans identifying with a political party declined by a sizeable amount:

1964	1966	1968	1970
75.3	69.8	69.4	67.9

Using the time series technique, one obtains the following *insignificant* results:

$$b = -1.13, \quad se = 0.38, \quad sig = 0.099, \quad N = 4$$

In contrast, if one combines the surveys from these four years into a single data file, and then calculates a regression model predicting identification with a party (coded 0,1) by year of interview, the following results are revealed:

$$b = -1.15, \quad se = 0.003, \quad sig = 0.0000, \quad N = 5925$$

The two methodologies thus give nearly identical estimates of the per annum changes because they are measuring the same trend over time. The time series analysis is not statistically significant because of the small number of surveys upon which it is based. In contrast, the analysis based on individual data has a much greater N, since it is based upon individual interviews rather than time-points—and thus the results are highly significant.

Some recent research on comparative public opinion trends uses the time series method (for example, Klingemann and Fuchs 1995; Dalton and Wattenberg 2000). If one had access to the raw survey data, we believe that it would be more appropriate to base the statistical analysis on the survey methodology. Unfortunately, we often did not have access to the raw data from all the national surveys analysed in this volume. In such a case, Benjamin Page and Robert Shapiro (1992: 44–5) suggest another alternative. They note that, with large sample sizes of approximately 1,500, a difference between two surveys of at least six percentage points would be statistically significant. We suggest this as a reasonable rule of thumb in judging the statistical significance of the trends discussed in this chapter and in other survey trends presented in this volume. In terms of the per annum change measures we present, a 6 per cent trend for two surveys over this period would be equivalent to a 0.300 per annum change coefficient over the typical time series span we present from the 1970s to the 1990s. In general, the longer the time series and the more observations it is based upon, the less the per annum change has to be in order to reach significance. We therefore offer this reference standard as a general guideline for readers to take into account when assessing significance in the absence of the best available data.

PART II

The Sources of Change

3

The Correlates of Political Support

THE public's growing scepticism towards politicians, political parties, parliaments, and other democratic institutions raises the question of whether advanced industrial democracies are facing a crisis of political support. The implications of these trends partially depend on what produced these shifts in public sentiments. For instance, if dissatisfaction has increased among lower-income individuals, it could signal that individuals at the margins of society are increasingly alienated from the political system. With some delay, we may now be witnessing the crisis of late capitalism that some scholars have long predicted (Offe 1972; 1984; Habermas 1975; Bobbio 1987). In contrast, other analysts suggest that a rising cohort of young, better-educated, postmaterialist citizens are dissatisfied with the current workings of the democratic process and are pressing for an expansion of the democratic process (Inglehart 1990; 1997*a*; Dalton 2000*b*). Indeed, if this were a mystery novel, there would be no shortage of suspects that have been mentioned by some observer or another (for example, Nye and Zelikow 1997). And each of these explanations holds different implications for the democratic process.

This chapter begins our examination of the correlates of political support. Because decreasing support is a common feature of most advanced industrial democracies, we examine explanatory factors that might generally affect the citizens of these nations. We also focus on cross-national patterns rather than specific nations. The evidence is drawn from the eight advanced industrial democracies included in the 1995–8 World Values Survey. We begin by determining whether people do distinguish between different levels of political support, as described in Chapter 2. Then we examine different theories that may explain the declines in political support.

DIMENSIONS OF POLITICAL SUPPORT

Can one distrust the President while still respecting the office of the presidency? Such questions were asked regularly during the Clinton impeachment debate, and they reflect an ongoing question about the dimensionality of political support. As we discussed in Chapter 1, political theorists maintain that political support is a multi-dimensional concept. We rely on David Easton's distinction (1965; 1975) between support for the authorities, for the regime, and for the political community. In distinguishing between different types of support, this framework highlights the separate implications for each level of support. Support for the authorities has limited political significance within a democracy because its major consequence may merely be the replacement of the incumbents at the next election. In contrast, declining support for the regime and the political community may lead to more significant calls for political reform and potential political unrest.

Despite these theoretically important differences, scholars of public opinion debate whether the average person can distinguish between authority support and regime support, or whether feelings of political trust develop from specific sources and are then generalized across different objects. Arthur Miller's and Jack Citrin's early debate about the decline in political support among Americans focused on this issue (Miller 1974*a*; Citrin 1974). Miller (1974*a*: 951) claimed that the decline in the American political trust questions indicated 'a situation of widespread, basic discontent and political alienation in the United States'. Citrin felt that Miller had overstated the data, arguing that the questions on political trust were simply measuring disenchantment with political authorities, not distrust in the system of American government. Citrin continued this criticism in his study of public opinion in the San Francisco Bay region, arguing that evaluations of the incumbents and political system were so highly correlated that it was difficult to disentangle the two empirically (Shanks and Citrin 1975).

Comparative analyses have similarly struggled with the empirical overlap between support measures. Gerhard Loewenberg (1971: 184) argued that separating dimensions of support posed 'insuperable problems of measurement'. In a series of articles, Ned Muller and his colleagues (Muller and Jukan 1977; Muller, Jukam, and Seligson 1982) tried to separate the dimensions of support in German public opinion. They concluded that traditional measures of political trust are highly correlated with systemic evaluations. Support seemed to be a generalized sentiment that flowed across different levels of evaluation. At the same time, when one did separate the two orientations, they had distinct behavioural correlates. Dieter Fuchs (1989) also distinguished between various levels of political support, but then found that empirical measures were strongly interrelated.

Our first task, therefore, is to determine whether the theoretical distinctions between different levels of political support are empirically observable in public opinion. The 1995–8 World Values Survey provides a valuable resource to address this question.[1] Because of the project's interest in comparing system orientations across a wide diversity of nations, the survey included many questions that were intended to tap different levels of political support. Hans-Dieter Klingemann (1999) has shown that separate dimensions of support emerge for the combined results of the more than 40 nations in the survey. We want to examine

---

[1] We analyse the 1995–8 World Values Survey because it is one of the rare cross-national surveys that include a large number of political support questions. Although many specific surveys done by the various national election study teams also contain a large number of questions, the specific items vary from nation to nation, and so cross-national comparisons are not possible. In Chapter 4, however, we examine longitudinal trends using the national election studies.

TABLE 3.1   *The dimensions of political support*

Variable	Institutions	Authorities	Democracy	Community
Confidence in parliament	0.77	0.31	−0.13	0.13
Confidence in parties	0.75	0.17	−0.06	0.12
Confidence in civil service	0.72	0.07	−0.03	0.10
Confidence in national government	0.70	0.42	−0.03	0.11
Confidence in legal system	0.54	0.21	0.01	−0.13
Incumbent satisfaction	0.23	0.72	−0.01	0.07
Rate political system today	0.27	0.64	−0.08	−0.02
Country run for benefit of all	0.14	0.70	−0.03	0.08
Extent of corruption	0.17	0.48	−0.10	−0.07
Democratic ideal	−0.10	−0.18	0.65	0.00
Democracy best	0.01	−0.23	0.61	−0.07
Army rule	0.01	0.13	0.65	0.20
Strong leader	−0.02	−0.01	0.70	0.09
Experts run government	−0.06	0.02	0.55	−0.20
National pride	0.05	0.04	0.02	0.77
Fight for nation	−0.04	0.22	−0.02	0.70
Social change	0.19	−0.12	0.01	0.36
Eigenvalue	2.70	2.16	2.04	1.41
% of variance	15.90	12.70	12.00	8.30

Note: Table entries are Varimax rotated factor readings of a principal components analysis (missing data were replaced by mean scores).

Source: 1995–8 World Values Survey (pooled results for Australia, Finland, West Germany, Japan, Norway, Sweden, Switzerland, and the United States).

the structure of opinion in the advanced industrial democracies, and for these nations additional questions are available. The 1995–8 World Values Survey includes eight advanced industrial democracies: Australia, Finland, (West) Germany, Japan, Norway, Sweden, Switzerland, and the United States.

In order to determine whether citizens distinguish between different objects of support, we factor-analysed the various political support questions for the eight nations combined (Table 3.1).[2] All of the support measures are positively inter-related, indicating that support tends to be generalized across levels.[3] The factor analyses, however, distinguish between different dimensions of support. The first dimension in the table reflects support for political institutions: parliament, political

[2] We used a principal components analysis to extract factors and a varimax rotation of the factor structure. We initially used pairwise deletion of missing data, but Table 3.1 is based on a substitution of the mean values for missing data in order to create factor scores for each respondent. The pairwise/mean score factor results were essentially identical.

[3] The unrotated solution yielded four dimensions using Kaiser's criterion for the eigenvalues (3.92, 1.36, 1.29, 1.02). All the questions loaded positively on the first dimension, indicating that feelings of support are partially a general orientation. The range of loadings on the first dimension ran from 0.2 to over 0.8. In addition, the second unrotated dimension had strong loadings for the democracy items, the third for community support, and the fourth for incumbent satisfaction. This led us to rely upon a rotated solution that emphasizes the distinctions across levels.

parties, the civil service, and the legal system. The second dimension taps authority support: satisfaction with the incumbents, the performance rating of the current government, and several standard political trust questions.

The third dimension measures support for democratic norms, including the question on support for the ideal of democracy and whether democracy is the best form of government (see Table 2.5). The fourth dimension includes two questions on support for the political community: national pride and willingness to fight for the nation.

These results are similar to Klingemann's (1999) findings for the larger set of nations in the 1995–8 World Values survey, except that, with more questions tapping the various elements of political support, we can separate incumbent and institutional support that formed a single dimension in his analyses. Because the variance in these variables is more restricted in the advanced industrial democracies (for example, democratic values are widely supported in all these nations), the similar results reinforce the view that these are separate dimensions of opinion.[4] For instance, some people are relatively supportive of political institutions, while remaining sceptical about political elites. Thus, contemporary publics do differentiate between levels of political support—these are not simply interchangeable formulations of a general feeling of political satisfaction or malaise.

Further evidence of the distinction between these four levels of political support appears if we compare opinions across nations. Figure 3.1 presents the national averages on the four factor scores created from the analyses in Table 3.1. It is important to remember that these are standardized factor scores in which the average score is calculated to equal zero (the average for all eight nations). Thus scores above the mean are balanced by scores below the mean. Even on support for democratic values, where the citizens of all eight nations are broadly favourable (Table 2.5), some nations will still score above or below the combined mean score.

The first column displays national scores on authority support. The Norwegian public ranks highest in government support at the time of this survey. For example, 86 per cent of Norwegians express satisfaction with the incumbents of government. At the other end of the continuum, the Japanese public was openly critical of their government in the mid-1990s. Only 11 per cent of Japanese expressed satisfaction with the incumbent government of Ryutaro Hashimoto. The other nations are arrayed along this dimension, varying significantly in their levels of authority support.

Sentiments towards political institutions are less varied across nations, ranging within a quarter-scale point of zero. Norway and Japan express relatively high levels of institutional support, and Finland and Australia fall below the average.

---

[4] We also conducted an oblique factor analysis, allowing the dimensions to be inter-correlated. This analysis showed that support for the authorities and for political institutions is most strongly interrelated (0.35). As theory would suggest, authority evaluations are much less connected to diffuse measures of political support such as democratic values (0.13) or support for the political community (0.06).

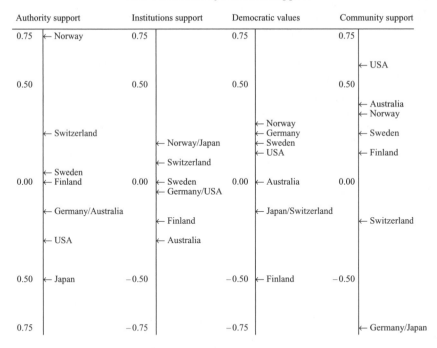

Authority support	Institutions support	Democratic values	Community support
0.75 ← Norway	0.75	0.75	0.75
			← USA
0.50	0.50	0.50	0.50
			← Australia ← Norway
		← Norway	← Sweden
← Switzerland		← Germany	
	← Norway/Japan	← Sweden	← Finland
		← USA	
	← Switzerland		
← Sweden			
0.00 ← Finland	0.00 ← Sweden	0.00 ← Australia	0.00
	← Germany/USA		
← Germany/Australia		← Japan/Switzerland	
	← Finland		← Switzerland
← USA	← Australia		
0.50 ← Japan	−0.50	−0.50	−0.50
		← Finland	
0.75	−0.75	−0.75	
			← Germany/Japan

FIG. 3.1. National scores on support measures

Note: Figure entries are mean scores for each nation on the factor scores computed from analyses in Table 3.1.

Source: 1995–8 World Values Survey.

The third panel in the figure describes national patterns on support for democracy. Norway, Germany, Sweden, and the United States score above the mean—and these values are lowest in the Finnish sample. One must remember, however, that the cross-national mean establishes a very high baseline. Even in Finland, for instance, 85 per cent of the public say democracy represents the best form of government and 76 per cent support the democratic ideal. The patterns in Figure 3.1 primarily reflect variations in the intensity of support for democratic values rather than outright opposition to democratic norms.

The fourth column in the figure presents cross-national differences in support for the political community measured by national pride and a willingness to fight for one's nation. As we saw in Chapter 2, national commitments vary considerably across this set of democracies. Americans score highest in national attachments: 79 per cent of Americans say they are very proud of their nation, versus only 46 per cent in the pooled sample. Americans are also above the norm in the expressed willingness to fight for their nation. At the other end of the continuum, the Japanese and Germans display the restrained sense of nationalism that other researchers have observed. The stigma of the Second World War remains a part of the political psyche in both nations. Only 14 per cent of Germans and 26 per cent of Japanese say they are very proud of their nation.

In summary, these findings tend to validate the distinctions between levels of political support that we derived from David Easton's typology (1965; 1975). Even though orientations towards different objects partially overlap, support for the authorities, political institutions, democratic values, and the political community are conceptually and empirically distinct in the minds of many individuals. Moreover, there is substantial variation across advanced industrial democracies in the patterns of support. Germany and Japan, for example, lack the feelings of national affect that some have argued are essential to a stable political order (Almond and Verba 1963), yet these are obviously well-established democracies whose citizens endorse democratic values and the institutions of democracy. Americans, in contrast, hold strong nationalist sentiments coupled with scepticism about the politicians who run the democratic process.

CORRELATES OF SUPPORT

This section examines some of the prominent explanations that have been cited for the growing distrust among contemporary publics—explanations that we can study with the 1995–8 World Values Survey.

Although idiosyncratic national factors are undoubtedly at play, we focus on general explanations that may apply across the advanced industrial democracies: (1) performance, (2) value change, (3) social capital, and (4) media effects. We will cautiously speak of the correlates of support rather than predictors, because the ability to explore causal relationships is limited with cross-sectional data. We are cognizant that many attitudinal measures have reciprocal effects, or arise from the spurious influence of another factor. Moreover, our real test of changing orientations must incorporate a dynamic perspective—something we pursue in later chapters. Still, these cross-sectional analyses provide an initial sense of the correlates of support and thus of where the sources of change might be concentrated, since most dynamic theories predict an unequal distribution of support across certain social groups. For example, if growing economic inequality explains decreasing political support, then we would expect to find significant differences in support by income level. The lack of relationships can be equally useful in eliminating theories where the present patterns of support are inconsistent with a specific causal process working over time. For instance, a theory explaining decreasing support in terms of the growing cynicism of the young would be open to question if age groups did not differ in their opinions.[5]

---

[5] At the same time, we recognize that even these cross-sectional relationships may yield incorrect evidence of longitudinal patterns. For instance, it may have been that the young were *more* supportive in the past, so the absence of age differences in contemporary data still reflects a change over time (see Chapter 4).

Performance

Democratic politics is first of all a social contract whereby government performs certain functions in exchange for popular support. David Easton (1986: 436), for example, notes, 'leadership assumes the responsibilities for tending to the problems of societies. In return the leadership gains the power to enable it to make and implement binding decisions, a power that it loses to an alternative set of leaders if it is unable to supply some average level of satisfaction to its supporters.' If governmental performance falls below expectations we might think that specific support for political authorities will suffer as a consequence. If these patterns continue for an extended period of time, the decline of support may generalize to broader evaluations of the regime and the political community.

Economic performance. One of the complications of the performance-based approach is that many different aspects of government performance might affect citizen evaluations. The narrowest definition focuses on economic performance. Often the research literature links the decline in support to economic decline or an economic crisis. For instance, the collapse of the Japanese economy in the 1990s is often tied to the public's decreasing faith in politics. The OPEC-induced world-wide recessions in the late 1970s and early 1980s is similarly linked to the public's growing concerns that government could not address economic needs and other policy demands (Alesina and Wacziarg 2000). The end of the post-war growth decades marked a new cynicism (or realism) about the limits of government. Indeed, this economic tale is repeated in the research literature of many nations.

Aggregate empirical analyses, however, provide limited support for economic explanations. For instance, Harold Clarke, Nittish Dutt, and Allan Kornberg (1993) find a modest empirical relationship between economic conditions and satisfaction with the functioning of the democratic process. Similarly, Ian McAllister (1999) concludes that economic factors have a limited influence on confidence in political institutions. In addition, growing public scepticism about politicians, parties, and parliaments does not match the general economic trends in these nations (see Chapter 6). Economic cycles have varied across nations, and are generally improving over time. For instance, after comparing US economic statistics with levels of political support, Nye and Zelikow (1997) discount economic factors as a major explanation for Americans' malaise. Americans had never experienced such prosperity and low employment as during the late 1990s, yet they simultaneously were cynical about the governing institutions that presided over this prosperity.

The strongest evidence of the economic performance theory might be found in individual-level relationships.[6] Individuals' economic satisfaction should be linked to their feelings of political support if economic performance is really the driving

---

[6] This, of course, does not resolve the aggregate-level problem that political trust does not track aggregate levels of economic confidence. For instance, consumer confidence in the United States hit new highs in the 1990s, even while political support remained far below its previous highs.

force posited by theory. Ola Listhaug (1995), for example, shows that evaluations of economic performance are significantly related to trust in politicians among Scandinavian publics. Following the logic of the Eastonian distinction between levels of political support, economic evaluations should have a greater impact on evaluations of authorities rather than of regime or system support (also see Kornberg and Clarke 1992: ch. 4)

Figure 3.2 describes the relationship between economic satisfaction and the four dimensions of political support. Financial satisfaction is moderately correlated with governmental support (r = 0.16), and has a slightly weaker relationship with confidence in political institutions (r = 0.14). Economic satisfaction is essentially unrelated to democratic values (r = 0.00) or community support (r = 0.05). (The general pattern is also repeated within each nation; see Appendix Table 3.A.) People do link their own economic concerns to their evaluations of governments—although the direction of any causal influence remains uncertain. Financial evaluations do not affect higher levels of political support.

Another dimension of the economic thesis is the debate over whether growing economic inequality has contributed to the current dissatisfaction with politics. The causes of this hypothesized relationship are varied, ranging from the negative consequences of globalization to the decommodification of peripheral economic groups in capitalist societies, but the implications are similar: the less affluent should be less supportive of the established political order that is worsening their social position.

The clearest test of this hypothesis correlates income levels with feelings of political support. In this case, the results are quite consistent: family income is virtually unrelated to political support (all the correlations are under 0.02). If economic

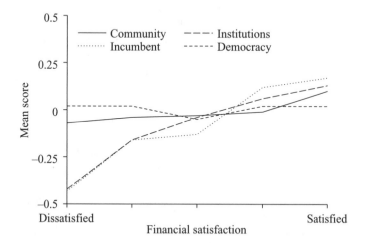

FIG. 3.2. Financial satisfaction and political support

Note: Figure entries are mean scores of the factor scores created from Table 3.1.

Source: 1995–8 World Values Survey.

conflict between the haves and have-nots was driving feelings of political distrust, we would expect stronger differences between high- and low-income groups. Moreover, the income relationship is highly variable across nations, and is even negative in some cases (see Appendix Table 3.A).

The different patterns of subjective and objective measures of individual financial conditions may explain why aggregate level analysis of economic influences yield only marginal results. Objective economic circumstances do not generate clear feelings toward the polity—these conditions are mediated by psychological judgements.

Policy performance.[7] Other performance-based theories maintain that evaluations of governmental performance should extend beyond the economic realm. Contemporary governments are now involved in a broad range of policy areas, and some of these new, non-economic domains may generate the public's declining political support.

When we search for systematic empirical data, there is again only mixed evidence that objective conditions track the aggregate declines in political support. In many areas, if not most, advanced industrial democracies have made considerable progress in improving the welfare of their citizens over the same period as support has decreased. The clearest evidence comes from Derek Bok's analysis (1997) of policy outputs in America. Bok concludes that the American condition in most areas has improved in absolute terms during the post-war period; and even relative to other OECD nations the United States has performed relatively well. The State Service Commission in New Zealand independently replicated Bok's analyses for New Zealand, and came to virtually identical conclusions (Barnes and Gill 2000). Indeed, the record of advancing incomes, spreading social security, improving civil rights, and other policy advances fits the post-war history of most advanced industrial democracies. A pure performance-based explanation would argue that a systematic decrease in support across the advanced industrial democracies would occur if all these political systems are worse-off than a generation ago. Some pessimists might claim this is so, but the empirical evidence in support of this proposition is very uncertain, especially as a general pattern for all advanced industrial democracies.

It is difficult to evaluate the policy performance hypothesis with cross-section survey data. A dynamic theory should be tested with longitudinal data: has the number of individuals who express dissatisfaction with specific government policies increased over time? Even with longitudinal data it is difficult to establish causality. Dissatisfaction with specific policies might be generalized into dissatisfaction with government or the political process. But it is also possible that people who are dissatisfied with government for other reasons will project this on to evaluations of specific policies. (Appropriate survey questions to assess policy performance are not available in the 1995–8 World Values Survey.) Thus, we will not formally

---

[7] While policy performance may potentially affect political support, other aspects of government performance may also enter into the public's calculus. The quality of leadership and the ethics of the governors, for example, are important in judging the performance of government. See the discussion of scandals presented in the media in the following section.

evaluate the policy performance thesis in this chapter, but it is a prime explanatory factor that should be examined with longitudinal data (see Chapter 7).

Ideology and policy polarization. Another group of scholars suggest that for a variety of reasons the representation gap—the difference between citizen preferences and government policy outputs—has systematically increased over time, and this erodes public satisfaction with the political process (Miller 1974*a*; Schmitt and Holmberg 1995; Borre and Andersen 1997; King 1997).

This argument is based on Downs's theory (1957) of rational political calculus, but there are sometimes contrasting assumptions about how these calculations are connected to empirical reality. For instance, Miller (1974*a*) claimed that increased polarization among the public stimulated distrust among Americans, while King (1997) maintained that growing polarization between the political parties is the cause. Similarly, the applications of this argument to Europe presume that dissatisfaction has increased at the political extremes as parties have converged on the centre; yet the evidence that party systems (or government policies) have generally converged remains uncertain. In addition, research that explicitly examines the linkage between party election promises and policy outcomes does not claim that the representation gap has systematically increased in advanced industrial democracies (Klingemann, Hofferbert, and Budge 1994).

Most tests of the policy polarization hypothesis compare levels of political support across various policy dimensions, normally with the expectation that individuals at the political extremes will display lower levels of support. In our initial mapping of these patterns, we use the left/right scale as a summary of policy positions. Figure 3.3 compares levels of support by position on the left/right

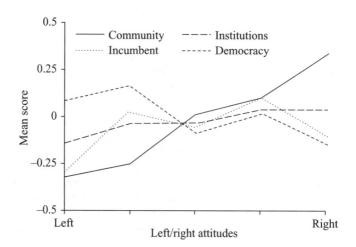

FIG. 3.3. Left/right attitudes and political support

Note: Figure entries are mean scores of the factor scores created from Table 3.1.

Source: 1995–8 World Values Survey.

scale. If political support is tied to ideology, then we would expect a systematic difference between leftists and rightists.

In actuality, there is relatively little left/right ideological polarization in support for the incumbent ($r = 0.04$), political institutions (0.05), or democratic values ($r = -0.06$). At the same time, there is a weak tendency for government support and democratic values to dip at the political extremes, but the magnitude of these effects are weak. The clearest instance of ideological polarization is the case where it should not exist: community support. Political culture research would suggest that community support should be a diffuse measure of system affect in a stable democracy: that is, not related to ideological competition. We find, however, that rightists are much more likely than leftists to express community support ($r = 0.17$) which suggests that nationalism has a strong ideological component.

This is one instance, however, in which aggregated cross-national analyses may easily be misleading. The partisan composition of governments varies across nations—some nations are headed by centrist governments, others have governments of the left or the right—and this should affect the ideological correlates of support (Anderson and Guillory 1997). Indeed, the separate national analyses show that government support is linked to ideology; conservatives are more supportive in nations such as Germany and Japan that were headed by a conservative government at the time of the survey, while leftists were more supportive of the left-leaning governments in Austria and Norway (see Appendix Table 3.A). When we expanded this ideological model to test for signs of party polarization, however, the difference from the simple left/right ideology model was minimal.[8]

In sum, the initial evidence suggests that ideological compatibility with the government influences governmental support, but the alienation of the political extremes is not a significant factor in governmental evaluations. It is also unclear how these patterns could explain a broad, long-term decline in political support in the advanced industrial democracies. Nearly all of these nations have experienced a rotation in governing coalitions—and trust still trends downward. This is an instance where a static relationship does not provide a dynamic explanation of decreasing support. We will explore the policy polarization thesis more directly with longitudinal analyses in Chapter 7.

Changing Values

Another explanation for the decline in political trust focuses on changing public orientations towards politics and expectations of the political process. With spreading affluence, Ronald Inglehart (1990; 1997a) shows that public priorities are

---

[8] To test the party polarization thesis, we conducted a regression model with a curvilinear estimation of the ideology relationship (government support = b1(left/right) + b2(left/right**2)). The following Multiple R correlations show only marginal increases over the simple correlations displayed in Table 3.A: Germany (0.25), US (0.04), Japan (0.23), Australia (0.13), Norway (0.08), Sweden (0.05), Finland (0.14), Switzerland (0.04).

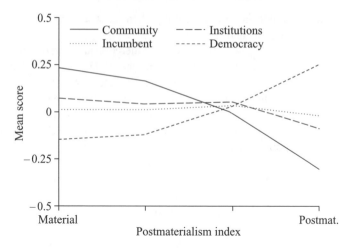

FIG. 3.4. Postmaterial values and political support

Note: Figure entries are mean scores of the factor scores created from Table 3.1.

Source: 1995–8 World Values Survey.

broadening to include a range of new postmaterial values, such as environmental quality, lifestyle choices, and consumer rights. Presumably because many democratic governments have been slow to respond to these new issue demands, postmaterialists are led to challenge governments through alternative political parties and movements. Ole Borre and Jørgen Andersen (1997), for example, find that support for postmaterial issues is strongly related to feelings of political trust in Denmark (while positions on traditional economic issues are unrelated to trust).

Inglehart (1999) and Flanagan (1987) also maintain that postmaterial values have a libertarian component that leads individuals to question authority. Postmaterialists often criticize the hierarchic and structured nature of contemporary representative democracy, and these values seem antithetical to the disciplined partisan politics that form the basis for parliamentary democracies. Thus, Dalton (2000*b*) shows that postmaterialists express less confidence in most institutions of government, especially those that emphasize authority and order (such as the military and police).

The spread of postmaterial values may therefore contribute to the general erosion in political support. To examine this question, we correlated postmaterial values with our four measures of political support (Figure 3.4).[9] The figure shows that post-material values have little independent effect on authority support (r = 0.00) and only weakly affect distrust of political institutions (r = −0.06). The national correlations indicate that this relationship also varies in polarity across nations. This indicates that postmaterialists are at least partially reacting to the partisanship

---

[9] The postmaterial variable is the twelve-item index of values which counts the number of postmaterial items selected from a mixed list of material and postmaterial goals (see Inglehart 1997*a*).

of the present incumbents, expressing more support when the left is in power and less when conservatives are in charge. At the same time, there is a consistent tendency for postmaterialists to espouse greater support for democratic values ($r = 0.15$). Expressed in simple percentage terms, 57 per cent of postmaterialists strongly supported democracy as a form of government, compared with 42 per cent of materialists.

Previous research has overlooked the strongest relationship that emerges from these data. Postmaterialists are significantly less supportive of the political community ($r = -0.20$). This correlation might occur because community support includes a willingness to fight for one's nation, something that postmaterialists likely avoid. Yet this same pattern persists if we correlate postmaterialism with national pride (data not shown). As Inglehart has shown (1997*b*), nationalism does not fit his general trajectory of postmaterial or postmodern value change, and this is reflected in our analyses.

Social Capital

Another explanation for declining political support is the supposed growth of social estrangement and social isolation in advanced industrial societies. Social mobility, geographic mobility, and other forces of modernization have supposedly weakened the ties between individuals and social communities, such as a class or religious groupings. More generally, Robert Putnam (1995; 2000) provocatively argues that social capital is decreasing as a result of these societal trends. Putnam shows that membership in voluntary associations is decreasing over time in the United States. Participation in such groups builds the social skills and norms that underlie many features of the democratic process. Other studies of political participation similarly draw attention to the importance of social group ties in stimulating political involvement (Verba, Nie, and Kim 1978; Verba, Schlozman, and Brady 1995). Putnam argues that the decline in social capital erodes political participation, interpersonal trust, and political trust.

Putnam's thesis that we are 'bowling alone' has generated substantial controversy in the research literature, and there is contradictory evidence that social capital may be increasing in other advanced industrial democracies (for example, Putnam 2002*a*; Hall 1999; 2002; Offe 2002; Pharr 2000). In addition, Kenneth Newton (1999; see also Newton and Norris 2000) questions whether interpersonal trust is related to trust in political institutions.

The 1995–8 World Values Survey can provide a direct test of the separate elements of the social capital explanation. The survey tapped membership in a diverse set of social groups as a measure of social capital. We counted the number of reported group memberships for each respondent, and correlated this with our measures of political support (Figure 3.5). Social group membership is positively related to all four dimensions, rising in influence as one moves from authorities (0.09), to democratic values (0.11), to community support (0.16). The direction of causality is unclear, but a correlation does exist.

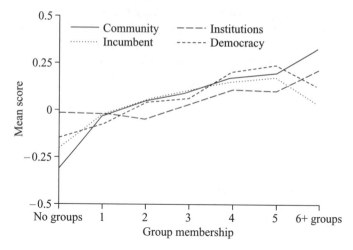

FIG. 3.5. Social group membership and political support

Note: Figure entries are mean scores of the factor scores created from Table 3.1.

Source: 1995–8 World Values Survey.

Another component of the social capital theory is the thesis that the democratic process is built upon the patterns of interpersonal relations among the citizenry (Eckstein 1966; Rueschemeyer, Rueschemeyer, and Wittrock 1998; van Deth 1999). Tocqueville (1960), for instance, argued that American democracy drew upon the social trust and collective cooperation of Americans. Putnam's (1993) research on the democratic process in Italy echoed these sentiments. From Tocqueville to Robert Dahl to Robert Putnam, analysts have argued that the creation of interpersonal trust facilitates the operation of the democratic process and the development of political trust.

Figure 3.6 displays the correlation between trust in other people and the four measures of political support.[10] Social trust is strongly linked to support for authorities (r = 0.19), political institutions (0.11), and democratic values (0.16). Support for the political community is not related to interpersonal trust, perhaps because the community is such an overarching concept that it is not seen as an extension of interpersonal relations.

These relationships are significantly stronger than what Newton and Norris (2000) report for all the nations in the World Values Survey. This difference may arise from a process that Dietrich Rueschemeyer (1998: 14) and others have observed. Participation in voluntary associations is more likely to encourage the formation of social capital and political trust when the activity occurs within a pluralist, democratic setting. Activity per se is less important than the qualities of that

[10] The question measuring interpersonal trust is as follows: 'Generally speaking, would you say that most people can be trusted or that you can't be too careful in dealing with people?'

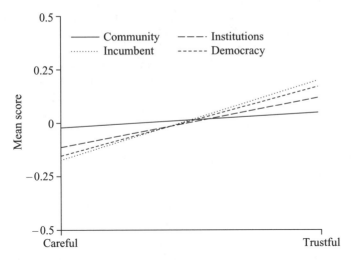

F IG . 3.6. Trust in others and political support

Note: Figure entries are mean scores of the factor scores created from Table 3.1.

Source: 1995–8 World Values Survey.

activity (Rueschemeyer, Rueschemeyer, and Wittrock 1998; Diamond 1994; Warren 2001). Trust in others can lead to cooperation on political matters within a demo-cratic setting, as Tocqueville argued, but it may have different consequences in less democratic environments. At the same time, it is not clear that social capital has decreased within the advanced industrial democracies leading to the declines in political trust we have observed (Putnam 2002a). Thus, this correlation may not signify a causal relationship that drives the longitudinal decline in political support.

Media Effects

The mass media, especially the rise of television, are often cited as a major fac-tor in reshaping contemporary politics and promoting distrust (see the review in Norris 2000a). Media effects can take several forms, and scholars are divided into several camps.

From one approach, the media in general, and television in particular, focus on scandals and report gossip that would not have entered the political discourse a gen-eration ago. This ranges from illegal behaviour to the private affairs of President Clinton and President Mitterrand. Attack journalism appears to be a new standard, in the American press at least, accompanied by changing journalistic norms about the role of the media (Sabato 1991; Fallows 1996). Longitudinal studies of media con-tent suggest that the news has become increasingly critical of politicians and the political process. Thomas Patterson (1993) found that over time the major American media have become more critical of politicians. Hans Mathias Kepplinger (1996; 1998) studied the treatment of politicians in three major German daily newspapers from 1951 to 1996, and found a substantial increase in negative comments about politicians. Other longitudinal studies find a growth in the number of political scandals reported by the press. Susan Pharr (2000) shows that reports on corruption in the Japanese newspaper *Asahi Shimbun* generally trended upward between 1948 and 1996, with peaks in the mid-1970s and in 1988–92 because of the Lockheed and Recruit scandals respectively. Donatella Della Porta (2000) found that cases of corruption reported in the Italian media slowly trended upward and then skyrocketed in the early 1990s. Two longitudinal studies of Swedish elections similarly find that the media have become more negative in their coverage of politics (Westerståhl and Johansson 1985; Asp 1991).

A less malevolent, but equally negative, interpretation of media effects is that the modern media simply violate Bismarck's dictum: 'people should not see how sausages and laws are made.' Many politicians have openly worried that the expansion of news information on television and the press has focused public attention on the conflictual parts of politics that normally were outside of the public view (*Washington Post* 1996). Similarly, a rancorous debate in the British House of Commons may be accepted as normal political sport by parliamentarians, but it may generate cynicism about politics in the average viewer. This pattern is exacerbated by the media's tendency to focus on conflict, failure, and the unusual.

Other analysts claim that the modern media place video style over substance, and encourage a change in the nature of political reporting that downplays the positive features of politics to the detriment of political elites and the democratic process (Patterson 1993; Cappella and Jamieson 1997). Criticisms of the media appear most often among analysts of the American media. Many analysts maintain that the commercial aspects of American television create commercial incentives to sensationalist reporting. At the same time, concern about the media's changing role is common in many other democracies (Dahlgren 1995; J. Langer 1998; Weymouth and Lamizet 1996; Holtz-Bacha 1990). Indeed, the concept of media-inspired malaise seems to appeal to nearly all audiences—political scientists, politicians, and their critics.

A very different approach argues that the media can be a positive force in developing better understanding and support for the democratic process, especially in democratic nations where television is managed as a public service. The media are a major source of information for contemporary publics; usage of newspapers, for example, is often related to greater political interest, high information levels, and greater political involvement (Norris 2000*b*). One can argue that access to CNN, C-SPAN, BBC World News, and other news channels should increase the political knowledge of contemporary electorates.

Finally, other scholars argue that the media are a relatively neutral transmission belt for information about politics. If the news is critical of politicians—such as the Watergate reporting or the recent exposés on British parliamentarians—it is not because the media are negative but because they are reporting on negative events that are occurring in the world. It is also possible that the media may be reacting to a changing public mood, not creating it. The public's new cynicism in the wake of political scandal may encourage the media to report events that reinforce this cynicism. In short, as Suzanne Garment (1991) has suggested, expectations are changing more than the reality of political scandals. After Watergate, it seemed that every journalism student wanted to be Woodward or Bernstein, and many Americans were receptive to stories that other politicians were betraying the public trust (though this explanation does not apply to the parallel trends observed in other democracies). In other words, media content may be both a cause and a consequence of the public's changing political orientations.

One indirect way to test whether media content is influencing opinions is to see whether media usage is related to political support attitudes. Before we proceed, we want to acknowledge that this is a partial and indirect test.[11] Communications research argues that the media can create norms and standards that diffuse through society, touching even those who are not regular consumers of the media. Opinion leaders may take their cues from the media, and then these norms are spread by other communication channels to the less attentive members of the public. With these caveats in mind, we would still argue that differences in orientation by media usage provide potential evidence of media effects.

The 1995–8 World Values Survey asked how often respondents watched television on a daily basis. Simple media usage does not consider the content of what is being watched; but if the media malaise thesis has an empirical base, people who watch television most avidly will be exposed to more critical reporting and thus may be less trustful of government.

Figure 3.7 compares feelings of political support by levels of television usage. Across these eight nations, high levels of television viewing are related to less incumbent support ($r = -0.09$) and lower support for democratic values ($r = -0.12$).[12] At the same time, regular television users are more supportive of the political community ($r = 0.10$). Furthermore, the national patterns of these correlations are quite varied. The United States is almost uniformly cited for the negative impact of television news reporting on political support, yet the US correlation for incumbent support is only -0.03 (see Appendix Table 3.A). Media correlations are stronger in Germany, Finland, Sweden, and Switzerland. Paradoxically, in these four nations the television networks in 1995 were still largely state-controlled, and thus presumably more deferential to politicians and the government than the US broadcast networks. Indeed, the rationale of a profit-driven exploitative media has been applied to the United States, but this model is much less accurate in describing of the electronic media in most other OECD nations.

---

[11] I want to thank Thomas Patterson for sensitizing me to this point, though the solution to this problem still eludes both of us.

[12] Unfortunately, the 1995–8 World Values Survey only contained a measure of television usage. Newton (1999) used the 1996 British Social Attitudes Survey to show that newspaper readership is actually positively related to political trust.

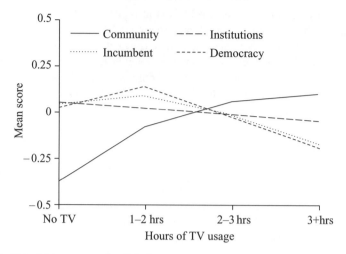

FIG. 3.7. Television usage and political support

Note: Figure entries are mean scores of the factor scores created from Table 3.1.

Source: 1995–8 World Values Survey.

Our findings thus parallel the results of previous studies (Norris 2000*b*; Holmberg 1999; Newton 1997). Although the media may contribute to—or reflect—the increasingly negative political climate over time, there is little evidence that media users are more sceptical about the political process. Indeed, the weak tendencies for television usage to depress trust in government and support for democratic norms is countered by media users' increased support for the political community. Furthermore, the decline occurs across nations regardless of the structure of the media (public or private) or the nature of political commentary about politicians in the nation, which suggests that the media climate is not a cross-nationally consistent factor. These results echo Pippa Norris's (2000*a*: 250) conclusion that 'we need to look elsewhere than television news for the source of our political ills'.

MULTIVARIATE ANALYSES

Many of the potential correlates of political support are themselves interrelated. Postmaterialists, for example, tend to have higher levels of social capital and to lean toward the left. Similarly, evaluations of governmental performance are often related to a respondent's ideology. Therefore, in order to separate the potential influence of each concept, we turned to multivariate analyses.

Table 3.2 presents the results of a multiple regression predicting the factor scores for the four dimensions of political support. In addition to the variables analysed above, we included several standard demographic variables as controls—education,

TABLE 3.2 *Multivariate models of political support*

Predictor	Incumbents		Institutions		Democracy		Community	
	β	b	β	b	β	b	β	b
Financial satisfaction	0.15	0.06	0.11	0.05	−0.03	−0.01	−0.01	−0.01.
Television usage	−0.02	−0.02	−0.02	−0.02	−0.09	−0.11	0.10	0.12
Left/right position	0.04	0.01	0.02	0.01	−0.03	−0.02	0.14	0.08
Post-material values	−0.02	−0.01	−0.06	−0.05	0.13	0.10	−0.16	−0.13
Group membership	0.00	0.00	0.04	0.02	0.06	0.03	0.11	0.05
Social trust	0.13	0.26	0.11	0.21	0.13	0.26	−0.01	−0.03
Education	0.00	0.00	−0.01	0.00	0.04	0.01	−0.05	−0.01
Age	−0.09	−0.01	0.04	0.00	0.13	0.01	0.10	0.01
Gender	−0.04	−0.08	0.02	0.00	−0.05	−0.10	−0.05	−0.10
Japan	−0.16	−0.47					−0.30	−0.91
Norway	0.28	0.85						
Constant		0.30		−0.02		0.23		−0.40
R		0.43		0.20		0.27		0.44

Notes: Table entries are the results of multiple regression analyses predicting the factor scores of political support constructed from Table 3.1. The first column of each model presents the standardized regression coefficient, the second column presents the unstandardized coefficient. Pairwise exclusion of missing data was used; Germany was not included in these models because of missing data on some predictors.

age, and gender—in order to see whether these social characteristics had an influence in addition to the attitudinal items. As well, because nations are pooled in these analyses, we compared the residual values for each nation to determine whether there was a significant misspecification by excluding 'nation' from the model. In two models this required the specification of a national dummy variable when the residual deviation was greater than 0.50. Most of the relationships in the multivariate model are modest, but the results generally resemble what we have seen in the bivariate analyses.

Several factors are correlated with support for political authorities. Financial satisfaction ($\beta = 0.145$) improves evaluations of the present government, implying that these evaluations are dependent on perceptions of economic performance. Feelings of interpersonal trust are also modestly related to government support ($\beta = 0.127$), providing evidence that substantiates the social capital argument. As noted above, Japan and Norway are the extreme cases, and both required a separate variable in the model. In contrast, ideological factors—left/right position and postmaterialism—are only weakly related to authorities support, which we attribute to the countervailing national patterns that depend on the partisan composition of the government (see Appendix Table 3.A).

Support for political institutions is not strongly linked to any of the predictors in this model. Financial satisfaction has a weaker effect than for authorities' support, as do most other predictors in this model. Ideological factors are essentially unrelated to institutional support. These patterns suggest that this support dimension is relatively diffuse, less connected to either performance or broad ideological norms.

The third set of columns in Table 3.2 presents the model for support of democratic ideals. Interpersonal trust again emerges as one of the strongest predictors. Indeed, in each model either interpersonal trust or group membership exerts a significant influence, which suggests social capital is a consistent correlate of political support. Postmaterial values are also correlated with democratic values ($\beta = 0.125$), even when one controls for the other eight variables in the model. Since postmaterialists are more critical on the three other dimensions of political support, it is significant that on the key dimension of democratic values they are actually stronger adherents of democratic norms.

Theory would suggest that attachments to the political community would be less dependent on performance criteria and other short-term factors, and more likely to be a diffuse orientation that arises from early socialization of political identities. We find, however, that left/right ideology is strongly related to community support ($\beta = 0.143$), despite being virtually unrelated to the other two dimensions of support. Postmaterial values are also correlated with lower support for the political community ($\beta = -0.158$). These patterns suggest that there is a substantial ideological component to the learning of these attachments, which is probably reinforced by current political debates over nationalism. These results show that broad feelings of attachment to the political community are not evenly distributed throughout the population.

PATTERNS OF SUPPORT IN ADVANCED INDUSTRIAL DEMOCRACIES

This chapter has mapped out the broad contours of political support in advanced industrial democracies, the patterns that can be generalized across nations relatively independent of the particular government in power or the recent political history of the nation. We should not stop here, but this provides a first overview of the factors potentially influencing the trends in declining political support.

It is theoretically important to distinguish between various dimensions of political support. Support for the incumbents of government, we argue, has potentially less political significance than public evaluations of system norms or attachments to the political community as a whole. While distrust in the incumbents might lead to a new government at the next election, distrust of the political process or rejection of democratic norms may undermine the vitality of the democratic process.

Data from the 1995–8 World Values Survey demonstrate that contemporary publics do make meaningful distinctions between the various objects of political support. Evaluations of the incumbents and political institutions form separate dimensions of political support, providing evidence that the theoretical distinction Easton (1965; 1975) presented is also observed by contemporary publics. Adherence to democratic principles represents a separate dimension, and support for the political community is yet another dimension.

The correlates of political support provide a first insight into the factors that might be changing citizen orientations towards the political process. We presume that a predictor may contribute to the decline in political trust if two factors are at work: (1) if the variable is related to political trust, and (2) we can shown that distribution of the variable has changed over time. If both conditions hold, then this becomes a possible explanation of the longitudinal trend. But if there is no relationship between these two attitudes, then a causal effect is unlikely.[13]

Support for political authorities is close to the type of specific support that Easton suggests can characterize these orientations. Governmental performance—measured by financial satisfaction—has a strong influence on evaluations of the incumbents and political institutions. As we move to higher levels of support—democratic norms or community support—the impact of performance declines. This suggests that performance factors may explain the declines in political trust and institutional confidence that we have observed if there is further evidence that contemporary publics have become less satisfied with economic conditions or other aspects of policy performance. This is a thesis we explore in more detail in later chapters.

We also find that social capital—either through membership in voluntary groups or through feelings of interpersonal trust—influences authority support and other dimensions of support. Group interactions apparently develop social trust that may

---

[13] Alternatively, even if the distribution of the predictor variable does not change over time, a shift in the relationship with political support may generate a trend.

carry over to the political process. Thus, the decline in social capital that Putnam (1995) observed for the United States may contribute to the declines in political trust. However, research suggests that the trends in social capital formation in other nations are varied, and often social capital is increasing (Putnam 2002*a*; van Deth 1999). Thus, social capital may be correlated to political support, but it seems an unlikely explanation for the longitudinal trends across advanced industrial democracies.

As I have argued elsewhere (Dalton 2000*b*), the spread of postmaterial values may have complex influences on political support. Postmaterialists (or manifestations of these values, such as in Green parties or new social movements) are often described as a new source of political cynicism in advanced industrial societies. These groups challenge the dominant social paradigm and are more willing to articulate their feelings through protests and other forms of direct action. There is some truth to these characterizations—postmaterialists tend to be more sceptical towards politicians, political parties, and parliaments—but at the same time they strongly support the democratic creed. In contrast, materialists are generally more supportive of contemporary democratic institutions, while displaying relatively less support for the ideal of democracy.

This tension between scepticism about democratic processes and commitment to democratic values evokes the image of the 'creedal passion' that Huntington (1981) saw as eroding the political harmony of American politics. I see the same data, but draw a very different conclusion. Postmaterialists are criticizing contemporary democratic processes, based on hierarchic authority, elite-based decision making, and the structures of representative democracy; but they are not questioning democracy per se. This is not an anti-system movement as characterized by other challenging political movements in the past, but a call for democracy to grow and progress. This value-based critique is, I believe, an important part of the process of political change that is eroding public confidence in politics, and fuelling calls for reforms to expand the democratic process towards its ideal. Such creedal passion has been the driving force behind democratic advancement throughout history.

The influence of the media is another factor that receives mixed support in our analyses. Although the content of the media has apparently become more critical of politicians and politics in many democracies, we find only modest differences in government support according to levels of television usage. The attention devoted to media effects in the literature warrants further study, but the initial empirical evidence fails to provide systematic evidence that media content drives trends in political support.

The last lesson from our analyses is that there is unlikely to be a single explanation for the declines in political trust. Our multivariate analyses, for example, demonstrate some empirical support for several possible explanations, but none of these effects is very strong. Similarly, even the bivariate analyses yield only modest correlations in most cases. Thus, declines in political trust may reflect a convergence of causes rather than a single explanation. Recognition of these multiple influences may be a first step in understanding why political support is changing among contemporary publics.

Appendix

TABLE 3.A *Correlates of political support by nation*

Predictor	GER	USA	JPN	OZ	NOR	SWE	FIN	SWI
Financial satisfaction								
Authority support	0.216	0.078	0.070	0.087	0.154	0.254	0.115	0.207
Political institutions	0.138	0.083	0.137	0.116	0.121	0.130	0.211	0.149
Democratic values	0.036	0.004	−0.005	0.041	0.047	−0.024	−0.022	0.017
Community support	0.054	0.069	0.071	0.064	0.057	0.056	0.088	0.049
Income								
Authority support	0.105	0.090	−0.031	0.130	0.190	0.278	−0.038	0.035
Political institutions	0.056	−0.090	0.023	0.055	0.047	0.080	0.082	0.047
Democratic values	0.181	0.157	0.058	0.132	0.119	0.128	0.075	0.090
Community support	−0.004	0.034	−0.045	−0.069	−0.059	0.014	0.011	−0.029
Left/right position polarization								
Authority support	0.268	0.002	0.086	−0.139	−0.051	0.129	0.105	0.097
Political institutions	0.082	0.042	0.197	−0.003	0.019	−0.023	0.095	−0.009
Democratic values	−0.189	0.015	−0.075	0.076	0.007	−0.095	−0.027	−0.166
Community support	0.352	0.118	0.270	0.158	0.154	0.010	0.165	0.265
Television usage								
Authority support	−0.068	−0.033	0.041	−0.011	−0.014	−0.072	−0.072	−0.074
Political institutions	0.036	−0.018	0.007	−0.027	0.002	0.000	−0.007	−0.110
Democratic values	0.217	−0.069	−0.011	−0.115	−0.103	−0.099	−0.015	−0.123
Community support	0.171	0.043	0.055	0.062	0.080	0.099	0.019	0.034
Post-material values								
Authority support	−0.142	−0.083	−0.001	0.061	0.049	−0.007	0.123	0.029
Political institutions	−0.047	−0.047	−0.178	0.030	−0.022	0.051	−0.061	−0.078
Democratic values	0.289	0.114	0.039	0.136	0.190	0.216	0.188	0.190
Community support	−0.384	−0.099	−0.097	−0.145	0.283	−0.130	−0.140	−0.270
Social group members								
Authority support	0.048	0.016	−0.048	0.040	0.091	0.082	0.116	0.071
Political institutions	0.137	0.092	0.121	0.106	0.099	0.113	0.093	0.089
Democratic values	0.115	0.014	−0.005	0.104	0.089	0.203	0.028	0.089
Community support	0.014	−0.019	0.077	0.0179	−0.007	0.016	0.017	0.071
Interpersonal trust								
Authority support	0.141	0.118	0.009	0.138	0.151	0.237	0.124	0.203
Political institutions	0.140	0.041	0.044	0.119	0.144	0.118	0.130	0.126
Democratic values	0.194	0.132	0.085	0.217	0.188	0.127	0.112	0.112
Community support	−0.183	0.020	−0.014	−0.009	−0.133	−0.104	−0.045	−0.093

Note: Table entries are Pearson r correlations computed separately for each nation.

Source: 1995–8 World Values Survey.

4

Social Change and the Accumulation of Incremental Effects

MOST Americans (as well as other democratic publics) began the 1960s with a generally positive image of their government and their nation's progress in addressing societal needs; over the next several decades many of these same individuals became disenchanted with politics. Even with the unprecedented affluence, peace, and security that Americans experience at the beginning of the new millennium, this malaise of the political spirit remains. What caused these changes?

This chapter compares the differential rates of decline in political support across specific social groups. There is no shortage of theories to explain the downward spiral of political support, and we introduced several of them in Chapter 3. However, it is difficult to evaluate causal processes with a cross-sectional survey. When those dissatisfied with government policy simultaneously express distrust of political institutions, we see a relationship but we cannot determine which attitude caused which. If specific causal forces are at work, however, they should leave their tracks in the longitudinal patterns of public opinion. For instance, if the growing alienation of youth that began with the student protests of the 1960s eroded political trust, then we should find specific and enduring generational patterns in political support over time.

Unfortunately, most prior longitudinal analyses have failed to find systematic social group differences in the patterns of decreasing political support. For instance, political support has been most extensively studied in the United States, but research generally stresses the uniformity of the decline. For example, Robert Lawrence (1997) presented a thoughtful discussion of how economic factors, such as slowing economic growth rates or widening economic inequality, may have increased the political scepticism of Americans. Then he actually tracked the political trust of various social groups over time. Lawrence concluded that the decline in trust was relatively uniform across social groups, without showing a pattern of group differences that would validate the various economic performance theories. Gary Orren (1997: 84) similarly concluded that Americans' growing 'cynicism cuts across all categories—black and white, male and female, rich and poor... Loss of faith in government has attached itself to every population group' (see also Alford 2001; Miller and Borrelli 1991: 153–6; Craig 1996: 51–4). Researchers in other nations find similar generalized patterns of decreasing trust across social groups (for example, Holmberg 1999; Listaug 1995).

It does appear that political trust is generally decreasing across almost all social groups—it is not a case of one group's trust increasing while another's is decreasing. Still, clues about the forces producing this decline may be found in the *differential rates of change* across social groups. Admittedly, studying longitudinal opinion change across demographic groups is a complicated analytical task. Explaining human behaviour is seldom simple, and many forces influence opinion trends over time. Tracking these influences is, as we will explain, like finding a needle in a haystack—there are often small effects that are difficult to examine in a short time frame. Studying changes in political support thus involves the art of finding small effects, which when aggregated over decades produce significant trends. Furthermore, without theoretical guidance on where to look, the researcher can lose small incremental effects in masses of empirical data. In short, without a map and good tools, the haystack may not yield the needle we seek. So even if previous researchers have not found clear evidence, I still believe that tracking longitudinal changes over time offers an opportunity to discover the causal forces producing these trends.

This chapter examines the longitudinal relationship between social status, age, and political support. We focus on these characteristics because they are often linked to theories of political change, and so can provide a surrogate measure of the forces that are supposedly transforming advanced industrial democracies. In addition, when we want to compare studies over a forty- or fifty-year time span, it is often difficult to find attitudinal items that were asked identically over time—most surveys include basic demographic characteristics such as age, education, or social class. These analyses can thus provide an introduction to the changing sources of political support over time.

THE ART OF FINDING SMALL EFFECTS OVER TIME

The declining public confidence in politicians, political parties, and political institutions is a significant development within the advanced industrial societies. Yet substantial total change comes from small effects that accumulate over decades. For instance, between 1958 and 1996 the proportion of Americans who said they mostly or almost always trust the government to do what is right decreased from 73 per cent to 40 per cent. This is a large change. But this trend occurred over 38 years, and the per annum change is slightly less than 1 per cent a year. Since the sampling error on most public opinion surveys ranges from 3 per cent to 5 per cent, even the shift from one presidential election to the next could easily be missed in the variability of sampling error. Indeed, without changes that accumulate over decades, most of the trends in this study would not look so impressive. The first challenge, therefore, is to be sensitive to the problems of estimating small effects.

The model for these analyses is Philip Converse's (1976) research on American partisanship. Converse showed that the substantial increase in the strength of partisanship by age was generated by a very small per annum coefficient. Thus, studies that tracked partisan learning over a relatively short time span had difficulty identifying the evidence of strengthening partisanship against the background noise of the random error in public opinion surveys and any short-term election effects. We have a similar problem in studying political support. The change in the mean score of the trust in government question from 1958 to 1996 was only 0.64. In per annum terms, this generates an annual change of -0.0168.[1] Thus, to identify systematic patterns over time, we need a long time span so that the cumulative impact of per annum changes is substantial.

This approach also applies to causal effects. If groups change at differential rates, the differences in their per annum rates also will be very small. If the per annum decrease in mean political trust is double the average rate for one group (-0.0336), and half the average rate of decline for another group (-0.0084), these effects might be difficult to detect with small surveys, a short time span, or few theoretical clues about where the needle might be found.[2] But if we study these cumulative differences over fifty years with a sophisticated statistical analysis, then we might be able to identify the different patterns of change.

A further complication involves shifts in the relative size of groups over time. Shifts in the size of groups may affect the level of political support, even if the pattern across groups is constant over time. For instance, we might compare the better and lesser educated on whether their opinions at the beginning of the time series differ from those at the end. In addition, there has been a marked increase in the number of better-educated citizens. A shift in the proportion of better educated could affect support levels even if the level of support across educational groups is constant over time. (This presumes that the better educated are less supportive, so a growing number of better-educated respondents would gradually lower support levels.) Thus, we have to be sensitive both to changes in how a predictor is related to political trust over time and to changes in the distribution of the predictor variable.

---

[1] Table 2.2 presents the per annum change in the *percentage* of trustful respondents over time, rather than the *mean score* on the four-point trust question. Thus, the table yields a per annum coefficient of -1.226 for the percentage change. This dichotomizing of the trust question into per cent trustful/non-trustful simplifies the presentation of data in Chapter 2, but it loses real variation across the four categories of the question. In order to find small effects in our data, we need to retain all the meaningful variance that is possible, and therefore we use mean scores where possible in this chapter.

[2] Another problem is the confounding effects of other variables. For instance, the next section will examine the changes across educational groups over time. We frame these analyses in terms of systemic changes in advanced industrial societies. But, as a measure of social status, the relationship between education and government support might also be affected by whether a left or right government holds power. These factors could be disentangled with a large number of time-points where the composition of the government varies, but these effects may be intermixed in our analyses of only two time-points.

All of these potential statistical problems take on added weight if we make the reasonable assumption that multiple factors drive opinions. The specific context of a campaign, or even the placement of a question in the election study, could influence the distribution of opinions separately from the trends we are observing.

The analyses use a two-prong strategy to address these potential problems. First, and more important, we develop specific theoretically based hypotheses about the expected patterns of change across social groups. Some of these hypotheses are admittedly contradictory—and the role of the data analyses is to test these conflicting claims. Theory is also valuable because it tells us where in the haystack the needle might be found. Second, we use a statistical approach developed in a related work on changing party attachments (Dalton and Wattenberg 2000: ch. 2). By combining theory and methodology focused on finding small effects over time, we can garner some evidence of why contemporary democracies have such dissatisfied citizens.

SOCIO-ECONOMIC CHANGE AND POLITICAL SUPPORT

Discussions of spreading political cynicism often link this trend to the socio-economic transformation of advanced industrial societies. The latter half of the twentieth century was a period of profound socio-economic change for advanced industrial democracies. Comparable to the industrial revolution, these nations experience a post-industrial revolution that reshaped the structure of the labour force, the nature of work, the lifestyles of their citizens, and basic economic conditions. These factors, it is argued, generated the decreases in political support—although researchers often offer different hypothesized causal processes.

The Negative Effects Hypothesis

To simplify the discussion, we divide the commentators into the negative effects thesis and the positive effects thesis. The *negative effects thesis* argues that the development of advanced industrial societies created new social and economic problems that have eroded the political support of the citizenry. Numerous commentators claim that social groups on the periphery of the economy, such as the unskilled, the unemployed, and the unemployable, are becoming marginalized by the labour structure of advanced industrial societies (for example, Bobbio 1987; Offe 1984). These marginalized or 'decommodified' citizens are seen as a potential source of social unrest and political discontent. From the quasi-Marxist perspective of these theories, these developments would lead to the eventual demise of 'late capitalist' economies as the marginalized sectors turn against the state.

More recently, the negative effects thesis has been linked to the new competitive pressures of international trade in a globalized economic system (for example,

Lawrence 1997; Scharpf 2000). One aspect of this approach suggests that globalization generally harms economies, fuelling a loss of political confidence. Alesina and Wacziarg (2000), for instance, suggest that globalization has led to slower post-1975 GDP growth rates, rising competitive pressures on wages and benefits, and the high unemployment rates currently found in most OECD nations. A related argument claims that globalization leads to a loss of political control, and this creates a dynamic whereby national governments are increasing blamed for policy outcomes that are beyond their control (Scharpf 2000). Robert Putnam (1996: 25) holds that 'transnational trends [such as economic globalization] increasingly escape control by any democratically constituted authorities. State boundaries no longer clearly define stable zones of political identity, economic activity, and military protection. National governments and the electorates to which they are responsible feel a very real "loss of fate control".'

As I noted in Chapter 2, there is only limited empirical support for the argument that aggregate economic trends have depressed political support. Analyses of aggregate opinion data, for example, demonstrate that economic conditions are only modestly related to various measures of political support (Clarke, Dutt, and Kornberg 1993; McAllister 1999; Kuechler 1991). I also agree with Katzenstein (2000) that it is difficult to identify empirical evidence to support the conclusion that globalization has hurt all OECD nations, and this in turn is linked to declining political trust.[3]

Another group of economic pessimists stresses the unequal benefits of global markets, and thus their differential effects on the populace (Lawrence 1997; Uslaner 1999). Lower-status individuals often bear the greater costs of economic competition, and share in a smaller proportion of the benefits. Indeed, contemporary political leaders (on both the left and right) frequently claim that globalization threatens the social benefits and wage levels of the industrial working class. At the same time, capital owners supposedly benefit from new investment opportunities, highly skilled workers often can improve their position because of new international markets, and high-income individuals find new tax shelters. Other research, including our analyses in Chapter 3, demonstrate that there is a cross-sectional relationship between feelings of financial well-being and political support (also see Listhaug 1995). In other words, it is claimed that increasing inequality in economic conditions may lead to growing cynicism among those at the lower end of the social status ladder.

The argument that lower-status groups may be more critical of government and political institutions is not novel. There are good reasons for expecting that those with lower incomes and lower-status occupations may be dissatisfied with their condition in life, and hold the government at least partially responsible for their individual condition. The economic pessimists, however, claim that these

---

[3] In the current context we are more interested in theories that suggest differential rates of change on population subgroups.

conditions are actually worsening, and this contributes to the decrease in confidence in politicians, parties, and democratic institutions.

If these economic arguments are correct, we should be able to observe the traces of these problems in the patterns of longitudinal change. The negative effects thesis implies:

H_1: The greatest loss in support should be located among those who are at the margins of the economic order: the less educated, the less skilled, and those with lower incomes. In contrast, upper-status groups also might have become more sceptical about government, but not to the same degree as lower-status groups.

Thus, we can broadly test the negative economic thesis by comparing social status differences in political support over time.

The Positive Effects Hypothesis

The *positive effects thesis* offers a very different accounting of this same period. The second half of the twentieth century was a period of rising affluence, expanding education, and improving social opportunities for most citizens. Even the 'economic downturn' of the post-1974 period was actually characterized by continued growth, albeit at lower rates of improvement. In addition, expanding access to education increased the educational levels and life skills of contemporary publics. Governments also addressed a host of new issues, such as the quality of the environment, the rights of women, and the rights of ethnic minorities. Many significant economic and social problems remain, but the OECD nations have made dramatic strides in addressing many of the traditional economic and social challenges that historically were the goals of government action (see, for example, Bok 1998).

Whereas the political culture literature once argued that the better educated and more affluent provided the core support for the political system in stable democracies (Almond and Verba 1963), several scholars now claim that social modernization is transforming the relationship between citizens and the state. Greater political skills and resources—that is, higher levels of cognitive mobilization—lead contemporary electorates to towards elite-challenging forms of political action, which often places them in conflict with politicians and government officials (Inglehart 1999: chs 10, 11; Nevitte 1996). In addition, these same individuals tend to be less deferential toward social and political authorities (Inglehart 1999; Dalton 2000*b*). In a different vein, Huntington (1981) argued that this group of better-educated youth endorse strong democratic ideals, which leads them to question democratic politics as it is currently practised. This is why the young and better educated have been the source of support for new social movements, such as environmentalism and feminism, that challenge both the values and the style of contemporary democratic politics.

In short, this perspective maintains that the development of advanced industrial societies is leading the better educated and the higher social strata to develop new questions about the democratic process, and thus the locus of change is centred among these groups. This leads to the following hypothesis:

H_2: The greatest loss in support should be located among those who are at the upper end of the economic order: the better educated, the more skilled, and those with higher incomes.

Both of these hypotheses are plausible, but they derive from contrasting processes behind the changing patterns of political support in advanced industrial societies. Therefore, we will judge their validity against the empirical evidence.

Testing for Change

Testing for the impact of socio-economic change involves the measurement of small effects, because social status differences in political support are very modest. But when accumulated over time, such modest effects may have a significant influence on the distribution of opinions.

The empirical analysis requires that we track changes in political support across as long a time span as possible. We start with a detailed analysis of the American pattern. Figure 4.1 illustrates the relative political trust of education

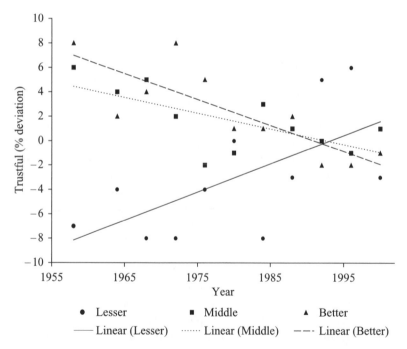

FIG. 4.1. Changing relationship between education and trust in the United States

Note: The lines represent the regression lines for the relationship between the three educational groups and trust in government question over time.

Source: 1958–2000 American National Election Studies.

groups over time. We initially examine education patterns because, when we turn to the cross-national analyses, most surveys include an education variable that is coded into comparable categories over time. It is more problematic to ensure this comparability with other social status questions, such as employment or income, which have different codings across surveys. To focus on the differences across educational groups, we detrend the series and express group values as deviations from the overall sample mean for each time-point.[4] The lines in the figure represent the proportion that trusts the government to do what is right most of the time. In the halcyon days of the late 1950s and early 1960s, better-educated Americans were more trustful of government (see also Stokes 1962). Over time, the trust levels of the better educated decrease at a steeper rate, and by the end of the 1990s the less educated are more trustful.

Today, better-educated Americans are more cynical about their government, despite their privileged social position. These results were further validated by examining occupational differences in political trust. Family income ranked by percentile is positively related to political trust in 1958 ($r = 0.10$), and negatively related in 1996–2000 ($r = -0.03$). Occupational status displays the same reversal of correlation between these two time periods. In summary, the erosion in political support has been more concentrated among the better-off in American society when judged against the baseline pattern in 1958.

The social change hypothesis implies that the changing influence of social status should affect other advanced industrial democracies, and not just Americans. There is not a single common question that has been asked over time in many nations, so the following analyses compare a few different items. We began with the 'don't care' question, including another indicator when multiple measures were available. In a few cases the 'don't care' question was not asked, so we used another trust item from Table 2.2. Not all the survey trends in Table 2.2 are publicly available in raw data form for analysis; we have acquired the survey data for only about half the nations from the table.[5]

To statistically test for the patterns shown in Figure 4.1, we combined a survey from the beginning of each time series and another from the end of the series. For each nation, political support is modelled as a combination of three factors: the

---

[4] For the United States we use the 'trust the government to do right' question because it is available for the longest time span. The 'few big interests' series only begins in 1964 and the 'don't care' item used in other nations changes wording in the United States.

Because we are looking for small effects, we have tried to maximize our N by coding only three educational groupings: (1) less than high school education, (2) high school degree, and (3) some college education or more. The results from pairs of adjacent election studies were combined to further increase the group Ns for the figure.

[5] To maximize the number of nations for analysis, we utilized additional data-sets when the national election surveys were not available. The pairing of the 1974–5 Political Action data with the 1995–8 World Values Survey provides data for Germany, Finland, and Switzerland, and one time-point for the British comparisons. These two surveys included the 'few big interests' question, as described in Figure 2.3.

TABLE 4.1 *The effect of education on political support*

Country	Constant	Time	Education	Interaction	Years
United States	2.822*	−0.406*	0.035*	−0.038*	1958–96/2000
Australia	2.341*	−0.642*	0.182*	−0.082	1969–98
Britain	3.789*	−0.157	0.292*	−0.122*	1974–2001
Canada	2.346*	−0.281*	0.139*	−0.066*	1965–97
Finland	1.294*	−0.029	0.058*	−0.054	1975–95
Germany	1.668*	−0.220*	0.011	−0.038*	1974–96
Japan	2.331*	−0.023	0.007	−0.066	1976–96
Norway	5.359*	−1.191*	0.347*	0.210*	1969–93
Sweden	4.406*	−1.330*	0.224*	−0.009	1968–94
Switzerland	1.673*	−0.210*	0.002	−0.018	1974–96

Notes: The British and Canadian results are based on an index of the 'don't care' and 'lose touch' questions; Sweden and Norway combined 'MPs don't care' and 'parties are only interested in votes'; the United States and Australia use the trust in government question; Germany, Finland, Japan, and Switzerland use the 'big interests' question. The table presents the unstandardized regression coefficients.
*Coefficients significant at the 0.05 level.

Sources: National election studies in the United States, Australia, Canada, Japan, Norway, and Sweden; Political Action study and 1995–8 World Values Survey for Finland, Germany, and Switzerland; Political Action and the 2001 British Election Study for Britain.

year of the survey, educational level, and an interaction term combining the two. The overall drop in political trust should produce a negative coefficient for the time variable. A positive initial relationship between education and political support is expected in each nation, which will appear as a positive coefficient for the education variable. Finally, if the decrease in trust is concentrated among the better educated, the education*time interaction coefficient should be negative, indicating that the better educated have become relatively more critical over time.

Table 4.1 presents the results of these regression analyses. As expected, in most nations the better educated are initially more supportive of the political system. In the United States, for instance, the reversal of the educational relationship can be seen in the two regression slopes derived from the pooled model:[6]

1958	Trust = 2.822 + 0.035*Education
1996–2000	Trust = (2.822 − 0.406) + (0.035 − 0.038)*Education
	Trust = 2.416 − 0.003*Education

[6] In more precise terms, the year of the survey is coded 0 for the first time-point and 1 for the second time-point. We then created an interaction term that multiplies education by this dummy variable. Thus, the equation can be interpreted as two separate models. First survey: a + b1 (educ); the other variables have a value of 0 in this year. Second survey: (a + b3) + (b1 + b2) (educ); b3 is from the interaction term and indicates the change in the intercept between time-points, and b2 is the adjustment of the education slope for the second time-point.

The pooled model shows that the drop in trust over time (-0.406) and the shift in the education relationship (-0.037) are statistically significant effects. Similarly, the impact of education weakens over time in all but one nation (the single exception is Norway). In the United States, Germany, Japan, and Switzerland, the shift is large enough to actually reverse the correlation between education and political support.

Are these significant differences? In mere numeric terms, the changes look quite small, and the relationship between education and political trust is modest at best. If one simply looked at the 1958 and 1996–2000 relationships in theoretical isolation, one would probably conclude that social status differences are not important in either period. Furthermore, the small changes in relative opinions across educational groups are not large enough to have produced the initial large drop in nations such as the United States, Britain, and Sweden during the 1970s— specific contextual effects clearly lowered trust during this period. But the slow reversal of social status differences also presses trust downward. The eventual trend reversal may explain why trust did not improve when the specific negative events of these decades ended, because the political system had lost the confidence of its upper-status citizens.

In addition to the reversal of these relationships, educational levels have risen considerably over time. In 1958 only 20 per cent of the US sample had at least some college education; by 1996–2000 this had increased to 49 per cent of the sample. If the initial relationship between education and political support had remained constant, this would have stimulated a further increase in trust, as the proportion of better-educated citizens increased. However, the reversal of this relationship magnifies the impact of education.

The United States data can be used to illustrate these effects, since the American data series is the longest and the interaction effect falls in the middle of the range in Table 4.1.[7] When these two factors are combined—a changing relationship and rising educational levels—the total shift in political support due to these effects equals approximately a fifth of the overall drop between these two periods.[8]

---

[7] In actuality, we consider the US a conservative estimate of educational effects. The interaction coefficient is higher in most other nations in Table 4.1; in addition, the rise in educational levels has been greater for most other nations over a comparable time period.

[8] Measuring effects is not straightforward because multiple factors are involved. We developed the following estimates based on what we felt were reasonable assumptions. The mean levels of trust dropped from 2.92 in 1958 to 2.41 in 1996–2000, for a change of 0.51. At the same time, the mean educational level increased from 2.81 to 4.11, for a change of 1.30. We used the results of Table 4.2 to estimate the impact of the changing relationship between education and political trust. If the educational relationship had remained as in 1958, then rising educational levels would have increased political trust by 0.045 (0.035*1.30). Instead, the negative relationship in 1996–2000 and the change in mean education lowered trust by -0.048 (-0.037*1.30). When both effects are combined, this produces a -0.093 shift in political trust, which is approximately a fifth of the total decline over time (-0.51).

The robustness of the cross-national pattern is also impressive evidence that systematic changes are occurring, because many of these time comparisons are relatively short and the confounding effect of other factors could affect these small social-status effects. For instance, changes in the partisan composition of governments could affect the relationship between education and political trust; or a unique change in the political context during one survey could disrupt the paired comparison.[9] Still, the general pattern of our results strongly indicates that higher-status groups have experienced a greater loss of support over time.[10]

There is an irony to these findings. The better educated (and upper social-status groups more generally) ostensibly benefit more from society. Because of their education, they should have better-paid careers and better life chances. This is why it was once common for upper-status groups to be more supportive of the existing political order. Nevertheless, scepticism about the political process has grown more rapidly among the better educated over the past generation. In several nations, this shift has been so large that today education is negatively related to support for the government and political institutions. Thus, when two factors are combined—the change in this relationship and rising levels of education—they are linked to a significant decrease in political support.

Moreover, the impact of these shifts is magnified because the better educated represent the pool of future social elites, serve as opinion leaders on politics, and are more likely to be politically active. If political systems normally expect greater allegiance from the upper-status groups—who diffuse these norms through their role as opinion leaders—then the reversal of this relationship could have equal effects in the opposite direction. The increasing cynicism of upper-status groups could contribute to a changing *Zeitgeist* about politics, with the cultural norms shifting from allegiance to criticism. Such cynicism could also generate a dynamic whereby additional scandals or negative news about government reinforce these impressions, while positive news about government is discounted. In the end, this process could produce the enduring negativism about government that we have observed, even when economic and political conditions are positive.

At the same time, because this decrease in political support is more heavily concentrated among future social and political elites, this dissatisfaction differs from the anti-system sentiments that typified earlier challenges to democracy

---

[9] For instance, the first time-point was during the Eisenhower administration, and the most recent data are from the Clinton administration. In a separate analysis of the ANES cumulative file from 1958–2000, we demonstrated that, even while one controls for the partisanship of the respondent and the party of the incumbent president, the effects demonstrated here are essentially unchanged. In addition, both education and age have significant independent effects in this multivariate analysis (Dalton 2004).

[10] The ideal analyses would replicate the detail of our US analyses across all the available time points in each nation. Assembling the national data series to replicate the analyses now possible with the ANES should be an agenda for future research. Still, the consistency of the results in Table 4.1 suggests the accuracy of the general pattern as a baseline for further detailed national analyses.

during the twentieth century. Would those who benefit most from the system because of their higher status really want to dismantle the system that assures them of these privileges? Thus, the fact that decreasing support is concentrated within this social milieu may explain why cynicism is focused on the individuals and institutions of the regime, and not the basic principles of the system. The current malaise of the political process is born amongst those who will sustain and lead the system.

GENERATIONAL CHANGE

Generational change has been another prominent element in the discussions of the political transformation of advanced industrial democracies. In the quieter, more halcyon days of the early 1960s, researchers maintained that the young began their political experiences with a positive orientation towards government that gradually faded with time (and presumably with the accumulation of less than idealistic political experiences) (Easton and Dennis 1969; Hess and Torney 1967). My, how things have changed!

College-educated youth often generated the first major public demonstrations against the working of the democratic process in the later twentieth century. In the United States, the Free Speech Movement and student participation in the civil rights movement and anti-Vietnam demonstrations presented some of the first radical critiques of democracy—from children raised under and benefiting from this same system, often those from the same supportive young generation that Easton and Dennis (1965) studied. The Events of May 1968 in France, the 1967 Provo movement in the Netherlands, and the student protests that spread across Europe in the 1960s and 1970s similarly stimulated new questions about the democratic process, and the development of alternative political visions. The faces of young college students were also prominent in the development of the environmental movement and the formation of new Green parties in the 1970s and 1980s, and the growth of the women's movement over this same time span.

The student protests proclaimed democratic values, and claimed that contemporary democracies did not match these ideals. This challenge to the political status quo was then enshrined in the counter-culture movement that spread across Europe and other advanced industrial democracies. The new German Green party, for example, mixed equal measures of political idealism and youth culture; and one of the party's founding principles was the call for more democracy. Even after the long hair has given way to buzz cuts, and VW vans have been replaced by BMWs, cynicism about politics remains a constant in the contemporary youth culture.

Ronald Inglehart (Inglehart 1977; 1990; Abramson and Inglehart 1995) has persuasively argued that the process of generational change has played a central role in transforming the politics of advanced industrial democracies. First, bettereducated youth exhibit a greater concern for new quality of life issues that often put them in conflict with the dominant political parties and existing government priorities. Second, this group more often favours more involvement in the decisions affecting their lives, which leads to greater support for participatory politics and corresponding criticism of the institutionalized structure of representative democracy (also see Dalton 2000*a*). Therefore, the group that is more likely to protest, join citizen groups and new social movements, criticize political parties, and generally challenge the established political order.

This logic leads to the expectation that there is a distinct generational component in the decline of political support:

H₃: The greatest loss in support should be located among younger generations.

Again, this implies that the very products of the political and social development of advanced industrial democracies are those who are becoming most critical of these political systems. Yet previous research has not identified generational change as a significant factor in decreasing support (Lawrence 1997; Owen 1997; Alford 2001). We believe a more thorough empirical investigation is needed.

Testing for Change

As a first test of this generational hypothesis, Figure 4.2 plots the trust levels of four generations over the time span of the American National Election Studies.[11] To again focus on the relative pattern across generations, we present these data as deviations from the average for each time-point. In 1958 there are modest generational differences, with the oldest cohort (born before 1910) expressing more distrust of government than subsequent cohorts; that is, there is a negative relationship ($r = -0.07$) between trust and age. Over time, trust decreases among all generations. But if one looks closely at the haystack of lines and time-points, one can see an additional pattern. Gradually the generational relationship reverses. The pre-1910 generation gradually becomes relatively less cynical of government; by the time that it leaves the electorate in the late 1980s, this generation is the most trustful. Conversely, the figure indicates that the youngest generation becomes relatively more distrustful over time. Thus, by the end of the series the age relationship is reversed: trust of government is greater among older Americans ($r = 0.05$). These differences are admittedly modest, but the incremental effects of generational change can have large cumulative effects, because over time older and more trustful citizens are gradually replaced by younger and more cynical individuals.

---

[11] Because we are looking for small effects, we have tried to maximize our N for each generation by coding for broad grouping: (1) born in 1909 or before, (2) born 1910–29, (3) born 1930–49, and (4) born 1950 and later. The results from two adjacent election studies were combined to further increase the group N for Figure 4.2.

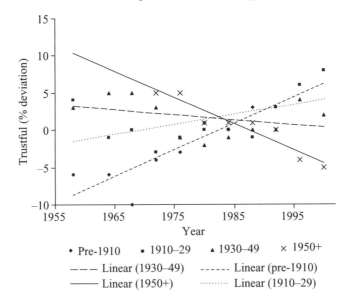

FIG. 4.2. Changing relationships between age and trust in the United States

Note: The lines represent the regression lines for the relationship between the four age cohorts and trust over time.

Source: 1958–2000 American National Election Studies.

We can also summarize these generational patterns with regression analyses of the age relationship across time (similar to the educational analyses above). The results in Table 4.2 generally confirm the theoretical expectations. As shown in Figure 4.2, the age relationship is negative among Americans in 1958 ($b = -0.0036$). The positive coefficient for the interaction term ($b = 0.0051$) means that by 1996–2000 older Americans are more trustful than the young. These results also show that the small patterns displayed in Figure 4.2 are statistically significant when their cumulative effects are calculated through longitudinal analyses.

Furthermore, this same pattern of generational change occurs in most of the other nations for which we have data. The age relationship is initially negative in Australia, Canada, Finland, Germany, Sweden, and the United States; and the interaction term is positive in these same nations. The exceptions are Japan and Switzerland, where the young were already more critical at the first time-point and there is not a significant change in this relationship over time. And in Norway, there is no age gap at the first time-point, but the older Norwegians are significantly more trustful at the later time-point.

All told, the long-term decrease of political support has been disproportionately greater among the young. One should note that in instances such as the

TABLE 4.2 *The effect of age on political support*

Country	Constant	Time	Age	Interaction	Years
United States	3.090*	−0.785*	−0.0036*	0.0051*	1958–96/2000
Australia	2.278*	−1.810*	−0.0152*	0.0244*	1969–98
Britain	5.006	−0.033	0.0039	0.0042	1974–2001
Canada	3.166*	−0.672*	−0.0056*	0.0051*	1965–97
Finland	1.546*	−0.180*	−0.0043*	0.0021	1975–95
Germany	1.722*	−0.495*	−0.0006	0.0039*	1974–96
Japan	2.574*	−0.111	0.0059*	−0.0007	1976–96
Norway	6.149*	0.719*	0.0017	0.0283*	1969–93
Sweden	5.985*	−1.445*	−0.183*	0.085*	1968–94
Switzerland	1.568*	−0.272*	0.0025	−0.0003	1975–96

Notes: The United States and Australia use political trust as the dependent variable; the British and Canadian results are based on an index of the 'lose touch' and 'don't care' questions; Sweden and Norway combined 'parties are only interested in votes' and 'MPs don't care'; Germany, Finland, Japan, and Switzerland use the 'big interests' question. The table presents the unstandardized regression coefficients.
* Coefficients significant at the 0.05 level.

Sources: National election studies in the United States, Australia, Canada, Japan, Norway, and Sweden; Political Action study and 1995–8 World Values Survey for Finland, Germany, and Switzerland; Political Action study and the 2001 British Election Study for Britain.

United States, the initial abrupt decline in political trust between the mid-1960s and late 1970s cannot be explained by generational turnover; the shift was greater than could be explained by generational differences, and generational patterns gradually evolved over a longer time span. But the cumulative forces of change over this period had their strongest effect on the younger generations. Consequently, the young are now more likely to display lower levels of political trust and greater cynicism towards politicians and political institutions. Members of 'generation X', for example, begin their political experience as cynics—and these sentiments might only strengthen with continued experience with everyday politics. The normal process of demographic turnover may therefore produce continued downward pressure on political support in the years ahead.

SOCIAL CHANGE AND POLITICAL SUPPORT

This chapter has produced some insights into the causes of decreasing political support by comparing how social groups have shifted over time. We focused on social status and generation as potential explanatory factors partly because there are strong theoretical reasons for selecting these items (although some theorizing leads to contradictory hypotheses) and partly because the dynamics of these variables could plausibly shift levels of political support over time. For instance, rising educational levels and generational turnover might systematically affect the distribution of opinions if education groups or generational cohorts varied substantially in their views.

Comparing the endpoints of several time series, political support has dropped disproportionately among the better educated and the young. At one time, the better educated and the more affluent were more supportive of democratic elites and institutions, and this was even seen as an essential element of a stable democracy (for example, Almond and Verba 1963). Today, in several nations the better-off have become more critical than the lesser educated and the less affluent. Similarly, at one time the young tended to be more supportive of government, but these relationships have also reversed. It is true that virtually all social groups are more sceptical about government today, but the decline has been disproportionately greater among the upper social strata and the young.

Although I believe the socio-economic development of advanced industrial democracies is producing these pressures on political support, there is not a simple, direct correlation between the distribution of these social traits and the decline in support. A simple social change model would imply that there is a slow and steady shift in political support as education levels rise or generational turnover occurs; but this does not fit the data. The national patterns of declining support are quite varied. In some nations, like the United States, the greatest decline in trust came during a short period beginning in the late 1960s; in other nations, like the Federal Republic of Germany, the decline is concentrated over the 1990s; while in yet others, such as Sweden, there has been a steady and relatively gradual erosion of support. Thus, the 40 per cent decrease in the proportion of Americans who expressed trust in government between 1964 and 1974 cannot be directly and narrowly linked to changes among the young and the better educated. But influence can work in other ways.

The forces of social modernization can change the *political expectations* of certain sectors of society. Heightened expectations, rather than specific social or political conditions, can contribute to the erosion of political support among these social groups. This premise is based on several considerations. First, the pattern of decline provides strong evidence that system performance was not the driving force behind these social patterns. Instead, support decreases among the social groups that arguably are the beneficiaries of the affluence, freedom, and opportunities that these nations offer.

Second, other research indicates that the rising educational levels, political sophistication, and democratic values of contemporary publics shifts public expectations of the relationship between citizens and the state (Inglehart 1990; van Deth and Scarborough 1995). Young, better-educated citizens are not as deferential towards politicians and political institutions; they are more likely to expect open government, accountability, and direct citizen involvement in the decisions affecting their lives. These groups are often vocal critics of the limitations of representative democracy. Jonathan Cohn (1992: 32) describes the feelings of this generation:

The mixture of idealism and political cynicism that many of us feel is inherently unstable; how long we can sustain it is difficult to tell. One thing is certain, however: With few exceptions, we have disengaged from politics, and that is something that should worry all Americans. Our disaffection should serve as an imperative for more inspiring national leadership—if not for the sake of progressive reform, then for the sake of democracy.

In addition to changing expectations, these social groups may also be more sensitive to the shifting political context of advanced industrial democracies. For instance, younger generations have been raised in a new media environment, and the changing style and content of the contemporary mass media may have more strongly affected their images of government. Similarly, the better educated both create the climate of opinion in a nation and are more sensitive to shifts in this climate. Thus, if political discourse among social commentators and political elites expresses greater cynicism about politics, then the better educated may be more cognizant of these changing norms. This is a rival explanation that we must consider as the analyses move ahead, but it makes the assessment of causality even more difficult. Are people more critical because they hear of more scandals and government mistakes from their televisions and daily newspapers, or has a more sceptical public created a new audience for such exposés?

The evidence of this chapter suggests that the process of social modernization is admittedly only a partial explanation, accounting for perhaps 20–30 per cent of the total decline. But it yields an important insight: democracies are not losing support from those at the margins of politics, but from the young, better-educated and upper-status citizens who have benefited most from social progress. These patterns typify the critical citizens or disaffected democrats that others have described as the source of political malaise.

5

Value Change and Political Support

Is political support a rational calculation of government performance—or a state of mind? The preceding chapter showed that dissatisfaction with the present political system has grown most rapidly among those who are primary beneficiaries of this system: the better educated, the more affluent, and the young. The explanation, we believe, is not that these individuals have suffered under the democratic process but that, as the beneficiaries of this system, their values and expectations have changed in ways that lead them to look beyond contemporary politics. Even if this is only a partial explanation, it is an important factor in explaining the decrease in political support.

This chapter focuses on the broad forces of social and political change that may be altering public values and producing these trends. We argue that changing public values, such as those described in Inglehart's theory of postmaterialism (1990; 1997), are altering citizen expectations about the democratic process. This affects images of the authorities and the institutions of representative democracy, and potentially the norms underlying the democratic process. This chapter determines the impact of these changing values and their implications for the function of contemporary democracies.

THE ROLE OF VALUE CHANGE

The modernization forces that created advanced industrial democracies have produced a slow evolutionary process. For several generations this process has been transforming the values of the citizenry, and thereby their relationship with the dominant social and political institutions. For instance, writing about Western democracies in the early twentieth century, Harold Laski (1931: 147) observed:

> The crisis of capitalist democracy is essentially a crisis of authority and discipline. The power to secure obedience to its principles has decreased because men increasingly refuse to accept its ends as obviously just...Disrespect for authority is not due to some sudden burst of enthusiasm for anarchy; it is rooted in a disbelief in the principles for which authority has been organized in a capitalist society.

This chapter draws upon my chapter in Susan Pharr and Robert Putnam's (2000) edited collection. I would like to thank Susan and Bob for the comments on that chapter, which have influenced the material presented here.

The liberalization of the period was partially reversed by the impact of the Great Depression and later the Second World War, but the initial signs of social change were apparent in the populist reform and democratic ferment early in the century.

During the second half of the century, the advanced industrial democracies experienced even more dramatic social change—perhaps the greatest advance in the human condition across history. The horrors of the Second World War were followed by an age of unprecedented economic growth and social change. By most measures, the citizens in these nations are several times better-off in their living standards than any pre-war comparison group. This economic miracle transformed living standards and life chances. No longer are the basic struggles for minimal sustenance and security a concern for most residents in these nations. This modernization process has brought concomitant changes in lifestyles, social stratification, and social relations. In addition, it has been an age of profound technological change, most clearly represented by the expansion of the electronic mass media, a theme that runs through many chapters in this book.

In writing about these changes, Ronald Inglehart (1977; 1990; 1997*a*; see also Abramson and Inglehart 1995) maintains that these societal changes are transforming the values of contemporary publics. Younger generations raised in the later twentieth century are shifting their social and political values away from the materialist and security concerns of the past—economic well-being, economic security, and personal safety—to a new set of *postmaterial* values. Postmaterial values emphasize goals such as protecting the quality of life, individual freedom, lifestyle choice, free expression, and participation. Indeed, a large literature has developed on the nature and impact of these value orientations on advanced industrial societies (for a review see van Deth and Scarborough 1995).

If public values are changing as Inglehart and others describe, then this has direct, albeit complex, implications for the democratic process. Changing values are expanding the boundary of politics, providing new rights to women, protecting our health and national heritage through environmental protection, and creating new opportunities for under-represented groups—hardly negative developments for democracies. The rise of Green parties, for example, may have caused some initial consternation to conservative political leaders (and academics), but most now realize that the green movement added a positive element to democratic politics.

More broadly, because of their emphasis on individualism and self-expression, postmaterialists are more likely to question authority and those who exercise authority based on status or political position (Inglehart 1999). Changing value orientations are thus diminishing deference towards social and political institutions (Nevitte 1996), and postmaterial values seem antithetical to the disciplined partisan politics that form the basis for parliamentary democracies. Instead, postmaterialists seemingly favour participatory political structures, collective decision-making, and consensus-building processes. The emphasis of Green parties on participatory decision-making and basic democracy illustrates the different principles of democracy and authority that many postmaterialists hold. These norms may place them in conflict with the institutions of representative democracy that emphasize governing power over citizen engagement.

In contrast, another group of scholars have presented a less sanguine interpretation of these value changes. In *The Crisis of Democracy*, Crozier (1975) held that societal changes were transforming the values of contemporary publics. Economic growth, for example, was expanding the political skills and resources of the public, as well as increasing the new political demands being placed on governments. Social mobility was weakening the bonds between individuals and social institutions, such as churches and unions. The mass media were creating a different relationship between the governed and the governors. Thus, changes in the values of contemporary publics were seen as eroding the governability of democracies.

> Behind all these governability problems of modern Western societies lie some more basic *problems of values*. Participation, people's consent, equality, and the right of the collectivity to intervene in personal affairs, and the possible acceptance of authority seem to be the preliminary questions to debate. (Crozier 1975: 39; emphasis added)

Echoing many of the points found in Laski's writings four decades earlier, Crozier discussed the role of changing values in more detail. He believed that changing orientations towards freedom, equality, order, and political opposition were creating new tensions that democracies were struggling to resolve. Increased public demands for political freedom, and the diminished appreciation for public order and stability, created governability problems for contemporary democracies.

Huntington (1975*a*) also argued that social and generational forces were transforming public values. However, Huntington seemed to emphasize only the negative aspects of changing public values. He believed that value change was leading to less respect for authority, decreased trust in public officials, and weakened bonds between the individual and political parties—generating governability problems. At the same time, value changes encouraged individuals to be more assertive in expressing their political preferences and less deferential to authority—another source of governability problems, in Huntington's opinion. Huntington (1975*b*: 37–8) saw these trends as creating a *democratic distemper*:

> The problem of governance in the United States today stems from an 'excess of democracy' ... the effective operation of a democratic political system usually requires some measure of apathy and non-involvement on the part of some individuals and groups. The vulnerability of democratic government in the United States comes ... from the internal dynamics of democracy itself in a highly educated, mobilized and participatory society.

Indeed, Huntington (1974; 1981) painted a fairly dark picture of what the development of post-industrialism and the concomitant process of value change meant for advanced industrial democracies.

From either prospective, this literature suggests that the process of value change may be a potential explanation of broad trends in political support. The percentage of postmaterialists is gradually increasing in these nations (Abramson and Inglehart 1995). For example, the percentage of postmaterialists in a set of European nations increased by nearly half between 1973 and the early 1990s (Inglehart 1997*a*: ch. 5). If postmaterialists do differ in their images of government, a shift in the distribution of values could contribute to the decline in political support. At the same time, others have questioned whether value change is actually linked to political support (Gabriel 1995; Fuchs, Guidorossi, and Svensson 1995). Examining this thesis is the primary goal of this chapter.

VALUES AND POLITICAL SUPPORT

As we have argued in previous chapters, orientations towards authorities, the political regime, and the political system have different implications for the democratic process, and each shows somewhat different empirical trends. Thus, we separately examine the relationship between postmaterial values priorities and these various objects of political support.

Authorities and the Government

Postmaterialism clearly represents a critique of the established political order. Postmaterialists and their representatives (Green parties, new social movements, and citizen action groups) criticize contemporary democracies for their corporatist tendencies and the lack of representation for minorities and counter-cultural groups. Empirical analyses generally confirm these expectations. For instance, Oscar Gabriel (1995: 366–70) found that in most European nations postmaterialists were slightly less trustful of government (as shown in Chapter 3). Similarly, Borre and Andersen (1997) found that postmaterialism was related to political trust in Denmark. Thus, our analyses make minimal assumptions: (1) that values are significantly related to trust over time, and (2) that the shifting distribution of values could therefore contribute to the decreasing trust of politicians and government.

To assess the influence of postmaterial values on the declining trust in politicians, we begin by tracking this relationship over time in the United States, where the longest data series exists. Then we extend these analyses to cross-national comparisons of political support over time.

From 1972 until 1992 the American National Election Studies have included Inglehart's simple four-item index of postmaterial values.[1] Across each election, postmaterialists are less trustful of the government (Figure 5.1). This relationship is also affected by the partisan composition of the government—that is, this

---

[1] Inglehart (1990: ch. 2; 1977) normally uses a four-item question to construct an index of material/postmaterial values. Respondents are asked to choose between two materialist and two postmaterialist goals; those that select two goals of the same type are coded as pure 'materialists' or pure 'postmaterialists'.

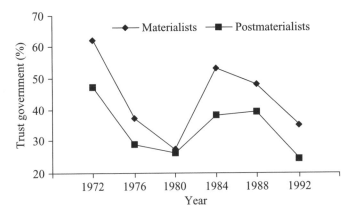

FIG. 5.1. Trends in political support by postmaterialists, 1972–1992
Source: American National Election Studies.

measure partially taps support for the incumbents of government. The gap between value groups is greatest at time-points when a Republican government is up for re-election (1972, 1984, and 1988), when conservative materialists are relatively more likely to be trusting and liberal postmaterialists are relatively more sceptical. Conversely, the value gap narrows when a Democratic administration is in office (1980) because values and evaluations of the incumbents may work at cross-purposes. Very similar results emerge when the survey question is used that asks whether government is run for the benefit of all (data not shown).

If we look beyond these inter-election shifts, however, these data suggest that the process of value change can make a modest but real contribution to the decline in political support. First, materialists and postmaterialists significantly differ in their trust of government, by an average of eight percentage points in the first three elections and eleven in the last three surveys. Second, there has been a considerable shift in the distribution of value priorities even over the relatively short time span covered in Figure 5.1. Over these two decades, the percentage of postmaterialists in the US doubled, while the percentage of materialists decreased by half.[2] Across a longer time span, such as the five decades analysed for demographic variables in Chapter 4, the shift in values would be considerably greater.

Thus, the combination of these value differences and a shift in the underlying distribution of value types leads to more postmaterialists in the electorate who are more critical of government. But, as we discussed for the demographic trend

---

[2] In the 1972 survey, fewer than 10 per cent of respondents were coded as postmaterialists, and this figure rises to 18 per cent in the 1992 survey. By the 1999 World Values Survey in the US, the number of postmaterialists had increased to 25 per cent.

analyses in Chapter 4, we would not link the distribution of values directly to the trends in political support. The short-term actions of government, as well as the composition of the government, heavily influence the shift in trust in government from election to election. Changing values cannot explain such short-term shifts. But values may indicate the shifting expectations of citizens over the long term, and these gradual changes can explain the long-term trend that underlies the short-term perturbations.

It is difficult to extend our analyses of US trends to other nations because there are few cross-national survey series that include both the postmaterial values question and an appropriate measure of political support. The best data sources for longitudinal analyses are the 1974–5 Political Action study and the 1995–8 World Values Survey that include both postmaterial values and political support. Since the coding of the values measure differs slightly between the two questionnaires, the results are presented separately for each study rather than merged together as in the analyses of Chapter 4.[3] This allows us to compare the four nations included in both studies, as well as the seven nations included in just one of the surveys.

Table 5.1 indicates that postmaterialists are slightly less trustful of government, which is consistent with other findings. The partisan composition of the government also affects these correlations, as seen in the US case. The relationship is normally weaker when the left is in power, and polarizes when there is a conservative government. In Germany, for instance, during the Brandt/Schmidt SPD administration postmaterialists were not significantly more critical of government as measured by the 'big interests' question (column 1), but they were much more critical than materialists during the conservative Kohl administration (column 2).

The relationships in Table 5.1 are consistent with the hypothesis that value change contributes to the growing political scepticism of contemporary publics. But value change apparently makes a limited contribution. Even though the distribution of postmaterial values changes significantly over time, the weak link between values and trust means that the potential impact on trust is mathematically limited. The impact of value change appears strongest in Germany because the shift in values and the shift in the relationship are exceptionally large.[4] In most other nations the effect is more modest. In short, the shift toward postmaterial

---

[3] In both studies the variable is a count of how often the five postmaterial items were selected as most important among the twelve items in the battery. In the Political Action study the respondent chose only five items; in the World Values Survey the respondent could choose six items. The scale thus runs from 0 to 5 in both studies, although the distribution of scores in each is not strictly comparable because of these questionnaire differences.

[4] Germany represents the maximal effects estimate: the mean score on the values scale shifts more than most nations over time (1.64 points between 1974 and 1995) and the relationship between values and trust changes substantially (−0.08). Multiplying these two factors yields a −0.13 shift in the predicted trust score. The actual shift in the two surveys was −0.33.

TABLE 5.1   *The effect of postmaterial values on political support*

Nation	1974–5	1995–8
United States	−0.031*	−0.023*
Finland	−0.008	0.024*
Germany	0.004	−0.079*
Switzerland	−0.069*	−0.035*
Austria	−0.006	n/a
Britain	−0.075*	n/a
Italy	−0.054*	n/a
Netherlands	−0.008	n/a
Australia	n/a	0.006
Japan	n/a	−0.021
Norway	n/a	−0.017

Notes: The analyses use the 'big interests' question as the dependent variable; an additive scale from the twelve-item values battery is used as the independent variable. The table presents the unstandardized regression coefficients.
* Coefficients significant at the 0.05 level.

Sources: 1974–5 Political Action Study and 1995–8 World Values Survey.

values appears to reinforce decreasing trust in politicians and the government, but this is only a partial explanation of the decrease in support.[5]

Confidence in Political Institutions

If postmaterialists are sceptical of politicians and incumbent governments, we might consider this a normal element of democratic politics that has positive benefits for the democratic process.[6] This may lead to changes in government and a new administration that is more attuned to postmaterialists' concerns. However, as the object of dissatisfaction broadens to political institutions, then the potential implications increase. And part of the postmaterial critique is aimed at the institutions and processes of representative democracy. What role has value change played in the recent decreases in confidence in political institutions?

[5] Although postmaterialists are less trustful of politicians and government, we should note that this does not reflect a general syndrome of low interpersonal trust, such as Robert Putnam (2000) has described in his research on social capital. Inglehart (1999) found that postmaterialists are more likely than materialists to trust their fellow citizens. In the US in 1990, for example, 43 per cent of materialists said 'most people can be trusted', while 63 per cent of postmaterialists expressed this opinion.

[6] People often become dissatisfied with political office-holders and act on these feelings to select new leaders at the next election. Dissatisfaction with authorities, within a democratic system, is not usually a signal for basic political change. Negative attitudes towards political officials can coexist with little loss in support for the office itself or the institutional structure encompassing the office.

Inglehart (1999) maintains that materialists value social order, structure, and hierarchy, which generates support for the dominant institutions of politics and society. In contrast, postmaterialists tend to reject authority, and this leads to decreasing support for the military, the police, churches, and other social and political institutions. Furthermore, materialists generally perceive political institutions as more responsive to their interests, while postmaterialists see the dominant social actors as rejecting their alternative values. The result, according to Inglehart (1999: 236), is that 'Governing has become more difficult than it used to be: the tendency to idealize authority that characterized societies of scarcity has given way to the more critical and demanding publics of postmodern societies. Authority figures and hierarchical institutions are subjected to more searching scrutiny than they once were.' Similarly, Flanagan (1987; see also Flanagan and Lee 1991) has shown how societal change is shifting priorities from authoritarian to libertarian values. In short, the decline in support for political institutions is seen at least partially as a consequence of the shift towards postmaterial values by contemporary publics (see also Chapter 3; Dalton 2000*b*).

We examine this question with data from the 1981–3 and 1995–8 World Values Surveys. The survey include a battery of items that tap support for a diverse set of social and political institutions. Indeed, these are some of the same data that led Inglehart (1999) to his conclusions about the impact of value change on political support (cf. Listhaug and Wiberg 1995).

Table 5.2 presents the correlation between postmaterial values and three indices of institutional support.[7] One index measures support for the political institutions of representative government: civil service, legal system, and parliament. The second index measures support for the institutions of state authority: the police and the military. The third social institutions index includes churches, the press, trade unions, and major companies.

Postmaterialists tend to be sceptical about social and political institutions, and nearly all of the correlations in the table go in this direction. For example, of German postmaterialists in 1995, only 43 per cent express a lot of confidence in the civil service, as opposed to 66 per cent among the most materialist category. Yet the results in this table also suggest caution in claiming that postmaterial values are inevitably anti-institutional. Postmaterial values are only weakly related to confidence in political institutions, and only slightly more correlated with social institutions. In some nations where the government has been relatively responsive to postmaterialist and New Left causes—such as the Netherlands and Sweden— postmaterialists are slightly more positive towards political institutions.

The scepticism of postmaterialists tends to focus on the institutions of authority and hierarchy: the police and the military. In every nation postmaterialists tend

[7] Because Inglehart (1999) and Listhaug and Wiberg (1995) emphasize the impact of postmaterial values on institutions identified with authority, we decided to separate the measure of political measures that Listhaug and Wiberg analyse into political and authority-oriented institutions. The following analyses validate this rationale.

TABLE 5.2 *Postmaterial values and confidence in institutions of politics, state authority, and society*

	1980s			1990s		
	Political	Authority	Social	Political	Authority	Social
Australia	n/a	n/a	n/a	0.03	−0.12	−0.05
Belgium*	−0.11	−0.17	−0.12	−0.08	−0.16	−0.07
Canada*	−0.09	−0.12	−0.15	−0.05	−0.13	−0.04
Denmark*	−0.03	−0.21	−0.10	−0.01	−0.18	−0.10
Finland	−0.02	−0.14	−0.06	−0.01	−0.14	−0.10
France*	−0.17	−0.29	−0.17	−0.10	−0.21	−0.08
Germany	−0.15	−0.25	−0.16	−0.08	−0.25	−0.06
Great Britain*	−0.04	−0.11	−0.03	−0.11	−0.16	−0.03
Ireland*	−0.10	−0.13	−0.12	−0.08	−0.12	−0.06
Italy*	−0.13	−0.24	−0.12	−0.04	−0.16	−0.11
Japan	−0.15	−0.16	−0.09	−0.14	−0.13	−0.06
Netherlands*	0.01	−0.18	0.00	0.08	−0.15	0.00
Norway	−0.03	−0.17	−0.05	0.00	−0.13	−0.08
Sweden	0.05	−0.09	−0.03	0.05	−0.10	−0.03
Switzerland	n/a	n/a	n/a	−0.08	−0.26	−0.05
United States	n/a	n/a	n/a	−0.05	−0.14	−0.09
AVERAGE	−0.07	−0.17	−0.09	−0.04	−0.16	−0.06

Note: Table entries are the correlation between the post-material values index and confidence in political institutions (civil service, legal system, and parliament), 'authority' institutions (police and the military), or social institutions (churches, the press, unions, and companies).

Sources: 1981–3 and 1995–8 World Values Survey; nations marked by an asterisk are from the 1990–3 World Values Survey for the second time-point.

to be more critical of these two institutions, and in some instances these relationships are quite strong. This is where the participatory and egalitarian norms of postmaterialists come into conflict with the norms of these institutions.

The variability of value effects across institutions is even more apparent in Figure 5.2, which displays the average correlation between postmaterialism and confidence in the various institutions included in the 1995–8 World Values Survey (these are pooled results for the eight advanced industrial democracies in the survey). Postmaterial orientations are strongly linked to negative evaluations of institutions that are identified with hierarchy, bureaucratic structures, and conservative orientations: the military, police, the church, and big business. These are the institutions of authority that Inglehart (1999) emphasized in his research. But the link between postmaterialism and other key institutions of democracy—such as parliament, political parties, the legal system, the civil service—is quite weak. In fact, postmaterialists display greater confidence in unions than do materialists. Furthermore, if we broaden our interests to include political movements and citizen groups, the pattern changes dramatically. On average, postmaterialists are *more*

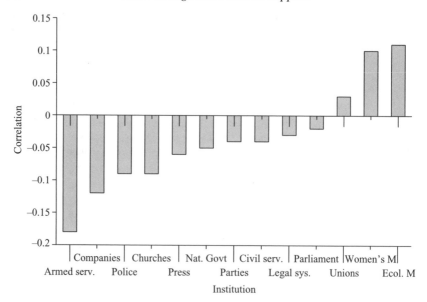

FIG. 5.2. Correlation between postmaterialism and institutional confidence
Source: 1995–8 World Values Survey (pooled results for eight advanced industrial democracies).

likely to express confidence in ecology groups and women's groups.[8] Thus, some political actors actually earn the confidence of postmaterialists.

In summary, these data modify previous arguments about the impact of postmaterial value change on contemporary democracies. The authors of *The Crisis of Democracy* and Ronald Inglehart (1999) maintained that the changing values of the citizenry are eroding respect for authority and thereby decreasing public confidence in political and social institutions. We believe the impact is not a general decline in confidence, but a shift focused on specific institutions. This implies that the factors that postmaterialists use to evaluate political and social organizations differ from the standards that materialists employ. In other words, the legitimacy of political institutions is not in question, but the source of legitimacy for political and social institutions may be changing. A Weberian legitimacy based on hierarchic authority patterns is no longer sufficient; support for organizations based on such structures is systematically weaker among postmaterialists. Thus, confidence in the armed services or the police suffers among postmaterialists, although these institutions never were shining models of democratic values. At the same time, postmaterialists display more confidence in their fellow citizens and in institutions that emphasize participation and the representation of public interests. *Legitimacy based on inclusion and participation is replacing legitimacy based on hierarchic authority.*

[8] There is a similar pattern for trust in human rights groups and civil rights groups in the 1990–1 World Values Survey (Dalton 2000b).

Support for Democracy

While postmaterialists might be sceptical about politicians and political institutions, their orientations towards the democratic system and its values is a more open question. On the one side, Inglehart's writings (1977; 1990) have emphasized how the social changes of advanced industrial societies are increasing the public's attachment to participatory values and encouraging greater tolerance and adherence to libertarian norms (see also Flanagan 1987). From this perspective, postmaterialists should be stronger advocates of the norms and values of democracy, even if they are critical of how contemporary democratic systems actually function.

The opposing view holds that postmaterialists are disenchanted with both the operation and the norms of the democratic system. The rise of radical leftist groups in the 1970s and 1980s represented a challenge to the political establishment, and postmaterialism and Green parties were initially portrayed by their critics as a threat to democracy. The Greens, for example, were characterized by some German politicians as watermelons: green on the outside but red on the inside. Indeed, embedded in much of the criticism of postmaterialists, yuppies, and the X-generation is a claim that these individuals lack an understanding and appreciation for the norms that underlie the democratic process. Individualism is seen as a cover for self-centredness; self-expression is seen as an excuse for self-indulgence.

This section thus considers whether postmaterial values reinforce or erode the principles of democracy. One way to approach this question is by examining feelings of political tolerance (Sullivan, Pierson, and Marcus 1982; McCloskey and Brill 1983; Gibson 1992). Tolerance of 'the other' is widely seen as an essential democratic value. Critics of the political establishment often embrace the call for tolerance in protection of their own interests. However, the crucial issue is whether one grants the same political rights to one's opponents. The 1995–8 World Values Survey included a tolerance battery that first asked respondents which was their least-liked political group from among a predetermined set. This was done so that respondents were judged by their tolerance of the groups they opposed, which could vary between materialists and postmaterialists.[9]

The survey then asked if the least-liked group should be allowed to hold political office, to teach in the schools, or to mount a public demonstration. Figure 5.3 displays the level of tolerance displayed by postmaterialists and materialists. One is first struck by the low level of tolerance displayed by all groups; the vast majority of respondents would limit the rights of disliked groups to hold office or teach, and a large majority even believes the rights to demonstrate should not be tolerated. But there are also clear differences between materialists and postmaterialists. Even when focused on their least-liked group, postmaterialists are considerably more likely to extend political rights to each of these groups. If we use opinions towards neo-Nazis as an example, among those citing this group as least liked postmaterialists are much

---

[9] Postmaterialists were more likely to cite neo-Nazis as the least-liked group; materialists were relatively more likely to name criminals, homosexuals, and immigrants.

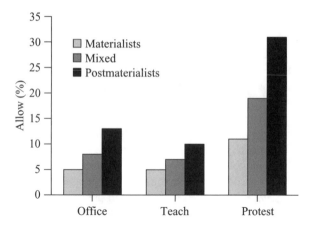

FIG. 5.3. Postmaterial values and tolerance of least-liked groups

Source: 1995–8 World Values Survey (pooled results for eight advanced industrial democracies).

more likely to tolerate political demonstrations by neo-Nazis (32 per cent) than are materialists (10 per cent). It is not that postmaterialists like neo-Nazis; postmaterialists are substantially more likely to rate neo-Nazis as their least-liked group. But still, these postmaterialists express support for the right to demonstrate even for those who they oppose. This is a positive reflection of postmaterialists' commitment to the democratic creed.

More broadly, the analyses of Chapter 3 (Figure 3.5) demonstrated that postmaterialists are *more likely* to express the belief that democracy is the best form of government and support democracy as an ideal. Inglehart (1999) has also demonstrated postmaterialists' greater commitment to democratic ideals—consistent with the participatory and egalitarian nature of these values. We certainly can be doubtful whether such expressed support for democratic principles will always be translated into democratic behaviour, especially when these principles are applied to specific cases. But the important point is that postmaterialists begin with these positive orientations toward democracy—without such norms the democratic process might be hollow.

The findings of this chapter thus describe a paradoxical pattern of how postmaterial value change is altering the political orientations of contemporary publics. This contrast can be seen by tracing the relationship of postmaterial values to political trust and support for the democratic ideal. Figure 5.4 indicates that postmaterialists are *less likely* than materialists to express confidence in government. Indeed, the postmaterialists' calls for political reform have partially fuelled present public doubts about politicians and political institutions. At the same time, postmaterialists are much *more likely* to support democratic ideals. For instance, only 39 per cent of the most materialist respondents in this subset of nations from the 1995–8 World Values Survey 'strongly agree' that democracy is

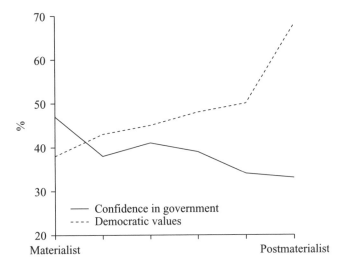

FIG. 5.4. Impact of values on support for democracy and confidence in national government

Note: Figure plots the % strongly agreeing that democracy is the best form of government and % having confidence in national government.

Source: 1995–8 World Values Survey (pooled results for eight advanced industrial democracies).

the best form of government, compared with 67 per cent among postmaterialists. In other words, materialists are satisfied with the present democratic state, but they have lower aspirations for democracy; postmaterialists are less satisfied with current democratic systems, partially because they have higher expectations.

These patterns again suggest that what is changing is, not so much the actual performance of contemporary democracies, but citizen expectations of what democracy should achieve. Postmaterialists have higher democratic ideals, and it is of this higher standard that contemporary politicians and political institutions fall short.

VALUE CHANGE AND POLITICAL SUPPORT

Postmaterial value change is affecting contemporary democracies—and it reinforces many of the political phenomena that preoccupy us in this book. Postmaterialists may be more cynical towards political authority and political institutions, especially certain institutions, but this reflects changes in the basis of legitimacy rather than an outright rejection of political and social institutions or the democratic process. Is democracy really in crisis if postmaterialists are more cynical about the police and more trustful of citizen-based movements? Moreover, postmaterialists express more support for democratic principles and processes than do materialists, and are more likely to trust their fellow citizens.

As part of the earlier *Crisis of Democracy* literature, Samuel Huntington (1975; 1981) argued that such orientations were threatening the democratic process.

He worried that such 'creedal passion' (that is, high expectations for the democratic process) were unrealistic and thus would inevitably generate dissatisfaction with reality. I do not believe that adherence to the democratic creed should be seen as a threat to democracy. The 'creedal passion' that so worried Huntington is actually a sign of the vitality of democracy, and a force that can generate progressive political reform. The development of Green parties and public interest groups, the expansion of participation opportunities, and other examples of modern democratic reform are the signs of progress that flow from such creedal passion. Similarly, earlier periods of creedal passion that generated the expansion of the franchise and the development of just voting systems were also periods of democratic development.

Michel Crozier (1975: 47) offered a more temperate reflection on political change than his coauthor Huntington, which captured the essence of changing citizen expectations that we have described in this chapter:

> What is at stake, therefore, is not the democratic creed and the Christian ethos, which are less directly threatened than they were for example in the thirties, but the contradiction between these core political beliefs and the principles of action that could make it possible to implement them.

The challenge of democracy is to move the process of democratic reform forward in reaction to citizens' changing expectations of government. In short, this chapter argues that changes in citizen expectations, rather than the reality of democratic performance, partially underlie the trends we have described.

It is possible that political systems can address these new concerns of postmaterialists by undertaking political reforms that open the democratic process, shifting away from the institutions of representative democracy towards forms of participatory democracy. I see strong parallels to present descriptions of value change and Laski's description of these value changes in the early twentieth century—at another time of democratic ferment when populist democrats pressed for reforms of electoral politics and the expansion of direct democracy. The present dissatisfactions with democratic government are similarly leading to calls for institutional reforms that expand the democratic process (Cain, Dalton, and Scarrow 2003; Curtice and Jowell 1997). We will examine this topic more extensively in Chapter 8.

Having documented the disaffection of postmaterialists, however, we should also realize that contemporary publics are characterized by a mix of value orientations. Responding to postmaterialists' calls for political reform may not be a solution to the current public dissatisfaction with government. While postmaterialists want the political system to change, materialists may become more dissatisfied by these same changes. While postmaterialists will applaud the development of participatory politics, materialists may lament the loss of governability that results from these same reforms. Perhaps the largest lesson is that there is now a conflict within contemporary publics on the meaning of democracy and how it should function. This conflict, itself, is likely to deepen public cynicism about the political process because it reflects different images of what democracy should be.

6

Economic Performance and Political Support

CHANGING citizen expectations might explain decreasing support for government, as we have suggested in the previous chapters. A more immediate explanation, however, focuses on the performance of government itself. For instance, the erosion of political support in Japan in the 1990s is routinely connected to the downturn in the economy during the decade (as well as political scandals); New Zealanders' frustration with government in the 1980s was attributed to the perceived policy failures of government; and the decline in political support among Americans is often explained in terms of the government's policy failures. Indeed, the separate national literatures on the decline in political support almost always link the trend to the specific policy problems or political scandals of the nation. The question is whether there are such commonalities in national experiences that, when accumulated over time and nations, may explain the general decline in political support across nations.

The 'performance hypothesis' linking government performance and evaluations of government is well ingrained in the political theory and political research on political support. As noted in Chapter 3, for instance, David Easton (1976: 436) laid out the logic that governments are (and should be) evaluated in terms of their performance—especially democratic governments (also see Citrin 1974; Wright 1976; Fuchs 1989; Weatherford 1992; Kornberg and Clarke 1992; Anderson and Guilloy 1997; Rohrschneider 2002). If governmental performance falls below expectations, specific support for political actors should suffer as a consequence. If the public is dissatisfied with the government's performance, the next election presents the opportunity to change the incumbents. If performance dissatisfaction continues for an extended period of time, the decline of support may become more generalized and affect evaluations of the regime and the political community.

This chapter examines the core of these performance theories, focusing on economic perceptions as a potential predictor of political support. Prior research often demonstrates a correlation between perceptions of economic conditions and measures of political support. We ask whether we should interpret this correlation as evidence of causal effects, or whether there are other explanations for it. Sorting out this relationship will demonstrate the potential of the performance hypothesis as an explanation for the trends in political support.

FOCUSING ON ECONOMIC PERFORMANCE

Despite the natural logic of the performance hypothesis, establishing the link between government performance and political support can be complicated. One complication is that governments are now engaged in a wide range of policy activities. Certainly any government is performing poorly on some dimensions, but performance may be better on other dimensions (see Putnam 1993; Bok 1998).[1] Ideally, citizens judge government performance as a weighted assessment of multiple policies, although we know citizens tend to specialize their interests on a few issues. Thus, the first question is what aspect(s) of performance determines citizen perceptions of government.

Whereas Chapter 5 discussed how new political values are affecting calculations of political support, this chapter focuses on economic performance as a crucial test of the performance hypothesis. We selected this issue because economic perform-ance is one of the main policy goals of government. The state of the economy con-tinues to be an important predictor of the fate of incumbent governments at election time, and economic policies dominate the political debate in most campaigns. Latent or manifest conflicts over economic issues are major factors dividing political parties and motivating citizens in their electoral preferences. Indeed, a large and rich polit-ical economy literature examines the impact of economic conditions and economic perceptions on voting choices (Anderson 1995; Lewis-Beck 1988). If government performance does substantially influence citizen support for political institutions, this should be readily apparent within the economic domain.

We also concentrate on economics because there is a rich literature claiming that economic factors contribute to the public's declining support for politicians, parties, and political institutions (see also Chapter 4). Alesina and Wacziarg (2000), for instance, suggest that deteriorating macroeconomic performance is prompting cit-izens to be more negative towards their governments. Similarly, Robert Lawrence (1997) presents a thoughtful discussion of how economic factors, such as slowing economic growth rates or widening economic inequality, may have increased the political scepticism of Americans. There is also a diverse literature theorizing that globalization, increased international competition, or growing economic inequality contribute to the declines in political support (for example, Offe 1984; Bobbio 1987; Uslaner 1999; Scharpf 2000).

As rich as these theories are, the difficulty is that there is only modest empirical support for their claims. One approach is to correlate national economic conditions with aggregate levels of political support. The most extensive analysis is Harold Clarke, Nittish Dutt, and Allan Kornberg's (1993) pooled time series modelling of two political support questions from the Eurobarometer surveys: satisfaction with the functioning of democracy and support for radical social change.

---

[1] In Chapter 7 we consider how multiple-issue interests and multiple dimensions of political competition may contribute to the decline in political support.

They found only a modest correlation between economic conditions (inflation and unemployment rates) and satisfaction with the democratic process, and an even weaker impact on the radical social change question. They concluded that economic conditions had a real but limited impact on political support, in part because the range of economic experiences among contemporary Western democracies generally lacks the economic disasters or economic miracles that might significantly shift levels of political support (Clarke, Dutt, and Kornberg 1993: 1015). Listaug and Wiberg (1995) found only a weak cross-sectional relationship between inflation rates and political trust for a subset of nations using the World Values Survey; unemployment displays a stronger, but variable, relationship. Ian McAllister (1999) also examined the cross-sectional relationship between aggregate economic conditions and support for political institutions in a larger set of WVS nations. He found a *negative* relationship between GNP levels and confidence in political institutions; and this negative relationship would appear in the time series correlations within most nations.[2] McAllister suggested that citizens in 'more affluent countries may...have higher expectations of their democratic institutions' (1999: 197), which is consistent with our rising-expectations argument in Chapters 4 and 5. Moreover, Chapter 4 demonstrated that political support is not decreasing disproportionately among lower-social status groups, as another version of the economic performance hypothesis would suggest. In short, there is limited systematic empirical evidence demonstrating that poor macroeconomic performance is driving down aggregate levels of political support across the advanced industrial democracies.

Not only is empirical evidence of the aggregate-level economic performance hypothesis lacking, I believe that this hypothesis cannot logically provide an explanation of the general decline in political support in the OECD nations. The breadth of decreasing political support almost necessarily excludes economic performance as a major causal force—unless everywhere economic conditions are worsening. Even when Alesina and Wacziarg (2000) present the economic performance hypothesis, their evidence is based on slower rates of growth among OECD nations, not actual decline. The standard indicators of economic well-being—such as disposable income, consumption, and wealth—have generally trended upward in these nations. Moreover, deteriorating macroeconomic performance may overlap with decreases in political support in some national contexts (such as Japan in the 1990s), but support levels also decline in nations where the economic conditions have improved over the same period. Moreover, when the economic cycle reverses and economic conditions improve, political support has not returned to its previous levels. The United States is a case in point. Economic conditions were relatively positive during 1965–74, when the first major drops in political trust occurred. Conversely, after the longest period of sustained economic growth in the nation's modern history during the

---

[2] For instance, merging the ANES and *New York Times* series on the 'trust in government' question reveals a strong negative cross-correlation with GNP per capita from 1958 to 2000 (r = −0.617, N = 42). Because political support is generally trending downward and GNP levels are generally trending upward, this same relationship should appear in most other OECD nations.

1990s, Americans remained sceptical about their politicians and political institutions. Thus, Nye and Zelikow (1997) discounted macroeconomic performance theories as an explanation for the declines in Americans' trust in government—and this logic generally extends to other advanced industrial democracies.

Another version of the economic performance thesis suggests that individual-level perceptions of economic conditions may exert a more direct influence on citizen images of government than aggregate economic statistics. If citizens are pessimistic (or optimistic) about the economy or their personal economic situation, then these perceptions may be linked to feelings of political support. In other words, *perceptions are reality* when explaining individual citizen behaviour.

Again, there is modest empirical support for this version of the performance hypothesis. Ola Listhaug (1995; see also Listaug and Wiberg 1995) demonstrated that perceptions of economic performance are significantly related to trust in politicians and political institutions for a set of European democracies. Several analyses have used Eurobarometer data to document a relationship between economic dissatisfaction and political alienation in Western Europe (Lockerbie 1993; Anderson and Guillory 1997). Several studies of American public opinion also found a correlation between perceptions of economic conditions and measures of political support (Lipset and Schneider 1987; Miller and Borelli 1991; Weatherford 1984). Similar patterns have been identified among Canadians (Kornberg and Clarke 1992: ch. 4), Germans (Fuchs 1989) and other nationalities (McAllister 1992).

Thus, research generally finds a relationship between an individual's perceptions of economic conditions and his or her evaluations of politicians and political institutions. This still leaves a number of important questions to address, however. Most important is the question of whether these correlations are sufficient evidence of causal influences. First, to explain the long-term decline in political support, citizen perceptions of economic performance would have to trend downward over time, which would then lower support. We expect that perceptions of economic performance have fluctuated over time without a consistent long-term downward trend. This is an empirical question that we can answer in the research presented below.

A second question is whether a correlation between economic perceptions and political support is actually a causal relationship or a spurious relationship—or even a case where the causal flow works in the opposite direction: cynicism of government leads individuals to be pessimistic about the economy as well. One example can illustrate this pattern. Before the 1992 US presidential elections, the ANES asked the public to judge whether the national economy would improve or worsen over the next twelve months. With George Bush in the White House, Republicans were more optimistic about the nation's future than Democrats by a 15 per cent margin. Immediately after the election, even before Clinton was sworn in, Republican optimism waned and Democrats became much more positive about the economy, by a 29 per cent margin. The reversal of the relationship between pre-election and post-election surveys illustrates the power of orientations towards the incumbent government to shape citizen perceptions of the economy. We hope to disentangle this relationship in the analyses that follow.

Finally, theory predicts that economic perceptions should have a varied impact on different levels of political support. In terms of the Eastonian framework, performance should be most relevant to evaluations of political authorities (incumbents and politicians as a group) and exert less influence on regime evaluations, while support for the political community should be relatively immune from short-term performance perceptions (Kornberg and Clarke 1992: ch. 4).[3] We uncovered such a pattern in Chapter 3. Financial satisfaction is moderately correlated with support for the incumbents (r = 0.16), has a slightly weaker relationship with confidence in political institutions (r = 0.14), and is essentially unrelated to democratic values (r = 0.00) or community support (r = 0.05). Where performance is compared across multiple dimensions of support, a similar pattern often appears (Clarke, Dutt, and Kornberg 1993; Kornberg and Clarke 1992: ch. 4). However, since most previous research examines only a single economic predictor or a single measure of political support, the variability of effects has not been clearly established.

In summary, a large research literature suggests that deteriorating government performance is a major contributor to the decline in political support in advanced industrial democracies. Indeed, it would be problematic for democracy if poor government performance did not generate dissatisfaction and pressure for political change among the public—this is the logic of electoral competition. But it is unclear whether the performance of contemporary governments has been so poor that this has eroded citizen confidence in political actors and institutions. By focusing on perceptions of economic performance, we have selected a policy domain in which the performance hypothesis is most naturally tested, and we can evaluate the contribution of performance to the decline in political support.

ECONOMIC PERCEPTIONS AND POLITICAL SUPPORT

There are good reasons to expect that economic perceptions may have a greater impact than objective economic measures on evaluations of government. Statistics on economic performance (GNP per capita, unemployment rates, and so on) follow a strongly autoregressive process that moderates change, but public perceptions of the economy are often highly responsive to short-term factors. For instance, the drop in objective economic indicators during the 1974–5 and 1980–1 OPEC recessions were fairly modest, but the drop in Americans' confidence about the economy was quite sharp. Furthermore, such subjective judgements may be exactly the type of

---

[3] In addition, it is not clear which aspects of the economy are most salient in judgements of the government. Citizens may base their evaluations on the performance of the national economy (sociotropic evaluations) or their own situation (egocentric evaluations). The political economy literature also asks whether the public judges government retrospectively or based on prospective expectations for the economy. See the discussion of these points in the next section.

forces that carry over to evaluations of the government, regardless of the objective economic circumstances.

Subjective economic perceptions also can be sensitive to different and multiple elements of the economy, whereas single economic indicators measure only one trait. For example, at one time the public may base their economic judgements on unusually high levels of unemployment, and at another time on the slow growth rates or high inflation rates. Correlating trends in political support with these separate series for unemployment, growth, or inflation may prove insensitive to the shifting bases of economic perceptions. Thus, economic perceptions should provide the best test of whether citizens use their evaluations of the economy to judge the performance of politicians and political institutions.

Since the richest data series to examine this hypothesis exists for the United States, we begin with analyses of the US experience. Figure 6.1 compares the levels of political trust between those with positive or negative expectations for their personal economic situation over the coming year. This measure of economic perceptions is available for the longest time span in the American election study series, and includes data from before the sharp drop-off in trust in government in the late 1960s. As in Chapter 4, to focus on the differences across groups, we detrend the series and express group values as deviations from the overall sample mean for each time-point.[4] The figure presents the percentage that trusts the government to do what is right, relative to the sample as a whole.

The overall pattern reaffirms the relationship between economic perceptions and political support. Across eight US administrations, those who are more positive about their personal financial condition are also more trustful of government. The magnitude of this relationship, however, is modest (averaging around $r = 0.10$); by comparison, it is smaller than the educational effects in Figure 4.1. In addition, there is a slight tendency for the gap between those with positive and the negative perceptions to narrow over time, although it would be more accurate to say there is no major change in this relationship over the thirty-four year time span of these data.

Another aspect of economic perceptions is whether one's financial circumstances have improved or worsened over the past year. Because these retrospective judgements are rooted in reality, and presumably are affected by governmental policies, these views may have a stronger influence on evaluations of government. A slightly shorter series of retrospective personal judgements is available from the ANES, and it demonstrates a nearly identical pattern (Figure 6.2). There is a consistent relationship between retrospective judgements and trust in government from 1966 until 2000. But these are modest differences, and they tend to narrow over time.

While personal economic circumstances are only modestly correlated with trust in government, the political economy literature often demonstrates that

---

[4] We use the 'trust the government to do right' question because it is available for the longest time span. The overall sample mean was subtracted from the percentage trustful among those thinking the economy was 'getting better' or 'getting worse' to produce the trends in the figure.

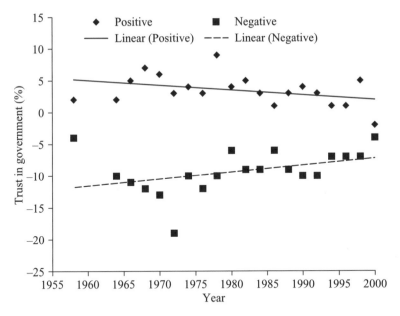

FIG. 6.1. The relationship between personal economic expectations for following year and political trust in the United States, 1958–2000

Note: The lines represent the regression lines for the relationship between the two economic perception groups and the trust in government question over time.

Source: American National Election Studies.

perceptions of the national economic condition (sociotropic perceptions) more strongly influence political support (Anderson and Guilloy 1997; Kornberg and Clarke 1992: ch. 4). The available time series of sociotropic perceptions from the ANES is considerably shorter, beginning only in 1980, and this post-dates the largest decline in political trust. These data, however, display a similar pattern to the personal economic measures. For instance, retrospective evaluations of the national economy are significantly related to political trust in the 1980 ($r = 0.18$) and 1982 elections ($r = 0.15$), and this relationship generally diminishes over time to present only weak correlations in 1998 ($r = 0.05$) and 2000 ($r = 0.07$). Prospective evaluations of the national economy follow a similar course.

This basic cross-sectional correlation is generally repeated across the advanced industrial democracies (Anderson and Guillory 1997). The relationships for a set of twelve West European nations are typical of these results (Table 6.1). The table correlates prospective perceptions of the family's economic situation and the national economy over the coming year with four measures of political support: trust in the government, trust in parliament, satisfaction with the functioning of democracy, and national pride. In all but one case, the correlations are in the

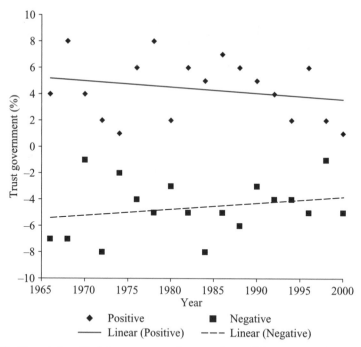

FIG. 6.2. The relationship between personal economic condition over previous year and political trust in the United States, 1966–2000

Note: The lines represent the regression lines for the relationship between the two economic perception groups and the trust in government question over time.

Source: American National Election Studies.

predicted direction. As noted above, perceptions of the national economy are more closely linked to trust in government (average correlation is 0.20), and the relationship with their personal financial condition is weaker (average correlation is 0.10). In other words, while citizens are more likely to hold the government responsible for the state of the national economy, they are less likely to generalize from their own financial circumstances to their evaluations of government overall. This same pattern exists across all three measures of political support for the government (authorities), the legislature (institutions), and the political process.[5] As theory would suggest, the last two columns of the table demonstrate that economic perceptions are not related to community support (national pride).

I do not question the existence of a relationship between economic perceptions and political support; the issue is whether this correlation is evidence of causation,

[5] Eurobarometer 42 included retrospective measures of family and national economic conditions. The average correlation between retrospective family conditions and satisfaction with the functioning of democracy was 0.13, the average correlation for retrospective national conditions was 0.18.

TABLE 6.1 *Correlation between economic expectations and political support*

Nation	Trust government		Trust legislature		Satisfied with democracy		National pride	
	Family	Nation	Family	Nation	Family	Nation	Family	Nation
Austria	0.20	0.26	0.22	0.25	0.30	0.30	n/a	n/a
Belgium	0.09	0.23	0.10	0.26	0.18	0.31	0.00	0.01
Britain	0.06	0.16	0.07	0.14	0.07	0.16	0.12	0.10
Denmark	0.06	0.16	0.01	0.16	0.01	0.10	0.03	0.00
Finland	0.15	0.22	0.10	0.20	0.17	0.25	n/a	n/a
France	0.10	0.28	0.10	0.27	0.11	0.25	0.09	0.11
Germany (West)	0.16	0.21	0.15	0.22	0.20	0.28	0.06	0.01
Ireland	0.08	0.12	0.07	0.16	0.07	0.11	0.02	0.07
Italy	0.04	0.27	0.05	0.24	0.10	0.34	0.06	0.13
Luxembourg	0.06	0.10	0.10	0.08	0.10	0.25	0.04	−0.05
Netherlands	0.17	0.22	0.16	0.21	0.11	0.20	0.00	0.03
Sweden	0.02	0.19	0.05	0.15	0.04	0.22	n/a	n/a
AVERAGE	0.10	0.20	0.10	0.20	0.12	0.23	0.03	0.05

Note: Table entries are tau$_b$ correlations between measures of economic expectations for one's family and the nation with political support questions.

Sources: Eurobarometer 48 (November 1997); national pride is from Eurobarometer 42 (November 1994).

especially for the long-term trend of decreasing support for politicians, parties, and political institutions. It is difficult to evaluate causal processes with a cross-sectional survey. When those dissatisfied with the government's economic performance simultaneously express distrust of political institutions, we see a relationship but we cannot determine which attitude caused which. The next section, however, uses longitudinal data to examine causal processes that are not apparent in a cross-sectional survey analysis.

TRENDS IN ECONOMIC PERCEPTIONS

In order to translate a cross-section correlation between economic perceptions and political support into a causal explanation of declining trust in government, we must assume that economic perceptions have deteriorated, and consequently citizens have lost faith in politicians, parties, and political institutions (see also Chapter 4).[6] Such a pattern would translate the cross-section correlation into a

[6] As we noted in Chapter 4, changes in the relationship between a predictor and the dependent variable over time may also alter the distribution of political support even if the distribution of the predictor variable remains relatively stable. That is, if negative economic evaluations exert a stronger impact on political support over time, this alone may erode the levels of support. But this pattern is not present in the United States (Figures 6.1 and 6.2), and analyses of the election study series in other nations also does not demonstrate a consistent pattern over time.

dynamic causal process in which a negative trend in economic perceptions contributes to the decline in political support.

The key question, therefore, is whether citizens are becoming more critical of economic performance—in terms of either their personal situation or the national economy—that might drive such a dynamic causal process. We maintain that objective economic statistics do not generally substantiate such claims, but perceptions of economic performance can be distinct from economic statistics.

The US Case

The available data series of economic perceptions are richest in the United States. If we begin with the measures of personal economic conditions from the American National Election Studies, there is considerable variability in opinion across elections. For example, positive views of the respondent's financial situation over the next year range from a low of 22 per cent in 1974 (the first OPEC recession) to a high of 46 per cent in 1964. Similarly, retrospective personal perceptions range from a low of 28 per cent in 1974 to a high of 52 per cent in 1998. However, neither time series demonstrates a significant negative trend in economic perceptions, as seen in the time trends in Table 6.2. Prospective evaluations display a slight downward trend from 1952 to 2000, but this is not statistically significant; retrospective evaluations actually display a statistically significant *upward trend* over time.[7]

More extensive data on Americans' economic perceptions comes from the University of Michigan's consumer sentiment surveys. Since 1960 this series has tracked American perceptions of the economy on a quarterly basis (and now monthly), and it is one of the most highly respected sources of consumer sentiments (Curtin 2002; Souleles 2003). The Michigan index of consumer sentiments is a combination of prospective and retrospective judgements about personal and national economic conditions, and thus is a very broad-based measure of economic perceptions.[8]

Between 1960 and 2000 this index has a considerable range, reacting to various ebbs and flows in economic circumstances (Figure 6.3). The dips for the 1974

---

[7] If we replicate the methodology used in Chapter 4, we can estimate the impact that changing levels of economic perceptions might have on political support assuming constant effects over time. There is a weak relationship between retrospective personal economic evaluations and trust in government in 1966 (b = 0.0872). Between 1966 and the peak of the economy under the Clinton administration (1998), the mean for the economic measure increased by 0.19. Thus, if the relationship had remained the same over time, rising economic perceptions would have increased political trust by approximately +0.02. In actuality, the mean on the trust question decreased by −0.41 over this period.

[8] For information on the index construction, see www.sca.isr.umich.edu/main.php. Information on the index is also available in Curtin (2002).

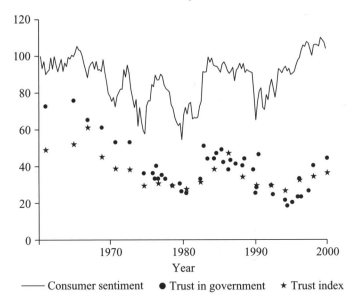

FIG. 6.3. Americans' consumer sentiment and trust in government, 1960–2000

Note: Trust in government: % saying they trust the government to do what is right some or all of the time (ANES and *New York Times* time series); trust index: composite trust index computed by ANES.

Source: University of Michigan Consumer Sentiment Index.

and 1981 recessions are clearly evident, as well as the economic slowdown in the early 1990s. Conversely, the decade of economic growth in the 1990s and the spurt of growth in the mid-1980s are also clearly reflected in the consumer sentiment series. More so than aggregate economic statistics, consumer sentiments are more responsive to shifts in the economic climate.

If one looks beyond these short-term economic swings, the overall trend is in the positive direction over the same period that political support has decreased substantially (Table 6.2). In a sense, Bill Clinton's optimistic 2000 State of the Union address was correct in the minds of many Americans, because consumer sentiment hit its highest peak in early 2000—despite Americans' simultaneous negativity towards their government.

Figure 6.3 also includes two measures of political support. The black dots represent the percentage of Americans who say they trust the government to do right, combining both the ANES time series and the *New York Times* time series to increase the number of time-points. In addition, the stars represent the percentage scoring as trustful on the ANES summary political trust index.

Consumer sentiment and trust in government are modestly related over this forty-year series (r = 0.233, N = 42), but the patterns in Figure 6.3 raise further questions about whether economic perceptions are a cause of decreasing trust in government.[9] The trust in government indicators generally trend downward between 1960 and 1980, paralleling the overall drop in consumer sentiment. But the direct relationship between the two series over this period appears quite tenuous. For instance, the peaks and troughs in consumer sentiments between autumn 1968 and autumn 1980 are not mirrored in the trust in government statistics, which rather seem to follow a steady downward slide over this period. The fit between both series since 1980 is also quite modest (r = 0.239). The upturns in economic conditions in the mid-1980s and the 1990s seem to be mirrored in citizen images of government, which rise by about 10 per cent during both of these interludes. But these are variations around a low baseline that is inconsistent with the overall levels of consumer confidence during the same period. Consumer sentiment had risen to its highest levels in the late 1990s, higher even than in the early 1960s— but political trust remains at half its 1960s level. Thus, while Americans were celebrating their self-identified best of economic times, this was among the worst of times in terms of their images of government.

The Cross-national Evidence

Moving beyond the US experience, we can test the core element of the performance hypothesis by determining whether perceptions of the economy have generally trended downward in advanced industrial democracies. In collecting such data, our goal was to have a long time series that substantially encapsulated the period when political support was decreasing in a nation. To meet this objective, we brought together a diverse set of data sources.

Since the early 1970s the European Union has conducted regular consumer sentiment surveys in the Member States that are separate from the Eurobarometer series (Commission of the European Communities, various years). Figure 6.4 tracks the consumer confidence index for the eight EU Members States during 1973–99.[10] Again, the most obvious pattern is the ebb and flow of consumer confidence rather than a distinct trend. Europeans' consumer confidence hit bottom in late 1974 and early 1975 in reaction to the global recession at the time, and then dipped again after the recession produced by the second round of OPEC price increases in the early 1980s. Another dip in confidence occurred in the early

---

[9] There is a stronger correlation with the ANES trust index (r = 0.397), but this is based on only 20 time-points. Using only the 20 time-points that include the ANES trust in government question also produces a stronger correlation (0.367).

[10] The EU Consumer Confidence Index is the arithmetic average of results for five survey questions: two on the past and future financial situation of the household, two on the past and future general economic situation, and one concerning expectations of major purchases (see Commission of the European Communities, various years). The eight nations included in Figure 6.4 are Belgium, Britain, Denmark, France, Germany, Ireland, Italy, and the Netherlands. We collected data only from the May and October surveys because in other research we have paired these data with opinions from the Eurobarometers that are collected in May and October.

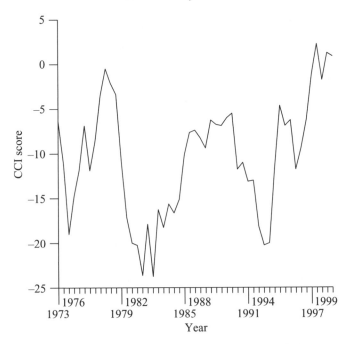

FIG. 6.4. European trend in Consumer Confidence Index, 1973–1999

Note: Averaged results for eight European Union members from the May and October consumer surveys of each year.

Source: Commission of the European Communities (various years).

1990s, but by the end of the decade sentiments had rebounded to their highest level over this time span. If one were to draw a straight trend line over this period, which is admittedly a poor representation of the dynamic patterns in these data, there is a statistically significant positive trend ($b = 0.271$, st. error $= 0.077$, $p < 0.01$). Certainly, if one picked a different time range there are periods for which consumer confidence has trended downward in Europe—and confidence will inevitably dip again at some time in the future.[11] (We also note that this time series begins before the first OPEC price increase and subsequent recession.) Thus, these data fail to show a clear downturn in consumer confidence that would be consistent with the argument that economic pessimism is afflicting political support.

To provide further detail on national patterns, we separated the trends in consumer confidence for the individual nations in the European Union series. In addition, we sought out separate time series of national consumer sentiment to validate these patterns, using possibly different time spans and different

---

[11] In fact, sentiments turned downward in many nations in the early 2000s, in reaction partly to economic recession and partly to the changing international order after September 11, 2001.

indices of consumer sentiment.[12] Table 6.2 reports on the time trends we have assembled—recognizing that linear trends are not an accurate description of the variability in these trends—but the coefficients simply summarize whether a long-term trend is present. Moreover, the results are naturally dependent on the choice of starting and ending points. A series beginning in the early 1970s catches most economies at a peak; a starting point a few years later would begin in the midst of the 1974–5 recession. To highlight the comparison of the economic and political trends, Table 6.2 also redisplays a measure of political support from Table 2.2, recalculating the time span of several trust items to generally match the period of the consumer confidence indicator.[13]

There are some clear instances in which both trends have declined over time: Japan is the most prominent example of both trends showing a statistically significant decline. But most of the comparisons in Table 6.2 fail to show this consistency. Sweden is a clear example. Except for the United States, the evidence of decreasing public support for politicians and political institutions is strongest for Sweden because the time series is longest and the overall amount of change has been considerable. Even if we recalculate the trust in government trend to begin in 1976, the consumer series trends upward (b = 1.361) while political support trends downward (b = −1.244). At the end of the 1990s, Swedish consumer confidence was close to its highest point of the last quarter century, but trust in government had dropped to its lowest point since the series began (Holmberg 1999).

Several of the nations in the table do show a significant downward trend in consumer confidence (such as Germany, Italy, and Japan). But more nations display a significant increase in consumer confidence over the span of the available data, such as Australia, Britain, Italy, Sweden, and the United States. And in this latter group of nations, the increase in consumer confidence runs directly counter to significant decreases in political support over approximately the same time span. At the least, one should conclude that these two time series are generated by different causal processes.

In summary, we have demonstrated a basic paradox in the time series data that test the performance hypothesis: over the last several decades political support has decreased in most advanced industrial societies, but this political negativity is not matched by public perceptions of national economic performance. Indeed, at the end of the 1990s citizens in many nations were often more positive about the economy than they were before the erosion of political support began.

---

[12] In most cases, the national election studies do not include long time series of consumer sentiment questions because their focus was on political behaviour. The additional data sources are: Australia, Wespac-Melbourne Institute surveys; Japan, consumer series available from www.economagic.com; Sweden, Statistics Sweden and GFK; and Canada, Conference Board.

[13] There are two nations in the EU data that are not included in the table because we lack long-term trend data:

Belgium	b = −0.001	st. error = 0.170
Ireland	b = 1.372	st. error = 0.360

TABLE 6.2 *Economic perceptions and political support trends*

Nation	Trend	(St. error)	Period	(N of time-points)
Australia				
Consumer sentiment-I	0.064	(0.101)	1974–2000	(266) W-M Institute
Consumer sentiment-II	0.388	(0.257)	1973–2000	(28) Ray Morgan
Trust government	−0.247	(0.333)	1969–98	(7) AES
Britain				
Consumer confidence	0.332	(0.194)	1973–99	(53) EU
Only interested in votes	−0.331	(0.185)	1974–2000	(8)
Canada				
Consumer confidence	−0.005	(0.166)	1965–97	(33) 6B
Govt. doesn't care	−0.611*	(0.157)	1965–97	(8)
Denmark				
Consumer confidence	0.415*	(0.145)	1973–99	(53) EU
Make right decisions	−0.169	(0.281)	1971–94	(11)
France				
Consumer confidence	−0.724*	(0.128)	1973–99	(53) EU
Govt. doesn't care	−1.685*	(0.280)	1977–97	(8)
Germany				
Consumer confidence	−0.434*	(0.178)	1973–99	(53) EU
Officials don't care (2)	−1.270*	(0.249)	1969–94	(5)
Italy				
Consumer confidence	0.342*	(0.153)	1973–99	(53) EU
Officials don't care	−0.451	(0.176)	1968–97	(5)
Japan				
Consumer confidence	−0.188*	(0.061)	1982–2000	(75) SA
Trust national politicians	−0.572*	(0.158)	1976–96	(5)
Netherlands				
Consumer confidence	0.871*	(0.240)	1973–99	(53) EU
Only interested in votes	0.785*	(0.200)	1971–94	(8)
Sweden				
Consumer sentiment	1.361*	(0.289)	1976–99	(99) SS
Political trust index	−1.244*	(0.148)	1976–98	(8)
United States				
Consumer sentiment	0.104	(0.080)	1960–2000	(164) UMCS
Personal finances past year	0.269*	(0.111)	1962–2000	(19) ANES
Personal finances next year	−0.111	(0.118)	1958–2000	(20) ANES
Trust government	−0.957*	(0.282)	1958–2000	(11) ANES

* Trends significant at the 0.10 level.

Sources: Political support trends were drawn from series presented in Table 2.2. Consumer sentiment series were drawn from multiple sources: EU, European Union. Australia: AES, Australian Election Studies. Canada: CB, Conference Board. Japan: SA, Economic.com. Sweden: SS, Statistics Sweden. United States, UMCS, University of Michigan Consumer Sentiment surveys. See n. 10 for additional information on the EU time series.

THE CONTRIBUTION OF ECONOMIC PERCEPTIONS

Government performance should be linked to citizen evaluations of their government. As Harold Wilson, a British Prime Minister in the 1960s and 1970s, once observed: 'All political history shows that the standing of a Government and its ability to hold the confidence of the electorate at a General Election depend on the success of its economic policy.'[14] When a government performs poorly, whether in terms of the economy or other policy areas, citizens should use this criterion in making their electoral choices. Indeed, there is a large and convincing literature demonstrating that economic conditions do influence electoral results.

The question facing us here, however, is whether negative evaluations of government performance have generalized to citizen images of politicians, political parties, and parliaments. We focused on economic policy as a test case because economic performance is purportedly a central focus of citizens' evaluations of their government, and there is a large literature claiming that poor economic performance contributes to the long-term decline in political support. If a relationship could be established for economic policy, then we might easily extend this same logic to other policy domains.

Even before beginning the analyses, however, there were reasons to question the performance hypothesis. By most objective economic measures, contemporary publics are better-off than they were a generation ago—affluence has increased, living standards have improved, social welfare provisions increasingly protect the disadvantaged—so positive performance should increase political support. In addition, Chapter 4 found that the greatest decrease in political support came from the better educated and the more affluent, which also argues against the economic performance hypothesis.

The empirical analyses in this chapter demonstrate the limitations of the performance model. Most cross-sectional surveys find a clear correlation between perceptions of the economy and political support—a pattern that generates claims that economic performance has a causal role in the decline in political support. But we find little evidence of such a causal relationship. Rather than becoming more pessimistic about their economic situation during the late twentieth century, contemporary publics often became more positive about their economic situation. In many nations, a simple application of the performance hypothesis to the empirical trends would predict an increase in political support over time. In broad terms, therefore, economic performance, whether measured in objective or subjective terms, does not appear to be a significant contributor to the long-term decline in political support during the later twentieth century.

These findings carry a mixed message for democratic theory and democratic practice. It would be problematic for contemporary democracy if citizens became

---

[14] Our thanks to Christopher Anderson (1995: 1) for drawing our attention to this quotation.

distrustful of political parties or sceptical about parliaments because of a short-term rise in unemployment rates or a slowdown in economic growth. The political culture literature argues that the reservoir of support for democratic institutions and processes should not be depleted by such specific economic effects (Almond and Verba 1963). And the downturns in economic conditions over the period of our analyses have (in most instances) not been dramatic. Thus, we should not expect that the economic trends of the past several decades have been a major and cross-nationally consistent source of decreasing trust of government.

Conversely, it is also be problematic for the democratic process if government performance did not factor at all into citizens' evaluations of their government. If poor economic performance—or poor performance in other policy domains—does not translate into a liability for the government, where is the accountability of the democratic process? Perhaps Japan represents the best current example. The recession of the Japanese economy during the 1990s should erode the public's evaluations of political actors, especially as successive governments fail to make progress in redressing that nation's economic woes. In such cases, democratic theory would predict a link between economic conditions and government evaluations; and this is one of the nations where both trends follow the same downward trajectory over time.

In most OECD nations, however, the link between economic performance and political support appears tenuous. We do not believe that this is because a linkage is non-existent. Rather, the range of experiences over this period is not sufficient to have a clear and direct role in decreasing political support. For performance dissatisfaction to become generalized to distrust in democratic institutions and democratic processes, it would require *major and sustained drops in the level of performance*. To restate the conclusion from Clarke, Dutt, and Kornberg (1993: 1015): 'barring extraordinary circumstances (e.g., economic disasters, major political triumphs or trauma), the political economy of public orientations toward polity and society in contemporary Western democracies is real but limited'. Economic perceptions thus apparently play a role in short-term perturbations around the long-term trend in political support, such as the slight rebound in Americans' confidence during the economic boom of the late 1990s. But economic performance per se does not appear to be a primary source of the long-term trend in declining political support in contemporary democracies.

7

Policy Preferences and Political Support

IF one sits down in a southern California coffee shop, a sidewalk café in Paris, or a pub in Australia, and strikes up a conversation with the person at the next table, I suspect that you would agree on the weather and that the government is falling short of your expectations. How is it that government can be performing so poorly in our minds, even while the 'objective' evidence suggests otherwise? One might at least expect that poor performance on some issues is counterbalanced by success on others. But (almost) everywhere, it seems, the public feels the government is falling short of our expectations.

The literature on declining political support frequently claims that governments are not meeting the public's policy expectations. Democratic governments are responsible for ensuring the general well-being of their citizens, which involves government in issues ranging from the provision of social services to the guarantee of human rights and to protection of the environment—as well as the economic outcomes examined in Chapter 6. Performance on these multiple dimensions may be, and should be, an important influence on citizen evaluations of government. The erosion of support in the United States, for example, supposedly began with the public's dissatisfaction with government policy on Vietnam and the civil rights issues of the 1960s; frustrations with government economic policy supposedly stimulated Japanese alienation from politics in the 1990s; and so forth. Indeed, such policy controversies, albeit with different policy focuses, are a standard part of accounts of declining political support in most nations. There are also strong theoretical and intuitive reasons to expect that policy considerations are at least a partial explanation of the trends in political support.

This chapter goes beyond the economic analyses of the previous chapter and examines the potential role of policy preferences in producing the downward trends in political support. It should be obvious from the outset that this is a complex relationship. A simple policy-based explanation of decreasing support is difficult to sustain unless all governments are generally performing more poorly over time and thus producing the decline in support. Moreover, such a pattern of policy effects would raise questions about the basic performance of democratic systems because elections should produce new governments that are more attentive to public preferences: this is the point of elections. To refer again to Citrin's sports analogy (1974), if the alternation of the players and managers over the past several decades has not improved the performance of any team, then something must be wrong with the game itself.

This chapter develops our theoretical and empirical understanding of how policy preferences may influence feelings of political support. We begin by outlining the basic Downsian model that links policy differences between the voters and political actors to dissatisfaction with the government. We then consider this model's presumptions of why political trust has decreased over the past several decades. The chapter assembles both longitudinal and cross-section evidence to test this model. This leads to a more complex interpretation of the role of policy preferences in changing citizens' images of government. We believe that policy concerns contribute to the decline in political support, but the workings of this process are different from that portrayed in prior research.

THE BASIC DOWNSIAN MODEL

Much of the literature on the relationship between policy evaluations and political support is based on a Downsian framework that implicitly calculates the policy distance between individuals and government policy (Downs 1957). Arthur Miller, for instance, attributed the early declines in Americans' political support to the widening gap between citizens' preferences and government policy on Vietnam and civil rights:

By 1970, Americans to a considerable degree had withdrawn some of their trust from the government because they had become widely divided on a variety of issues, for in the normal attempt to satisfy the greatest numbers, the government had generally followed a more or less centrist policy which in reality appears to have displeased a substantial proportion of the population. (1974*a*: 963)

In other words, Miller observed a bipolar distribution of opinions on these issues, with the government pursuing a centrist position: this created 'cynics of the left' and 'cynics of the right'. More generally, Miller presented evidence that the *distance between* an individual's own policy preferences and the parties' positions on a range of policy issues was strongly related to political trust. Those individuals who saw a larger gap between themselves and the nearest political party tended to be less trustful of government.

In contrast to Miller's cynics of the left and right, David King (1997) explains contemporary American distrust of government in terms of this model of 'cynics of the center'. King cites data of a growing policy polarization between the political parties in Congress, that moves both parties away from the median American voter (also see Dionne 1991). The result, he argues, is a decrease in political trust:

As the parties have polarized, more and more Americans have seen the parties drift away from their centrist preferences...The more distant the parties are from respondents, the more likely respondents are to say that they mistrust government. (King 1997: 176)

Other studies have found patterns similar to either Miller or King in other nations. For instance, Miller and Listaug (1990; 1998) demonstrate a relationship between dissatisfaction with government policy and political distrust (see also Erber and Lau 1990). Ole Borre (2000; see also Borre and Andersen 1997: ch. 11) similarly finds a strong correlation between Danes' distrust in government and the perceived difference between their own policy positions and the position of the Social Democratic government. Schmitt and Holmberg (1995) cite growing policy differences as a reason for decreasing public satisfaction with political parties and government. Listaug (1995: 288) presents evidence of a strong relationship between Swedes' evaluations of the policy performance of the government and their general level of political trust, even while controlling for partisanship. Our analyses in Chapter 3 (Figure 3.3) also provide some evidence that policy polarization is related to political support—with the extreme leftists and rightists often expressing less support. This relationship seems to be a common pattern in public opinion surveys. Indeed, the absence of a relationship would be surprising on theoretical and empirical grounds, because of the presumption that evaluations of government are based, at least in part, on citizen judgements about how close the government is to one's policy preferences.

These basic Downsian models are based on a set of simplifying assumptions for spatial analyses (Hinich and Munger 1997; also Alesina and Wacziarg 2000). The model normally assumes that there is a single, ordered dimension along which all voters assess the government (or political parties). Even if there are multiple issues involved in policy-making, the model assumes they can be summarized into a unidimensional scale, such as left/right position. If V_i represents the position of voter i on this dimension, and P represents the position of the governing party on the dimension, then:[1] Policy Dissatisfaction $(PD)_i = |V_i - P|$. Large gaps between the positions of voters and the governing party would produce high levels of policy dissatisfaction. The persistence of policy dissatisfaction, or severe levels of dissatisfaction, could then generalize into diminished support for politicians, parties and the institutions of representative democracy:[2] Political Support $(PS) = f(PD)$.

These assumptions are necessary to yield a stable mathematical solution to predicting choices along a policy continuum.[3] We will proceed on the basis of these assumptions, but in a later section we consider the implications if these assumptions are violated.

---

[1] There are also questions of whether individuals evaluate the government alone or make a relative judgement between government and opposition parties (see, for example, Citrin 1974). We address this topic later in the chapter.

[2] Again, this is a very simplified statement of the relationship. We expect that the link between specific support for the policies of government have a lagged and imperfect relationship with measures of system support (see, for example, Easton 1975). In addition, the relationship would be more direct for lower levels of support, such as evaluations of politicians and parties, than for higher levels, such as political institutions or the political system.

[3] The spatial modelling literature makes additional assumptions about the behaviour of the actors and the calculus of the voters (for example, Hinich and Munger 1997: ch. 2), but these are not as directly relevant to the analyses that follow.

While the formal logic of such a Downsian model is readily apparent, its empirical contribution to declining political support is uncertain. The model presumes that the level of policy dissatisfaction has increased over time, fuelling citizens' distrust of government. This would imply that nearly all governments are generally doing worse than they used to—or at least citizens feel this is so—and so trust has decreased. This contrasts with the evidence we have previously cited on government performance (for example, Bok 1998; Barnes and Gill 2000). Our specific test of economic perceptions in the preceding chapters also failed to find evidence that perceptions of performance are worsening. Thus, one must question whether citizens in most nations perceive a generally widening gap between their policy preferences and government policies.

Explanations based on this model of rational political calculus also are sometimes based on contrasting assumptions about how the voter–party relationship creates distrust of government. For instance, Miller (1974*a*) claimed that increased *polarization among the public* in the late 1960s and early 1970s stimulated distrust among Americans; conversely, King (1997) maintains that growing *polarization by the political parties* is the cause. Thus, the actual relationship between parties and their supporters remains an open empirical question.

This is also an instance where cross-sectional relationships may be misleading. A correlation between policy dissatisfaction and trust in government may exist in a cross-sectional survey, but this might reflect democratic politics in an equilibrium state. Supporters of the incumbent party are routinely more favourable towards government, and possibly more trusting of government, than are supporters of the opposition parties (Anderson and Guillory 1997). In fact, Chapter 3 showed that government support is linked to partisanship; conservatives are more positive about the economy when their party heads the government, while leftists are more supportive when there is a left-leaning government. When the government changes, the partisan composition of the satisfied and dissatisfied groups might switch, but their rough numbers would be approximately constant (since roughly half voted for the new government). For the Downsian model to explain decreasing trust, we need to show how this equilibrium has changed systematically over time in a manner that would erode generalized support for the political process. This might mean that either the level of policy dissatisfaction has increased or the relationship between policy dissatisfaction and general political support has systematically changed.

Finally, the direction of the causal relationship that links policy dissatisfaction and political trust is unclear in a cross-section analysis. Citizens who see a gap between their policy preferences and government policy may be distrustful of government, but the underlying causal relationship can run in either direction. It might be that policy dissatisfaction diminishes trust in government; this is the logic of specific political evaluations generalizing into system support. But it is also possible that distrust of government or political institutions that was produced by other factors leads individuals to become more sceptical about the specific policies of government.[4] Thus, a static relationship does not provide a dynamic explanation of decreasing support, and we must track both trends over time before we can begin to speculate on causality.

In sum, the initial evidence suggests that policy dissatisfaction is correlated with support of politicians, parties, and political institutions, but we need to marshal additional evidence that considers whether this relationship explains a broad, long-term decline in political support across the advanced industrial democracies.

PRIOR EVIDENCE ON PARTY CONVERGENCE/DIVERGENCE

Our ultimate objective is to determine whether the policy distance between the median voter and government has systematically increased in advanced industrial democracies, which could then lead to decreased trust in the government. While the research question can be easily stated, the empirical data to answer this question are not easy to assemble.

We might start by asking whether the political parties, and thereby the government and the political opposition, have become more polarized over time (as implied in the logic of the 'cynics of the centre') or become more similar in their policies. It is not easy to answer this question with prior research. To begin with, the issues of political competition constantly change over time, so one cannot simply compare polarization on a single issue across elections. The policy controversies of the 1960 US presidential election are quite different from the issues of debate in the 2000 election. Furthermore, long-term survey data on policy preferences are quite limited, especially if we wish to compare a large number of advanced industrial democracies. Therefore, we draw upon a diverse range of evidence to see whether a consistent picture of changing policy polarization emerges in advanced industrial democracies.

One source of data comes from a pair of relatively recent elite studies, which asked experts to position the political parties in their respective nations along several policy continua. Both Peter Mair (1995) and Oddbjørn Knutsen (1998) trace party movements from the early 1980s to the early 1990s and find evidence of convergence. Mair (1995), for instance, finds that the ascribed policy distance between the major left party and the major right party has decreased in eleven of thirteen European democracies. Although the time period is very short, this is suggestive cross-national evidence.

Another approach to studying the changing policy space utilizes party programmes, which can generate long data series across many nations. Early codings of party platforms by David Robertson (1976) and John Thomas (1979) suggested that the basic policy positions of political parties are generally converging in

---

[4] In a similar vein, Page and Jones (1979) find evidence of both causal flows in their analyses of issue voting with similar policy difference measures. They distinguish between issue differences that are projections of voters' previous partisan preferences and partisan preferences that are a rationalization of issue perceptions.

advanced industrial democracies. They attributed this to the emerging consensus on the economic and welfare state issues that had long provided a basis of party competition. More recently, Miki Caul and Mark Gray (2000) used data from the Comparative Party Manifestos Project (Budge, Robertson, and Hearl 1987; Klingemann, Hofferbert, and Budge 1994) to track party positions for nearly all the OECD democracies. They combined a variety of traditional economic issues with some of the new policy controversies of advanced industrial societies to create a summary left/right measure. Caul and Gray show that the left/right distance between the major parties decreased in 9 of 15 nations; in addition, in 11 of 15 nations the overall left/right polarization of the political parties decreased (in no nation was there a significant increase in polarization between the 1950s and the 1980s).[5]

The expert evaluations and party manifesto data thus point to the gradual decrease in party polarization during the late twentieth century. If we assume that public preferences along the overall left/right dimension are distributed as a normal bell curve, then this would imply that parties are moving closer to the median voter and thus political support should be increasing. But this is clearly not the case—something is missing from these statistics.

Frankly, I am sceptical about using data from the Comparative Party Manifestos Project (CPMP) to track party policy positions over time, even if aggregated to a single broad left/right scale. One problem is that the project does not measure positions along a policy continuum, but simply counts the salience given to each policy in the party programme (that is, the percentage of the party programme that discusses the issue, regardless of the context of the discussion) (see, for example, Harmel, Janda, and Tan 1995). In addition, the CPMP devotes little attention to how separate issues are combined to measure the left/right dimension. The project assumes that a constant set of items tap a broad left/right dimension, but factor analyses do not yield such a clear empirical structure among these items. Moreover, a single, constant measure does not accommodate the changing meaning of left/right over time. For example, while economic and welfare state issues may have divided political parties in the mid-twentieth century, by the end of the century a new set of cultural and quality of life issues had joined the political agenda. In sum, the CPMP data might not be sufficient to determine systematically how party positions have changed over time.

Another way to answer our question is to ask the public. In fact, regardless of what the parties are doing, the important question is whether the public perceives a changing gap between the parties that might increase the distance from the median citizen. In other words, citizen perceptions are the reality that we need to measure.

Some relevant opinion trends are available from several national election studies. The American National Election Study has the longest time series of relevant data. Since 1952 the ANES has asked whether voters 'think there are any important

[5] Consistent with King (1997), the United States is among the minority of cases in which party polarization is increasing. The other clear example on both measures is France.

differences in what the Republicans and Democrats stand for'. One is struck by the seeming independence between this perception and expert interpretations of various US presidential elections.[6] For example, more people perceived important differences in the 1992 (60 per cent) and 1996 elections (63 per cent) than in the highly polarized contests of 1964 (55 per cent) and 1972 (46 per cent). At the same time, there is a weak trend of more Americans perceiving important party differences over time.

The British Election Studies also include a long series on perceived party differences (Evans, Heath, and Payne 1999: 97). Election-specific effects are strongly present in these data. British voters saw the greatest differences between the Conservative and Labour parties during the 1983 and 1987 elections, when Thatcherism was transforming the nation. The smallest perceived differences are during the 1997 election, when Blair's New Labour pursued a distinctive centrist strategy. But, across these dramatic ebbs and flows in perceived party differences for specific elections, British voters tend towards seeing greater party differences over time. For instance, in 1964 when class voting differences and presumably the economic policy differences between the parties were considerable, 45 per cent of the British public perceived 'great' differences between the parties, but 55 per cent gave the same reply in 1987 even though class differences had narrowed substantially.

A similar question was asked in the 1967 Australian National Political Attitudes Survey and in several election studies in the 1990s. The number of Australians who see 'some' or 'a good deal of' difference between the parties has generally increased over time.[7] Even more striking is the public opinion data from Sweden. In 1973, 39 per cent of Swedes perceived at least 'fairly big' differences between the parties; in 1991 40 per cent held the same opinion. This pattern is surprising, since the sharp erosion of class voting in Sweden is generally interpreted as evidence of the convergence of the major Swedish parties on the key economic and welfare state issues that historically structured party competition, but voters did not perceive a broad convergence.

The findings in this section produce an intriguing paradox: the 'objective' evidence (elite assessments and party manifesto data) suggest that party differences are generally narrowing in advanced industrial democracies. In contrast, the subjective evidence from the electorate in four nations suggests that people perceive constant or increasing differences between the parties.

[6] These data are available at www.umich.edu/~nes/nesguide/toptable/tab2b_4.htm.

[7] The Australian data are given below:

	1967	1993	1996	1998
Good deal	33%	44%	31%	30%
Some	24%	39%	44%	46%
Not much/none	42%	17%	25%	25%

Admittedly, the data on public perceptions of party differences is limited. Most national election study series do not include the necessary questions or the wording changes over time. The inconsistencies between data sources may arise from the fallibility of one or more measures. Until opinion trends are located for more nations, we cannot tell whether this pattern is common across advanced industrial democracies. However, we lean towards treating the evidence of public perceptions as more definitive. Citizens are apparently perceiving a widening gap between the party choices being offered. This suggests that a further analysis of these perceptions is warranted.

MEASURING POLICY DIFFERENCES

The title of this section might better read: 'The complexity of empirically testing a simple theory.' The Downsian model has intuitive appeal because it reflects a calculation that most policy analysts, and presumably many voters, make in judging governments: how close are government policies to my own preferences?

The difficulty comes in translating this Downsian logic into an empirically testable model. The American case seems like a simple example. If we assume there is a single policy continuum, two major parties compete for votes along this dimension. However, Figure 7.1 uses data from the 2000 American National

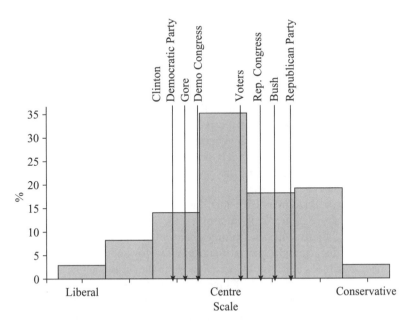

FIG. 7.1. Location of US voters and political actors on liberal/conservative scale, 2000

Note: Respondent self-placement and mean placement of political actors.

Source: 2000 American National Election Study.

Election Study to illustrate the complexity that can enter into judgements about policy agreement. The actual distribution of voters along the liberal/conservative scale is depicted by the bars in the figure, which describe a rough bell-shaped curve. (Virtually all the cross-national data of this type describe the national distribution of opinions as a single-peaked preference distribution as in Figure 7.1.) Most American voters position themselves near the centre of the political spectrum, and the dispersion of voters has not dramatically changed over the past three decades.

The complexity of model estimation arises because voters have many political actors who can serve as reference points in judging policy agreement. The voters may compare their own policy location along the liberal/conservative scale to those of the presidential candidates; in 2000, for example, the average voter (mean = 4.28) was closer to George W. Bush (mean = 5.01) than to Albert Gore (mean = 3.16). Another alternative is to compare one's liberal/conservative position to the congressional candidates running in the district. These are the politicians who will actually represent the voter in the legislature; congressional evaluations also are based on a large number of politicians, and so these calculations may better represent the broad orientations of each political party. Or one might simply compare one's own position with the perceived positions of the political parties, as represented by the location of the Democratic and Republican parties in Figure 7.1. It is relatively easy to see how these different frames of reference may alter the ultimate calculations, especially if the frames change over time. Moreover, how does one evaluate congruence with government policy when we move from a period of unified party government to divided government?

When researchers are studying voting choices, this Downsian framework is still relatively straightforward to apply; the distance between the voter and the designated political actor is calculated, and this distance is used to predict voting choice. But is this the appropriate calculation for judging government performance? In other words, should the perceived policy distance from either Bush or Gore be an indicator of agreement with government policy-making? Many Downsian-style analyses of political support rely on this logic.

If we think of political support as linked to retrospective judgements—what has the government done lately?—then assessing policy agreement with the candidates who will assume office after the election is not appropriate. Rather, as we suggested above, voters ask themselves how the *incumbent government* has been doing, and these policy-based judgements then may influence political support. In 2000, for example, the relevant question for political support was, not what the public thought Bush or Gore might do in the future, but how they judged the prior accomplishments of the Clinton administration.

This is a somewhat unconventional application of the Downsian model, but we believe it comes closest to tapping the inherent logic of political support within a Downsian framework. When the election studies ask voters to judge whether they trust the government or whether politicians are interested in what they think, these are judgements about how the government has performed in the past, not prospective judgements about future political office-holders. Indeed, elections can at least temporarily renew the public's optimism that a new set of officials will be better than the incumbent one. But if the next election comes along, and performance has not improved, then negative judgements about politicians and parties may deepen. Fans of the Chicago Cubs may gain solace from the eternal hope that next year will be better, but democratic citizens ask what the current governing team has accomplished.

Thus, there are good reasons to expect that evaluations of government performance are more strongly tied to retrospective evaluations of the incumbent government than to prospective assessments of what the current candidates might accomplish. To use the Clinton administration as an example: Clinton was seen as a more desirable candidate by a plurality of voters in 1992. Clinton thus began his administration with positive expectations that his administration would perform better than the Bush administration. Over time, however, the reality of any incumbent administration probably falls short of citizen expectations.[8] So, by the time an incumbent leaves office, perceptions of policy performance are probably less positive than when he or she first assumed office.

This pattern, of course, will vary with the characteristics of the incumbent. An incumbent administration that loses an election is generally viewed more negatively than one which wins the election. If performance evaluations are influencing political support, it would imply that there is a general decline in policy evaluations of incumbent governments over time. In other words, is the policy performance of successive administrations generally viewed more negatively by the American public?

Figure 7.2 presents data from the United States to illustrate this point. It presents the average difference between the respondent's self-placement on the liberal/conservative scale and their placement of the incumbent president. The growing distance between the American public and their government is unmistakable. For instance, each time an incumbent administration is voted out of office (Ford in 1976; Carter in 1980; Bush in 1992; Gore in 2000), the gap between the voter and the administration was wider than the previous episode. In addition, the policy gap even widens across incumbent administrations that are successful in winning re-election (Nixon in 1972; Reagan in 1984; Clinton in 1996). One suspects that, if comparable data were available for the halcyon 1950s, the American electorate would display far more policy agreement with the Eisenhower administration than the data show for US administrations since 1972.

These trends might reflect a general disenchantment with politicians that arises from sources other than policy distance eroding support. Thus, as a

---

[8] In addition, this may have occurred because some citizens misperceived the policies of a Clinton administration in 1992, projecting their own hopes on to an untested government, and because candidates promise more than they actually can or intend to deliver.

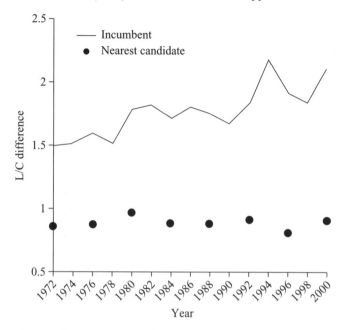

FIG. 7.2. Average distance between US voter and incumbent president and nearest presidential candidate, 1972–2000

Note: Incumbent party is represented by the liberal/conservative position of the incumbent president.
Source: American National Election Studies.

control for such effects, we also calculated the average distance between the voter and the nearest presidential candidate at each election (represented by the circles in the figure). The distance from the nearest candidate is always smaller than distance from the incumbent president, because some voters support the opposition candidate. It is noteworthy, however, that the distance from the nearest candidate does not increase over time (the same pattern applies for congressional candidates). Consider what this means. At election time, voters see choices that they perceive as relatively close to their own position. By the end of the electoral cycle, however, impressions of the incumbent government are generally worse. Moreover, over the past three decades there is a tendency for each successive administration to be viewed as more distant from the voter than its predecessor.[9] Successive governments receive lower marks over time.

[9] The reader may suspect that this is an artefact of changes in the distribution of voters or candidates along the Liberal/Conservative spectrum. In terms of the voters, there is a slight shift toward the Conservative pole over time, but there is not a significant change in the dispersion of voters. The average standard deviation of respondent self-placement on the liberal/conservative spectrum is 1.35. From 1972 until 2000, all the elections are +/− 0.10 of the average standard deviation.

How much might these performance evaluations contribute to the trend of decreasing political support? Using the estimation methodology we presented in Chapter 4, our calculations suggest that 10–20 per cent of the decline in the United States might be explicable by the increasing policy gap.[10] Of course, there is a potential reciprocal nature to this relationship. Growing cynicism of politics may prompt voters to see governments as more distant from their policy priorities. Such effects are likely present in the data to an indeterminate degree. Our measurement of the policy gap, however, is not a simple reported assessment of agreement or approval that might more easily generate such projections. By focusing on liberal/conservative positions, this should emphasize the policy content of political evaluations, which then might generalize into feelings of political support. So we believe that more than projection is involved.

The importance of policy differences would gain further support if we could demonstrate that this is a general pattern in advanced industrial democracies. The most appropriate data would examine nations with a large long-term decline in political support to see whether perceptions of policy agreement follow the same pattern. With a long series one can begin to disentangle the long-term trend from the short-term patterns of incumbent victory/loss in a specific election. Unfortunately, there are few nations that fit this profile and for which a long-term series of left/right scales is available.[11] The most extensive non-American series exists for Sweden. Since 1979 the Swedish Election Studies have included a measure of the respondent's self-placement on the left/right scale as well as placement of the major parties. The Swedish political system presents another potential analytic problem, however. Since most governments over this period have been based on multiparty coalitions, assessment of 'the incumbent' is uncertain. Is the incumbent government the average of all the coalition parties, a weighted average, or the position of the dominant partner? To have a straightforward, albeit imperfect, measure of incumbency, we use the party of the prime minister. Even if this is not the most precise measure, it enables us to track broad trends.

Figure 7.3 shows that Swedes' evaluations of the distance between their left/right preferences and the incumbent government have widened over time.

---

[10] The relationship between policy distance and distrust is roughly constant over time. We estimated the slope (b) as -0.08 with 'trust the government'. Between 1974 and 1994 the mean policy distance had increased by 0.56 and trust had dropped by -0.21. If we use these statistics, then the predicted impact of the changing policy distance would be: $-0.08*0.56 = -0.033$. This is about 15% of the total decline of -0.21. Using other political support measures as the dependent variable yields results that range around this estimate.

[11] To the best of my knowledge, the major British academic series do not ask a left/right question over a long time span; the Canadian election studies asked a seven-point left/right scale in the 1979 and 1984 surveys, but these were not replicated until 1997 when this study used a ten-point left/right scale; comparable French trends are not available; and a long-term series of left/right questions are not available in the Japanese election studies. The left/right series is available for the Netherlands, but this is one of the few nations where political support measures are not generally declining. In other nations where these questions may have been asked, I did not have access to the raw data for the surveys.

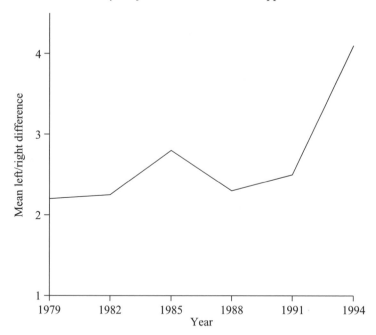

FIG. 7.3. Distance between voters and incumbent party in Sweden, 1979–1994

Note: Figure represents mean difference between position of voters on the left/right scale and position of incumbent; incumbent party is represented by position of party of incumbent prime minister.

Source: Swedish Election Studies.

When conservative governments stood for re-election in 1979 and 1982, the distance between the prime minister's party and the average voter was relatively small, even when the incumbents lost in 1982. After the Social Democrats regained office in 1982, policy distances rose as they won re-election in 1985 and 1988. And perceived policy differences spiked up as a conservative coalition government was turned out of office in 1994. Like Americans, the Swedes perceive a widening policy gap between themselves and their government.

The German election studies also include measures of left/right attitudes in several surveys. The series is too short, however, to clearly separate election-specific effects from a potential long-term trend.[12] The series also stops in 1990

---

[12] The following table presents the average difference on the 10-point left/right scale between the voter and the incumbent party for those time-points where a pre-election survey is available:

1976	1980	1983	1987	1990
2.79	2.46	2.68	3.12	2.58

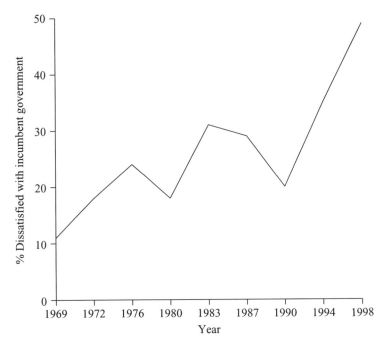

FIG. 7.4. Dissatisfaction with incumbent government in Germany, 1969–1998

Note: At least two pre-election polls were combined for each time-point.

Source: German Election Studies.

in the midst of the atypical election of German unification. However, the German election studies also ask a question that specifically measures evaluations of the incumbent government. Pre-election negative assessments of the government demonstrate an unmistakable increase over time (Figure 7.4). In the divisive elections of 1972 and 1976, barely a fifth of the public expressed dissatisfaction with the incumbents; this group gradually increases until it has doubled in size by the last two elections of the 1990s.

Certainly, these few opinion trends are a weak base for assessing broad changes in advanced industrial democracies, though this is all the presently available evidence.[13] If we accept that this might be a general pattern across these nations, what might explain it? The most direct explanation is that governments are failing to respond to the left/right policy preferences of their citizens: people are criticizing governments for these failures, which appears in declining political support. A host of voices sing this refrain—and there are obviously many examples of government

[13] There are three time-points available for Australia, but these span barely a decade and the coding of the left/right scale changed from ten categories to eleven. Still, there is some evidence that the policy gap had held stable or even increased between 1987 and 1996/98.

failure to illustrate this trend. But I hesitate to accept such a direct explanation, for several reasons. First, I doubt that policy performance is decreasing everywhere, and the analyses of Chapter 6 demonstrate that this explanation does not fit the economic domain. Second, Chapters 4 and 5 showed that the greatest declines in political support have not come from those at the margins of politics and society, but from the very groups that have benefited most from their nation's advances: the young, the better educated, and the postmaterialists.

Another possible explanation is that voters are making poor choices, and paying for these choices in diminished policy performance. Let me give an example. To the extent that politics is becoming candidate-centred, this means that more voters may be making electoral choices based on personal characteristics or video style instead of policy congruence. If the media reinforce these themes in their reporting, then elections are becoming less a policy mandate and more a popularity contest (Patterson 1993). Indeed, a simple policy distance model would predict that a majority of the US electorate would have voted for Carter in 1980 (and Bush in 2000). When voters instead chose Reagan in 1980, it was no surprise that the policies of the new administration were less in tune with the policy preferences of the public. (And when Americans re-elected Reagan in 1984, the policy gap could remain wide.) This is an explanation that needs further research. However, to the extent that perceived policy distances generally grow across the OECD democracies—even where there are systems of strong party government that limit candidate-centred politics—this suggests that candidate-centred voting is not a general explanation. Moreover, my own view is that voters have become more rather than less sophisticated and demanding about policy voting (Dalton 2002).

This draws us back to an explanation based on the changing expectations of contemporary publics. Were the Bush and Clinton administrations really so much more out of touch with Americans' policy preferences than the Nixon, Ford, and Carter administrations?[14] Remember, in the midst of President Carter's term he lamented that the erosion of citizen trust posed a fundamental problem for American democracy; and the Nixon administration was a source of this erosion. Or are we seeing a process whereby changing citizen preferences create higher expectations of government, or perhaps even expectations that governments cannot achieve? This might lead to a spiral of decreasing satisfaction with the government. Citizens elect a new government because they expect it to be more responsive to its policy preferences, but in four or eight years' time the dissatisfactions are still there and they try a new government. Thus, cynicism may grow from replacing Republicans with Democrats, and then Democrats with Republicans, and still feeling that the government is not effectively addressing

---

[14] Two other trends from the American national election study display this same pattern. Based on judgements of government performance on the most important national problems, positive evaluations of the incumbent government have trended downward since the 1960s. In addition, approval of the incumbent president has also trended downward since 1972 (see Abramson, Aldrich, and Rohde 1999: ch. 7).

one's preferences. The following section offers an explanation for this possible downward spiral in political support.

THE EXPECTATIONS SPIRAL

Let us return to the anecdote at the start of this chapter, where we suggested that a conversation with a typical citizen in California, Paris, or Sydney would find agreement on the poor policy performance of government. If one pursued the conversation, however, I think certain differences would appear. You both might agree that government is performing poorly, but when you talk about specifics you would probably find that you have different policy examples in mind. While one person is concerned with the government's shortfalls in social programmes, the other might feel that not enough is being done to protect the environment, or that taxes are too high, or that the government is not correctly dealing with globalization issues.

This description illustrates what I believe is a major factor contributing to the decrease in political support in advanced industrial democracies (and many of the patterns we have described in this book). Over the past half century, the traditional class and economic issues that historically structured partisan competition have been joined by a set of new postmaterial, cultural, and social issues (Inglehart 1977; 1984). These new issues did not replace the traditional issues with another set, but added new issues to the policy agenda. In addition, these new issues often are inconsistent with existing party alignments on traditional left/right issues. Political parties have difficulties responding to their traditional constituencies and finding compatible positions on these new issues. For instance, demands for economic growth compete with new calls for environmental protection; so Labour parties are divided between representing labour unions and environmental interests. In short, governments are being asked to do more things—and not just to do more on a constant set of goals.

As these new issues emerged in most advanced industrial democracies during the later twentieth century, they created a new dimension(s) of political competition. Issues of environmental protection, women's rights, greater individual freedom, and related issues jointly reflected an alternative political ideology that cut across the traditional left/right framework of Western democracies. Scholars of American electoral politics, for example, tracked the emergence of this 'New Politics' cleavage beginning in the 1960s. Herbert Weisberg and Jerold Rusk (1970; Rusk and Weisberg 1972) described how this cultural conflict introduced a new dimension of political cleavage, as represented by dissident Democratic candidates such as McGovern on the left and George Wallace on the right (see also Miller and Levitin 1986). This began a series of new Democrats who championed a New Left perspective, such as Gary Hart in 1984–8 or Jerry Brown in 1992, and then conservative counter-movements (Miller and Levitin 1986; Dalton 2002: ch. 7). This development was not limited to the United States; a New

Politics cleavage was developing independent of the traditional left/right divide in most Western democracies (Inglehart 1984; Knutsen 1987).

Because these new issues are not easily accommodated in the traditional left/right framework, this created new volatility in electoral politics (Dalton and Wattenberg 2000: ch. 3). Eventually, these issues spawned new political parties to represent these views. The first wave included environmental parties, such as the Green parties in Germany and France or left-libertarian parties; then a counter-wave of New Right parties emerged, such as the National Front in France or the Republikaner in Germany. Similarly, there has been a proliferation of new citizen interest groups and social movement organizations that are policy advocates on these new issue controversies (Berry 1999; Meyer and Tarrow 1998).

Thus, a common theme in almost all advanced industrial democracies is the expansion of the political agenda over the past several decades, and the emergence of new political actors to represent the new issues. This is often presented as the development of a new cleavage dimension that runs orthogonal to the traditional left/right dimension; a New Left advocates issues of environmental protection and women's rights, and a New Right offers a conservative response on issues of cultural change. Indeed, this two-dimension space has been described in electoral studies of many democracies (for example, Rusk and Weisberg 1972; Inglehart 1984; Flanagan 1984; McAllister 1992: ch. 5; Borre and Andersen 1997: ch. 2; Dalton 1984*b*; 2002).[15] Similarly, Robert Dahl (1994: 1) has observed that 'government policies are made in response to a greater number and variety of conflicting and substantially independent interests(s)'.

In fact, rather than a two-dimensional space, it is probably more accurate to discuss the fragmentation of policy interests across multiple issue dimensions. One set of voters tell politicians they will be judged on their policy towards abortion, the next group says social security is the litmus test, the next emphasizes educational policy, and so forth. One of the common experiences of advanced industrial societies is the rise of such single-issue politics over the past generation. Consequently, separate groups of voters evaluate the performance of government in terms of distinct sets of issue concerns. These patterns of increasingly fragmented issues interests would be recognized by politicians speaking to voters in southern California, Paris, or Sydney.

---

[15] Some scholars argue just the opposite. For instance, Jacques Thomassen (1999: 54) claims that 'political cleavages in western societies have become more and more one-dimensional in the sense that the left-right dimension has gradually absorbed other conflict dimensions'. Gabel and Huber (2000) have recently categorized Western political parties along such a single left/right scale. Indeed, the left/right dimension includes elements of both old and new political conflicts (Inglehart 1997*a*; Dalton 2002). Thus, the literature on the changing meaning of 'left' and 'right' signifies the existence of multiple political dimensions at the present time. If the left/right dimension has a different meaning to different individuals, this indicates that there are multiple dimensions of political competition embodied in this measure rather than a single dimension.

The Downsian model is useful in understanding how this broadening of the political agenda may affect political support. The Downsian model is analytically appealing because it provides a simple way of viewing political choices that is derived from strong logical and mathematical principles. The model assumes, however, that political competition can be represented by a single dimension.[16] What happens when politics functions within a multidimensional political space? The spatial modelling literature demonstrates that in a two-dimensional space it is difficult for any single government or political party to adopt a policy programme that represents the median voter (Riker 1982; Hinich and Munger 1997: chs 3, 4). In simple terms, this is because there is no single equilibrium point in a two-dimensional space that represents the median voter. Rather, there is a mix of policy choices, some of which are preferred on one dimension, but not so appealing on the other—and vice versa. This produces an indifference area of equally acceptable policy mixes rather than the single policy solution predicted in the one-dimensional space. Thus, whatever position a government takes, there is another policy mix that is preferred by an equal or larger number of voters. If the opposition assumes this second policy set, then there is another policy set that is preferred by an alternate set of voters. In short, if political actors (parties or governments) try to maximize voter satisfaction with a specific programme in a multi-dimensional space, they find that *this is an impossible task.*[17]

The situation is even more complex. If voters differ on the importance they attach to each dimension, this further alters the structure of the political space. Donald Stokes (1963), for example, discussed how multiple dimensions and the varying salience of policy dimensions can reshape the indifference area in the policy space and thus the preferred policy goals. Thus, if one issue becomes salient, a certain party is seen as closer to one's position; but as another issue becomes salient, perceptions of which party is closest may shift. Alternatively, two voters may see the same relative position of the parties, but because they attach a different salience to the two dimensions, their distance from the closest party differs. Neither the voters or the parties are shifting positions; it is merely a change in the salience of policy conflicts. Stokes's insightful observations have often been overlooked in the simplified Downsian analyses which ignored these complications.

Even the assumption of two dimensions is a major simplification of contemporary policy-making. The increasing fluidity of electoral choice encourages opposition parties to search for new issues that might give them a competitive advantage over the incumbents (Petrocik 1996). Often these issues are new expressions of the underlying ideological framework of politics, whether a left/right framework

[16] At times, perhaps most times, this is a reasonable approximation of political competition in a nation, such as the class coalitions that structured many Western party systems during the twentieth century. The 1860s, 1890s, and 1930s realignments of the American party system also illustrate periods when party politics can be well-represented by a single left/right dimension.

[17] See Arrow (1951), Riker (1982), McGann (1999).

or a New Politics framework. Sometimes these are orthogonal issues, such as the role of the European Union or the personal attributes of candidates, that represent a new and temporary dimension of political choice.[18] New issues create a more complex policy space that gives more room for manoeuvre and strategic action by the opposition, but manoeuvring is possible by all political parties. After describing politics in a multidimensional space, Hinich and Munger (1997: 71) conclude 'the effect is to release the genie of chaos from its bottle'. A stable and effective representation of public policy preferences becomes nearly impossible in such an environment.

Complex public choice calculations lie behind the processes we have described, but the implications for evaluations of political support are fairly straightforward. If governments and political parties strive to represent public policy preferences within a multidimensional space, it is difficult to adhere to a broad policy programme that consistently satisfies the median voter. After an election the new government can pursue its election programme and make real progress towards its goals; but the fragmentation of policy interests means that the government must cater to distinct and often conflicting policy preferences of its diverse constituencies. No mix of policy action may be able to maximize support for an extended period of time because each group sees an alternative policy mix that is preferable. The government may even shift its policy emphases or positions while in office in reaction to these tensions—although this may breed more discontent by alienating those who elected the government in the first place (remember the Clinton administration, which first attempted to implement a major expansion of the social services through health care reform, and then dramatically reduced the social welfare programme). Consequently, this multidimensional space may create a 'cycle of policy jumping' or a shifting emphasis on different policy dimensions that further distances government from its citizens.

In short, in a multidimensional policy space a government can satisfy most people some of the time, or some people most of the time, but not most of the people most of the time. Even if the government performs well, it cannot consistently represent the ideal point of most voters. When government performance falls short of expectations, a chorus of critics often blames special interests or insensitive politicians for the shortfall. The proliferation of public interest groups has both increased the number of voices that may join such a refrain and further increased the number of distinct issues being represented within the policy process. The simple reality may be that in such an environment even the best government cannot represent an ideal policy mix that most voters will consistently endorse.

One intriguing bit of evidence that supports this explanation of declining political support comes from Durr, Gilmour, and Wolbrecht's (1997) study of popular

---

[18] There are also some indications that policy distances on such new issues are more strongly related to levels of political support than policy distances on the long-standing issues of the traditional left/right dimension (Borre 2000; Miller and Listhaug 1998).

approval of the US Congress. They assembled an impressive longitudinal database on public attitudes towards Congress and measures of Congressional activity. At first glance, their results appear counterintuitive: 'While pundits and polls often portray declines in Congressional approval as indications of that body's failings, if not a crisis of the political order, our research suggests that decreases in Congressional approval are, in part, simply a reaction to Congress doing its job.' They continue to explain that the passage of major legislation and the override of presidential vetoes lowers approval ratings because Congress is functioning in an environment where a majority of interests cannot be simultaneously satisfied (Durr, Gilmour, and Wolbrecht 1997: 197). Furthermore, they find that the most obvious indicators of negative behaviour by Congress—political scandals involving House members—had a negligible impact on approval of Congress. Evaluations of Congress appear to suffer more from the body's positive actions than from its failures.

TESTING THE EXPECTATIONS EXPLANATION

We believe that the logic of a multidimensional Downsian model can help to explain why citizens are becoming more critical of government as a result of the changing issue space of contemporary politics. The development of new dimensions of political competition creates the potential for citizens to feel their expectations are unfilled, which may generalize into an erosion of political support. While successful administrations may temporarily resist this trend, the logic of multidimensional political competition suggests continuing downward pressure on political support within advanced industrial democracies.

This theoretical model is intriguing, but can it be verified empirically at the micro level? A simple cross-sectional relationship that measures the policy gap between voters and the government, as was done earlier in this chapter, is but a partial test. First, these analyses assume that there is a single left/right dimension along which policy distances can be measured. Measuring policy distances in a multidimensional space is not as direct. Second, the dynamic aspect of a policy jumping cycle may deepen feelings of policy dissatisfaction, but this cannot be assessed in a single survey. Voters dissatisfied with successive governments may come to the conclusion that elections do not select a better government but just a different government that struggles with the same policy challenges. This dynamic itself creates the potential for substantial negativity towards the politicians, parties, and parliaments that are making government policy.

While one can construct a mathematical proof of the argument we have proposed, there is little appropriate longitudinal evidence from public opinion surveys to test this hypothesis. For instance, data from the Federal Republic of Germany indirectly illustrate the process we are describing. Figure 7.4 depicts Germans' evaluations of government policy in a way that allows citizens to combine multiple issue dimensions—and dissatisfactions with incumbent governments have increased over time. But the lack of policy specificity in this question also may allow voters to project their general distrust of government on to this question about governmental performance.

Another approach is to ask about the policy performance of political parties across multiple issues. In a one-dimensional space citizens will generally see their preferred party as better able to deal with the salient issues, since these issues are related to a single dimension of cleavage. In a multi-dimensional space it is possible that citizens will see different parties as closer to their interests on issues tapping different policy dimensions. We can test this idea with data from the German Election Studies, which over a long period of time have asked respondents about the importance of various issues, and then asked which party is more competent to deal with each issue. Is the increasing complexity of the issue space leading citizens to see that there is not a single party that best represents their mix of preferences?

To control for the possible influence of party preferences on party images, Figure 7.5 presents perceptions of issue competency separately for SPD partisans and CDU/CSU partisans.[19] In the early 1960s, more than two-thirds of both partisan camps believed that their party alone was most competent to deal with the majority of the issues listed in the survey. Gradually these perceptions of party competence weaken, so that by the 1994 and 1998 elections only about a third of CDU/CSU partisans and SPD partisans think their party is more competent on the majority of issues. If these assessments of competency decrease for supporters of the major parties that have alternated in government over this period, the trend is undoubtedly stronger for adherents of minor parties and non-partisans. In other words, partisans once viewed their own party as offering a package of policies that represented their preferences, but now they fail to see this clear policy fit. Instead, some issues are seen as better addressed by another party or neither party, or voters cannot differentiate between the parties. In a complex, multi-dimensional issue space, such a lack of congruence can easily develop.[20]

Only a short series (1990–8) exists from the Australian Election Studies.[21] In 1990 Bob Hawke's Labor government was returned to office, but after three

[19] Because the exact list and number of issues vary across elections, and there has been a change in question wording, we advise the reader to treat these data with some caution. In analysing these data, we first assume that the issues in each election study are a comparable set of the important issues of the day. Second, to adjust for the changing number of questions, Figure 7.5 presents the percentage of partisans that rated their party as most competent on at least half the issues in the survey. Third, the format of the question response options changes between 1969 and 1980. Because the trend seems to span this full time period, we do not believe that questionnaire change produced the trend.

[20] Even this test is more indirect than ideal, because we expect that the public is divided into different issue publics that focus on different subsets of these issues. Still, the overall pattern of issue competence indirectly validates the point we are making.

[21] The 1990 survey included nine items, and we counted the percentage of partisans who ranked their party as competent on five or more. The 1998 survey included thirteen items, and we counted the percentage that ranked their party as more competent on seven or more.

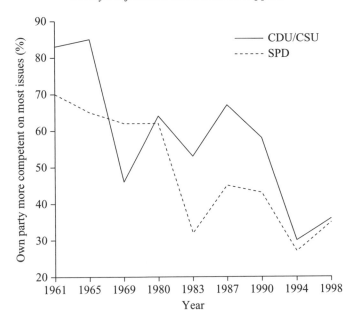

FIG. 7.5. Decreasing attribution of party competency by SPD and CDU/CSU partisans, 1961–1998

Note: Figure represents % partisans saying own party is the more competent on most issues included in the competency battery. Pre-election surveys were used at each time-point.

Source: German Election Studies.

previous terms only 52 per cent of Labor Party identifiers felt their own party was most competent on the majority of issues listed in the survey; Liberal/National Coalition identifiers were more supportive of the Coalition in opposition (59 per cent rated the Coalition as more competent on most issues). These patterns were essentially reversed in 1998. Even though Coalition leader John Howard won re-election, only 52 per cent of Liberal/National Coalition identifiers gave high competency ratings to the Coalition; Labor partisans were slightly more supportive of their own party, which lost the election (58 per cent rated it as most competent on the majority of issues). There is no clear trend across the short time span of the 1990s, but this pattern of lower competency ratings by the supporters of the incumbent (and victorious) party illustrates how governance leads the public to see that parties cannot achieve all they claim.

To a limited degree, the American National Election Studies also suggest a similar pattern of decreasing party competence. The ANES asks respondents to name the most important problem facing the nation, and then asks which party can best deal with this problem. At the start of the series in 1960 and 1964, most Democrats and Republicans felt their own party was better able to deal with the most pressing problem (Figure 7.6). But since 1972 most time-points show that less than half of both partisan groups view their own party as more competent. There are also the short-term ebbs and flows of failed incumbents and successful challengers that produce bounces in this trend. These inter-election shifts illustrate the cycle of unmet expectations we have described. When Reagan ran for office in 1980, Republicans were momentarily optimistic that their party could solve the nation's most pressing problem; Republicans' self-image declined sharply by 1984 and fell below 50 per cent in 1988. Democrats then had high hopes in 1992, but by 1996 only 38 per cent thought their party was better able to handle the nation's most pressing problem. In 2000 neither major party won the confidence of a majority of its own partisans.

We cannot probe the multiple issue images of Americans with the available survey data, as was possible with the German and Australian surveys. However, since less than half of partisans feel their own party is most competent on even the single issue rated as most important, we suspect that the feeling of party competence would likely decrease further if multiple issues were considered. Furthermore, other evidence indicates that more American voters are crossing party lines and

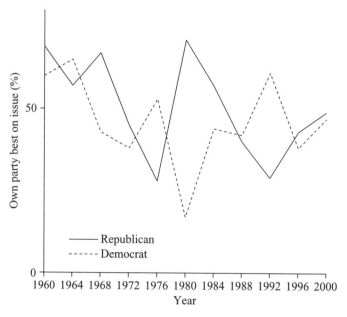

FIG. 7.6. Decreasing attribution of party competency by Democrats and Republicans, 1960–2000

Note: Figure represents % partisans saying own party is the more able to handle the most important national problem.

Source: American National Election Studies.

splitting their ticket between the parties (Dalton and Wattenberg 2000: ch. 3); such patterns suggest that confidence in one's own party has deteriorated over time.

Since I have not been able to identify comparable data series from other elections studies, these results from Germany, Australia, and the United States only suggest what might generally be occurring in advanced industrial democracies.[22] But, paired with the formal logic of the Downsian model, this generates strong evidence that this factor contributes to the public's growing frustration with their government.

To summarize, if partisans have lost faith in their own team, it is not surprising that their faith in the game of politics has also eroded. This process must be even stronger for non-partisans, who lack the emotional bond to root for the home team. Furthermore, there is a strong relationship between perceptions of the government's issue competence and measures of political support. In the 1990 German elections, for example, competence ratings of the governing party (as measured in Figure 7.5) are strongly correlated with satisfaction with the workings of the democracy system ($r = 0.26$). Similarly, perceptions of issue competence for the incumbent Liberal/National government in 1998 were strongly related to Australians' belief that parties were doing a good job ($r = 0.28$), that parties care ($r = 0.21$), and that politicians know what people think ($r = 0.22$). Perceptions of the government's policy performance matter, but in complex ways.

GOVERNING IN A COMPLEX WORLD

Lyndon Baines Johnson told what became a famous story about the relationship between citizens and their government. In the story, Congressman Johnson returns from Washington to campaign for re-election in his Texas district. He meets an old friend, and reminds him of the help Johnson's office had provided over the years: helping with one government programme after another, and acting as an ombudsman for the constituent. Johnson's expectation was that this recital of constituency service would guarantee the voter's support, and was shocked to hear the voter was wavering. The reason? The constituent asked: 'What have you done for me lately?'

In an overly simplified way, this story summarizes part of the findings of this chapter. Citizen dissatisfaction with government has increased because the gap between reality and expectations has increased. It is not so much that governments produce less, but that citizens expect more.

The overload literature similarly suggests that citizens' expectations are the source of eroding faith in government (for example, Huntington 1981). In one sense, the average citizen may expect the government to do more—after all,

---

[22] Since 1979 the Swedish Election Studies have included questions on parties with 'good' and 'bad' policies across a set of policies. However, because of the multiparty system and the coding of responses, it is difficult to assess how party perceptions have changed over time.

the government *is* doing more. The scope of government grew dramatically during the later twentieth century in virtually all advanced industrial democracies. So one can legitimately expect governments to be responsible both for promoting the economy and for promoting a large array of non-economic issues that have entered the government's policy agenda.

The crucial factor, however, is not that citizens are expecting government to do more in absolute terms on all these issue domains—at least, relative to the expansion of government resources to address these issues. Rather, *the expanding diversity of policy goals* may create a dynamic in which dissatisfaction easily develops. Spatial analysis of social choice suggest that, as politics becomes more complex and the government must act on several distinct policy dimensions, this makes it difficult for the government to find a median position on an overarching programme that simultaneously satisfies most voters. For instance, during a legislative session the US government might address the social security interests of the American Association of Retired People (AARP), then the concerns of environmental groups on Alaskan oil drilling, and then deal with trade liberalization advocated by a business association—even if each interest group is satisfied in its own issue domain, the majority of the American public may be dissatisfied with this policy mix. And each of the three groups involved in this example may criticize government actions in the other two policy areas, leading to a general cynicism about government. Thus, if governments and political parties respond by a cycle of policy jumping—trying to satisfy one interest this month, another interest the next month, and so forth—the result may be that everyone feels short-changed, asking 'what have you done for me lately?'

This chapter cites the evidence that most advanced industrial democracies are experiencing this multidimensional policy space as new issues of environmental quality, minority rights, cultural issues, and other matters have entered the political agenda. This multiplication of separate interests provides the context in which dissatisfaction with government might develop. And even the temporary renewal of political support in the United States following the September 11, 2001 terrorist attacks may provide the contrary evidence that actually reaffirms this interpretation.[23]

The development of complex issue spaces is not a sufficient explanation for declining support for politicians, parties, and parliament. There have been other periods in recent electoral history in which elites responded to such cross-cutting

---

[23] The epilogue to Chapter 2 presents data on the rise in political support among Americans after the terrorist attacks of September 11, 2001. In addition to the shock evoked by these events and the feelings of national pride during this period of threat, Americans' singular focus on the terrorism issue pushed other issues into the background and thus temporarily diminished the processes of multidimensional policy comparisons discussed in this chapter. Even in the midst of the post-9/11 surge of support, more differentiated analyses showed that Americans trusted the government on responses to the terrorist attacks, but continued to distrust the government on the range of normal domestic policies (Langer 2002*a*). As the singular focus on terrorism diminished and politics returned to more normal processes (and the terrorist threat declined), overall trust in government also eroded.

issue dimensions without eroding system support.[24] I believe that the increasing complexity of the policy space erodes political support because there has been a concomitant change in the pattern of interest representation in democratic societies. In the past generation, a myriad of special-interest groups and single-issue lobbies have assumed a greater role in representing the public's expanding political interests (Berry 1999; Meyer and Tarrow 1998). The proliferation of such groups partially reflects the modernization process in advanced industrial societies, both in the increasing diversity of citizen interests and in the public's tendency to engage in independent political action. As these new interests find voice within the political process, the boundaries of democratic politics expand.

At the same time, the rise of an interest-group polity creates a new dynamic in the democratic process. The expansion of interest representation encourages individuals and groups to think in terms of their specific interests. Like the constituent in LBJ's story, each asks what have you done for me lately. Each group claims that its desires should be fully met, and anything short of this is often cast as a failure of the political process.[25] Even the collective decision-making process of elections is diminished, because interest groups often distance themselves from partisan politics and cast aspersions on all political parties. Environmentalists, for instance, criticize the policies of both Republican and Democratic administrations, or both Conservative and Labour governments. Even when government passes new environmental legislation, the normal reaction from environmental groups is to stress the remaining shortfalls of the legislation. Half a loaf is never sufficient. In theoretical terms, there is a weakening of the processes of interest aggregation that encourages individuals and groups to subsume their specific interests in a general government programme, understand the necessary trade-offs in making public policy, and accept government policy as a political compromise among these diverse interests.

An indication that Americans feel these tensions comes from a survey of Americans conducted by the Council for Excellence in Government (1999). The survey found that most Americans felt disconnected from the institutions of government, even while expecting that government would have a growing impact on their lives in the future (and that the government should do more). Most directly related to our concerns, when asked who is responsible for what is wrong with

---

[24] The literature on partisan realignment, for example, discusses how cross-cutting issues have often emerged in democratic party systems. Sometimes the parties have successfully integrated this issue into the previous political structures, sometimes they have colluded to remove the new issue from the space (such as the race issue in America), and sometimes new groups have emerged to successfully represent the new cleavage.

[25] Additional indirect evidence of this process comes from a Kaiser Foundation (1996) study of American trust in government. Asked why people do not trust the government, a substantial number of Americans said it is because the government spends the money in the wrong places (79%) and because special interests have too much influence (65%). People may simultaneously hold these two views because policies that address the needs of others are not appreciated and policies that address one's own preferences fall short of expectations. As the vernacular has it: 'the other guy's interests are the special interests'.

government today, respondents did not nominate politicians or political parties or even the media as the primary culprit. A plurality of Americans (38 per cent) said that 'special interests' were primarily to blame. The quandary is that when people cite 'special interests' as the problem, they mean the groups that represent others—not the groups that represent their own interests. As the number of competing interest groups grows in contemporary democracies, and interest articulation becomes more intense within policy-making, there are more of these 'others' groups that erode public faith in the process.

Moreover, the ascendancy of interest-group politics is coming at the expense of political parties that traditionally were the major actors in the democratic process and primary agents of interest aggregation. There is mounting evidence that parties are losing the support of contemporary publics, whether measured by affective party attachments or by formal party membership (Dalton and Wattenberg 2000). The proliferation of interest groups diminishes the parties' role as a vehicle for political voice. This proliferation of groups with independent voice and standing within the political process makes it difficult for parties to act as interest aggregators and to provide the basis for developing consensus around the policies of government. Indeed, it appears that many political parties have responded to these trends by attempting to insulate themselves from them, such as through the development of cartel parties (Katz and Mair 1995). In a similar vein, Farrell and Webb (2000) describe how parties are shifting their campaign strategies from presenting broad programmatic alternatives to offering short-term options tied to current public preferences—but such narrow-casting cannot broadly satisfy the public over a long period.

The declining political role of parties and the increasing importance of interest groups reinforces the difficulties in satisfying the public in a complex political space. For instance, after elections most party elites (the majority that won the election) trumpet the strength of the democratic process and what the new government will achieve. It is in the interest of the party majority in government to stress the accomplishments of government. Special interest groups are seldom fully satisfied, however, and generally benefit from criticizing the government for its shortfalls. Similarly, a majority of party actors in a legislature normally proclaim that a new legislative act is good for the nation (since a majority voted to pass the legislation), but routinely the affected interest groups stress how the legislation does not do quite enough for them. If the democratic process stresses interest articulation and interest maximization over the aggregation of interests into a collective programme, then growing scepticism about government action may be inevitable.

One cannot fault this evolving pattern of interest articulation, because it brings legitimate new interests and groups into the democratic process. This is the ideal of democracy, and so expanding access and influence should be encouraged and applauded. But these changing patterns of citizen interests and interest articulation create new challenges for democracy to find ways to balance the tensions inherent within the democratic process in this new context. Dissatisfaction with the political process is a signal that the current processes are not seen as equal to this challenge.

PART III

The Effects of Change

8

The Consequences of Political Support

WHAT does it mean if more citizens are becoming more suspicious of political elites, more distant from political parties, and more sceptical about governmental institutions? There are legitimate reasons to worry that such trends may erode the vitality of democracy, or eventually may undermine the democratic process itself. Indeed, the history of democracies seems to be punctuated by political analysts raising such concerns, even before there were public opinion surveys to provide supporting evidence (Laski 1931; Lippman 1922; and review in Mueller 1999).

The consequences of eroding political support are likely to appear in a changing relationship between citizens and their government, and in changing expectations of government. But the evidence that political support affects citizens' attitudes and behaviours is mixed. The late Warren Miller, one of the co-founders of the American National Election Study, reputedly said that the decline of political trust is the most dramatic trend in American public opinion...that has no apparent effect on citizen behaviour. More recently, David Moore (2002), senior editor of the Gallup Poll, claimed that the decline of political trust was a myth because it lacked any apparent impact on the American political process! A cross-national review of the correlates of political support found generally weak relationships for several behaviours that are routinely discussed as affected by political support (Norris 1999b). If the trends in political support are real, there should be demonstrable consequences.

This chapter examines the impact of political support on the behaviour of contemporary publics. We review the theoretical literature on what effects should be expected, and why. Then we marshal a diverse array of evidence to test these hypotheses. Some of this evidence comes from examining the individual-level correlates of political support. In addition, we assemble aggregate data from the US states to demonstrate the systemic consequences of support levels. The results, we believe, provide a basis for discussing how citizens' changing political attitudes are likely to affect the functioning of the democratic process in contemporary societies.

THEORIZING ABOUT CONSEQUENCES

Ultimately, political support is important if it affects the pattern of human relations and, in our case, political relations. We might theorize that trust facilitates political cooperation, that it encourages compliance, and that it strengthens political loyalties. But, unless these and other connections can be demonstrated, then the real-world importance of declining political trust is limited (or even the evidence of decline might be questioned).

Political support can have a range of effects that are aligned along multiple political dimensions. Many of these effects function at the individual level, influencing how citizens interact with government and participate in the political process. Other effects are systemic, meaning that the pattern of political relations differs in systems where the aggregate level of trust is low (for example, Putnam 1993; Inglehart 1997*a*). This chapter stresses the behavioural consequences of support rather than effects on other attitudes and values.[1] Feelings of national pride, for example, are likely linked to attitudinal expressions of national identity, but stronger evidence of effects would involve demonstrable behaviours, such as participation in patriotic events or actually flying the flag on holidays. This avoids the potential circularity of studying attitude-to-attitude relationships, and enables us to determine whether there are behavioural implications of the trends described in this volume.

One approach to theorizing about the consequences of political trust builds upon the rational-choice literature in economics. I will label this the *evaluative dimension* of political support, similar to Russell Hardin's (1998; 2002*a*) concept of trust as common, encapsulated interests among actors (Table 8.1). This literature argues that trust facilitates transactions: it is easier and more efficient to do business with someone you trust, because this reduces the need to monitor compliance or develop enforcement mechanisms (Fukuyama 1995; Arrow 1972). Since politics is also a social exchange, the decline of political support should lessen voluntary compliance with government directives (Hardin 1998; Tyler 1990; Uslaner 1999; Kornberg and Clarke 1992: ch. 7).

For example, John Schloz (1998; see also Schloz and Lubell 1998) demonstrates that trust in government increases voluntary compliance in paying taxes, even while other factors such as civic duty, perceptions of tax fairness, and fear of prosecution are controlled for (see also Song and Yarbrough 1978; Norris 1999*b*). Other research suggests that the use and evaluation of government service are coloured by an individual's initial trust in government (Bouckaert and van de Walle 2001). If we generalize this finding to voluntary compliance with government regulations, then a large part of contemporary public policy becomes at least partially dependent on trust in the processes and institutions that generate these regulations.

Between 1958 and 1998, the percentage of Americans who thought that people in government waste a lot of tax money increased by almost half. It should not be

---

[1] We also expect that there are strong attitudinal effects of political support. For instance, Lacy (1998) shows that support for the Reagan tax cuts was greatest among those with lower trust in government. Political support should generally be related to attitudes towards government action. But, to show 'harder' evidence of the effects of political support, we focus on behavioural consequences.

TABLE 8.1   *The potential consequences of political support*

Nature of effects	Type of consequence	Examples
Evaluative	Compliance	Voluntary tax reporting Willingness to serve on a jury Respect for the law Bribery Lower political transaction costs
Affective	Allegiance	Voluntary campaign contributions Provide information to government Voluntary service Expressions of national pride Willingness to work for government
Cognitive	Information heuristic	Vote for the incumbent Interpretation of politics Policy positions
Participation	Conventional political action	Turnout in elections Campaign activity Participation in political groups
	Protest	Complaints to government agencies Protest activity Membership in 'challenging groups'
Institutional	Structural changes	Institution of term limits Support for institutional change

surprising, therefore, that compliance with income tax laws has decreased over this same period in the United States, or that attacks on the Internal Revenue Service have become common among some politicians. If minorities distrust police, if conservatives distrust the IRS, if people are generally sceptical about government, this has real consequences for policy. These examples highlight a particular feature of democracy: democracy functions with minimal coercive force because of the legitimacy of the system and the voluntary compliance of the public. Declining feelings of political trust and political support can undermine this relationship and thus the workings of democracy.

Another potential compliance consequence of political support is the willingness to work for a government agency. For example, the Council for Excellence in Government (2001) surveyed non-federal employees in the United States; it found that trust in government was significantly related to willingness to work in the public sector. Government will not employ the best and the brightest if they are sceptical about the government (Haque 1999).

A second aspect of political support involves *affective orientations* or psychological dispositions that are not fully captured by exchange theories of political support. Trust in government is more than a calculation of an expected exchange between a citizen and a political actor; it represents affective orientations that might be socialized early in life or generalized from other experiences. Indeed, the political culture literature stresses the affective base of political support as an important aspect of political culture (Almond and Verba 1963). More recently, Jane Mansbridge (1997) discussed political trust as based upon moral or altruistic values, and Claus Offe (1999) described trust as a categoric trait that develops separately from evaluative judgements.

The affective elements of support may stimulate *allegiant* behaviours that are non-instrumental expressions of this support. Attendance at a Fourth of July parade in the United States or a Bastille Day celebration in France is a demonstration of political support that is not dependent on instrumental calculations. Even the willingness of an American taxpayer to check off the presidential campaign contributions box on a tax return may be a more affective expression than a calculated one. In other words, if the evaluative aspects of political support lead to compliance and the avoidance of sanctions, the affective aspects of support may generate acts of allegiance without either real or implied coercive threats.

Attitudes towards government may also involve *cognitive effects*. Trust in politicians and confidence in political institutions can be important pieces of information that help guide individual action. For instance, Marc Hetherington (1999) describes trust as a heuristic that helps American voters make choices between candidates at election time. Lack of trust in government often generates support for the challenger, especially when there is a significant third candidate in the presidential election. Hetherington also argues that growing media attention to issues of trust and competence increases the worth of these traits as a basis of understanding and interpreting politics. Underscoring this point, many election surveys now ask about the perceived trustworthiness of candidates, presumably because this is considered a relevant trait as voters make their decisions.

Russell Hardin (2002) extends the discussion of the cognitive element of political support to stress that knowledge of expected outcomes is necessary to allow a citizen to trust a politician or a political institution. Thus, embedded within a rational-choice interpretation of political support is information on past patterns of action that generate feelings of trust or distrust towards political actors. The existence of this knowledge then may influence attitudes towards, and evaluations of, these actors or their actions. For instance, a citizen lacking confidence in government may be more open to conspiratorial interpretations of public policy making or to claims that 'special interests' determine government policy.

Even though we believe cognitive effects are potentially important consequences, we do not explicitly examine them in this chapter, partly because cognitive effects often depend on the national context, which makes it difficult to assemble consistent cross-national evidence. In addition, identifying the cognitive elements of support may require a more fully specified model of a specific behaviour—such as voting choice—that goes into more detail than is possible here. The interested reader might consult Hetherington (1998; 1999) or Kornberg and Clarke (1992: ch. 6) for further evidence on the cognitive effects of political support.

The evaluative, affective, and cognitive aspects of behaviour are potentially significant consequences of political support. In addition, the literature has focused so much attention on the relationship between political support and participation that this topic warrants separate attention. There are, of course, long-standing debates on whether political support stimulates or discourages conventional political activity (Norris 1999*b*). On the one hand, there is an argument that those who feel supportive are more likely to participate in the political process, while the alienated will be less likely to turn out. Political trust may encourage participation in politics as another expression of this support—much as sports fans come to the park to root for their team. On the other hand, there are claims that political alienation stimulates attempts to vote the incumbents out of office and to take other actions to change the course of government.

Both effects are theoretically reasonable, and their joint presence in contemporary political behaviour may explain why there is not strong evidence of either (for example, Farah, Barnes, and Heunks 1979; Verba and Nie 1972; Verba, Schlozman, and Brady 1995). As a starting point for our research, we distinguish between two different types of political participation. First, Table 8.1 suggests that conventional forms of political action may be more common among those who trust government and are supportive of the regime. This logic is embedded in the political culture and democracy literature (for example, Almond and Verba 1963; Inglehart 1997*a*: ch. 6; Putnam 1993). In contrast, the lack of support may more often stimulate unconventional political action that challenges established political elites. Muller and Jukam (1977), Sniderman (1981), and Kornberg and Clarke (1992: ch. 8) found that criticism of the political regime was strongly related to unconventional political action, but the cross-national consistency of this relationship is uncertain. Our research will empirically test these ideas for a wide range of advanced industrial democracies.

Finally, many of the consequences we have discussed assume that the democratic 'rules of the game' are fixed, and citizen behaviour may change within these structures. An alternative assumption is that public dissatisfaction can lead to reforms that restructure the political process (Cain, Dalton, and Scarrow 2003). There is strong micro-level evidence of such a relationship. For example, John Curtice and Roger Jowell (1997) show that British political dissatisfaction generated support for the institutional reforms that became part of the political programme of New Labour. Scholars cite popular dissatisfaction as a prime factor in recent restructuring of the electoral systems in Italy, Japan, and New Zealand (Vowles et al. 1995; Shugart and Wattenberg 2001). Recent calls for campaign finance reform and term limits in the United States undoubtedly draw support from a dissatisfied public (Karp 1995). A lack of public support for government can generate, and has generated, calls for constitutional change in contemporary democracies. We examine these potential effects in a final empirical section of this chapter.

Although we have discussed these effects as consequences of political support as a general phenomenon, it is also important to recognize that there may be differential effects according to the level of political support (Fuchs 1989; Easton 1975; Kornberg and Clarke 1992: ch. 4). For instance, attitudes towards the regime may exert substantial influence on voluntary compliance with laws and regulations. This is where the evaluative aspects of trust in political actors seem most relevant. In comparison, orientations towards the political community or regime values may have a stronger influence on allegiant behaviours, such as expressions of national pride. And, in general terms, support for authorities might influence electoral choice, but one would hope that paying taxes, following the law, and other such acts are not closely tied to incumbent evaluations. This chapter thus examines how different levels of political support may vary in their effects.

INTRODUCING A NEW DATA SOURCE

Most of the analyses in this chapter rely on a variety of cross-national and single-nation surveys to examine the potential effects of political support (also see Norris 1999b). It is difficult to assemble the breadth of cross-national and cross-temporal evidence found in many of the previous chapters because few studies have asked questions about the consequences of support, and the potential consequences often differ depending on the national context. Yet the available data provide rich examples of how political support affects the behaviours and attitudes of contemporary publics.

To go beyond these survey data, we also examine the impact of political support through aggregate-level analyses. Political trust is a state of mind for individuals, but it is also a characteristic of a polity. When most people trust (or distrust) the government, the style of political discourse and behaviour should reflect the shared values of the public. If trust matters, then it should also be apparent at the system level in the patterns of governance and government.

The literature on political culture and the more recent literature on social capital stresses the system effects of citizen values (Almond and Verba 1963; Putnam 1993; Inglehart 1997a). Ronald Inglehart (1997a: ch. 6) demonstrates that a supportive public is strongly related to the stability of a democratic system. Putnam's (2000) recent research on social capital demonstrates very strong relationships between the social capital of US states and a variety of state characteristics, such as educational achievement, health statistics, economic well-being, and effective government. John Pierce, Nicholas Lovrich, and David Moon (2002) extended these analyses to a sample of US cities, describing a strong relationship between a composite indicator of social and political trust and several measures of city government performance. Newton and Norris (2000: 71) analysed social and political trust cross-nationally, and concluded that the relationship is more evident as a systemic characteristic than as an individual-level relationship.

When a community is largely populated by individuals who trust the government, this not only affects those individuals but creates a climate of opinion that may modify the behaviour of the non-trusting. For example, if one sees others willingly supporting the state with their taxes and civic engagement, the sceptical citizen may begin to conform to these behavioural patterns, even if they remain sceptical about government. In a similar vein, Putnam, Pharr, and Dalton (2000: 26) suggest that social trust in a community affects the behaviour of people who are neither socially engaged nor trustful of other people. In other words, the contextual effects of community-level trust cannot be reduced to the simple sum of the individual-level effects.

It is difficult, however, to assemble cross-national aggregate statistics that reliably tap either the predictor or the consequences in such hypothesized relationships. Therefore, this chapter includes a comparative analysis of political support across the US states. In addition, a variety of state-level aggregate statistics are available to assess the purported consequences of support.

MEASURING POLITICAL SUPPORT AT THE STATE LEVEL

To assemble state-level data, we used a set of surveys conducted to predict election outcomes based on exit polls of voters. At both the 1990 and 1994 elections, there were large national exit polls as well as separate surveys of most states.[2] On the positive side, these surveys yield relatively large samples for most of the states, and the survey contained the standard trust in government question ('How often can you trust the government in Washington to do what is right?'). In addition, they come from two elections in which the partisan composition of government differed (a Republican president in 1990 and a Democrat in 1994) and thus any partisan effects will tend to balance out. On the negative side, these data are based on exit polls, which by definition excludes non-voters, and only a single measure of political support is available. We also expect that specific state-level effects, such as the performance of the incumbent administration or a local political scandal, could affect these state estimates. Ideally, one would seek multiple measures of political trust, over a substantial time period, before one could definitively characterize the

---

[2] While national survey data exist in abundance in the United States, measures of state-level public opinion are fairly rare. The large area-probability in-person national surveys, such as the ANES and GSS, use a clustered sampling process that means separate states are not representatively sampled. These two studies were obtained from the Inter-university Consortium for Political and Social Research (ICPSR 9602 and 6520). The 1990 exit poll included 19,888 respondents, the 1994 poll included 11,308 respondents. These surveys yield state samples ranging from 49 (Alaska) to 1,286 (California) in the 1990 survey, and from 31 (Delaware) to 1,192 (California) in the 1994 survey. The distribution of cases across states was not directly proportionate to total population because the survey over-sampled in some states with important statewide races. The median number of cases per state was 278 in 1990 and 197 in 1994.

trust culture of the American states.[3] Still, we believe these data give us a credible first estimate of political support across the US states, and part of the verification comes from the analyses that follow.

We combined the results of both the 1990 and 1994 surveys to provide a summary measure of political support (Table 8.2).[4] The levels of political trust vary across states, but some general tendencies emerge. Trust in the national government tends to be higher in the states that are more affluent (r = 0.41) and that have more educated citizens (r = 0.34). This demonstrates the separation between individual-level effects and systemic patterns, because we have shown that these patterns are much weaker, and in the opposite direction, in our individual-level analyses of political support (Chapter 4). Based on the state measure of liberalism from Erikson et al. (1993), trust in the national government is also higher in more liberal states (r = 0.31). Phrased in different terms, trust tends to be lower in southern states (r = −0.32) and in states with a large rural population (r = −0.17).

For the sake of comparison, political trust is significantly related to Robert Putnam's (2000) state-level comprehensive indicator of social capital (r = 0.31). There are some notable differences between political trust and Putnam's state-level patterns of social capital, however. While Putnam identifies the upper Midwest as a well-spring of social capital, states such as Wyoming and Idaho rank low on political trust (North and South Dakota are not included in the state-level database), and a state such as Utah, which is high on social capital, is nevertheless low on political trust. Both social and political trust are higher on the East Coast; citizens on the West Coast (California, Oregon, and Washington) are more sceptical towards the federal government.

We expect that other measures of political support may show different patterns across the states. For instance, feelings of national pride and attachments to the political community might be distributed quite differently from trust in federal government; national pride is presumably higher in the American South and the more rural areas of the nation. Some of the other dimensions of political support we described in Chapter 2 and analysed with national survey data also might show a different distribution across the US states. But this measure of trust in the federal government has been central to our analyses in earlier chapters, and clearly demonstrates the decline in support for political authorities and the government that we have documented. Thus, we will use this measure to determine whether the different trust contexts of the American states are significantly related to politics.

---

[3] To partially validate our 1990–4 measures, we followed the same procedure to construct a state-level measure using the 1988 exit poll data. These 1988 and 1990–4 state scores are correlated at 0.55.

[4] For seven states, only 1990 data were available (Alaska, Kentucky, Louisiana, Montana, Rhode Island, Vermont, and West Virginia). In these cases we estimated the values expected in 1994, and then averaged the 1990 data and the 1994 estimates.

TABLE 8.2   *State rankings in political trust*

State	Trust score	State	Trust score
Delaware	2.40	Iowa	2.23
Minnesota	2.39	Nevada	2.23
Hawaii	2.37	Arizona	2.22
Oklahoma	2.35	California	2.22
Maryland	2.33	Vermont	2.22
Maine	2.32	Massachusetts	2.21
Nebraska	2.32	Colorado	2.20
Pennsylvania	2.32	Oregon	2.20
New Hampshire	2.31	Tennessee	2.20
Montana	2.30	Kansas	2.19
New Jersey	2.29	Washington	2.19
Alaska	2.28	Kentucky	2.18
Texas	2.28	Michigan	2.18
Connecticut	2.27	New Mexico	2.18
South Carolina	2.27	North Carolina	2.18
Wisconsin	2.27	Virginia	2.15
Illinois	2.26	Arkansas	2.14
Ohio	2.26	Idaho	2.12
Florida	2.25	Wyoming	2.11
Georgia	2.25	Missouri	2.10
New York	2.25	Utah	2.10
Mississippi	2.25	West Virginia	2.08
Rhode Island	2.25	Louisiana	2.06
Indiana	2.23	Alabama	2.05

Note: Table entries are the mean scores on the four-point trust measure: from (1) never trust the government to (4) always trust the government.

Sources: 1990 Voter Research and Surveys, CBS News and *New York Times* General Election Exit Poll; 1994 Voter News Service General Election Exit Poll; North and South Dakota are not included in either exit poll.

POLITICAL SUPPORT AND COMPLIANCE BEHAVIOUR

One of the strengths of democracy is the principle that government of, by, and for the people is the basis of our political system. To the extent that political support represents a belief that government can and will act in one's interest, this encourages a belief that government actions are legitimate and should be followed (Braithwaite and Levi 1998; Hardin 2002). Thus, voluntary compliance with laws and regulations becomes the expected mode of behaviour: 'good' citizens pay their taxes, follow government regulations, and do not jaywalk. This increases both the freedom for the citizen (if these laws were made with the consent of the governed), since it lessens the need for government monitoring and coercion of the population, and the freedom of political elites to act with a presumption of legitimacy.

The 1995–8 World Values Survey contained a battery of items to tap individuals' willingness to obey the law. Respondents were asked whether it was justified to: (1) claim government benefits to which you are not entitled, (2) avoid a fare on public transportation, (3) cheat on taxes if you have a chance, (4) buy something you know is stolen, or (5) accept a bribe in the course of one's duties. Most of these items involve a temptation that most citizens have experienced. It is striking, however, that more than a third of the respondents say that none of these actions is ever justified (the extreme answer on the ten-point scale) and very few individuals believe each item is justified.

We should, of course, expect that willingness to obey the law is at least partially dependent on citizen orientations towards government, but one should also distinguish between different levels of political support (Easton 1965; 1975; Chapter 2 above). We do not expect support for authorities to strongly affect compliance, because losing at the polls should not be a justification for ignoring the law. However, evaluations of the regime and the political system may carry over to citizen opinions about the legitimacy of government, and thus a willingness to comply with the law. In other words, there would be dire consequences for contemporary democracies if law-abiding behaviour were dependent on support for the political incumbents. If citizens saw dissatisfaction with Bush (or Clinton) as justification for cheating on their taxes or abusing government programmes, then democratic governance would be chaos. But if citizens begin to distrust the institutions of government or the political system as a whole, there are theoretical and political reasons to expect that this might erode compliance with government actions.

We created a willingness-to-obey-the-law index, and correlated this with the four indicators of political support we developed in Chapter 3: authority support, institutional support, democratic values, and community support.[5] The four support dimensions are created through a factor analysis, and therefore they are statistically independent. Table 8.3 indicates that each dimension is correlated in the expected direction with voluntary compliance with the law, but there is a systematic difference across the four dimensions. As we expected, support for authorities is very weakly related to compliance. Rather, support for political institutions and the political community more strongly affect compliance. To give a better feel for these correlations, we can use the Swiss survey as an example. The Swiss are a generally law-abiding citizenry; however, among the Swiss who have a great deal of confidence in the parliament, 71 per cent say it is *never justified* to cheat on one's taxes; among those with little or no confidence in parliament, 50 per cent say cheating is never justified. Multiply this by millions of tax returns, and the financial costs of declining trust in government becomes very real.

Additional cross-national evidence comes from the International Social Survey Program (ISSP). The 1998 survey asked whether it was wrong to report less income in order to pay less tax or to falsify information to claim government benefits. In overall terms, most citizens endorse compliance: over 70 per cent say it is wrong to

---

[5] Factor analysis indicated that the five items loaded strongly on a single dimension, explaining over half of the total variance. We therefore created an index as a simple additive summary of the five items.

TABLE 8.3   *The effects of different levels of political support*

	Obey the law	Party activity	Protest
Incumbent support	−0.02	−0.01	0.02
Institutional support	−0.11*	0.10	−0.01
Democratic values	−0.05*	0.10	0.25
Community support	−0.16*	0.14	−0.07
R	0.20	0.20	0.26

Note: Table entries are standardized regression coefficients predicting each variable.
* Coefficients significant at the 0.05 level.

Source: 1995–8 World Values Survey for the eight advanced industrial democracies.

TABLE 8.4   *Correlation between trust in government institutions and compliance*

Nation	Tax reports		Government benefits		Obey law
	Parliament	Courts	Parliament	Courts	
Australia	0.08	0.09	0.03	0.01	0.11
Austria	0.12	0.12	−0.02	0.15	n/a
Britain	0.07	0.09	0.01	0.07	0.14
Canada	0.08	0.08	0.01	0.00	0.03
Denmark	0.10	0.16	0.07	0.15	n/a
France	0.08	0.10	−0.01	0.04	0.03
Germany (W)	0.10	0.11	0.02	0.07	0.08
Ireland	0.15	0.17	0.15	0.16	0.13
Italy	0.06	0.06	0.01	0.01	0.12
Japan	0.04	0.04	0.01	0.05	0.14
Netherlands	0.10	0.08	0.07	0.07	n/a
New Zealand	0.09	0.13	0.06	0.06	0.04
Norway	0.11	0.14	0.09	0.12	0.10
Sweden	0.13	0.10	0.08	0.08	0.10
Switzerland	0.10	0.09	0.02	0.04	n/a
United States	0.03	0.06	−0.01	−0.02	0.05

Note: Table entries are the tau$_b$ correlation between confidence in each political institution and belief it is wrong to falsify tax reports or information for government benefits; the last column is the correlation between trust in government index and belief that citizens should obey the law.

Source: 1998 International Social Survey Program; last column from 1996 International Social Survey Program.

misreport income and over 85 per cent say it is wrong to falsely claim benefits. Each of these opinions is consistently related to trust in parliament and the courts, especially for tax compliance (Table 8.4). These effects may appear small because the size of the correlation coefficients is attenuated by the skewed distribution of these sentiments, but in percentage terms the differences are often quite substantial. For example, among Swiss respondents who have a great deal of confidence in the

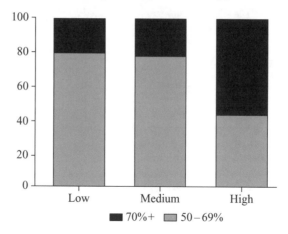

F IG . 8.1 US state level of political trust and voluntary census return rates, 1990
Source: Census return rates collected by the author from the US Bureau of the Census.

courts, only 6 per cent say it is not wrong to falsify tax information, but 36 per cent express this opinion among those who have no confidence in the courts. These patterns would strike terror into the hearts of tax collectors.

Another item from the 1996 ISSP asked about the principle of obedience to the law.[6] There is a consistent relationship between trust in government and the belief that one should obey the law without exception (the last column in Table 8.4). The British survey results can illustrate the differences summarized by the correlations in the table. Among those who express the least trust in government, 30 per cent say one should obey the law without exception. In comparison, among those British respondents who are most trusting of government, 58 per cent say one should obey the law without exception.

Admittedly, the measurement of compliance behaviour in an opinion survey is difficult because of the tendency for individuals to give socially expected responses, which inflates the evidence of actual compliance. By turning to aggregate statistics, however, we can observe patterns of actual behaviour. One available indicator measures compliance in returning census forms across the states. Census returns are a reasonable first indicator of voluntary compliance because returning the census form is a legal requirement.

Figure 8.1 describes a weak relationship between the level of trust in a state and the return rate for the 1990 Census. Of US states where the public expresses limited trust in government, 21 per cent had census return rates of 70 per cent or more, and

---

[6] The question asked: 'Would you say that people should obey the law without exception, or are there exceptional occasions on which people should follow their conscience even if it means breaking the law?'. In most nations about two-thirds of the respondents favour the second position.

this rises to 31 per cent within the high-trust states. This is one of the weakest relationships we describe in this chapter (r = 0.10), but it does run in the correct direction.

Behaviours we have described in this section also appear to parallel the decrease in political support over time. Although it is difficult to objectively measure compliance with government regulations, there are indications that tax evasion is a growing problem in most advanced industrial democracies. Anti-tax sentiments in the United States have become so intense that the Internal Revenue Service uses its website to counter bogus claims that citizens are not legally required to pay taxes. Similarly, voluntary compliance with the US Census has trended downward since 1970; in 2000 Census compliance became another target of anti-government sentiment. Multiplied across the expanding range of government regulations and activities, diminished levels of compliance represent a significant cost of decreasing public trust in government.

POLITICAL SUPPORT AND ALLEGIANT BEHAVIOUR

While voluntary compliance may be a rational effect of political support, these feelings should also generate affective consequences in areas where coercion and compliance are not relevant. For example, Americans who have pride in their nation should be more likely to fly the flag on the Fourth of July and attend parades on the holiday. Supportive Canadians celebrate Canadian Day on July 1, Australians celebrate Australia Day and Anzac Day, and so forth.

In addition, political support should generate other allegiant behaviours that have a more direct relevance to the political process. For instance, the annual tax forms in the United States include a check-off box for making a voluntary contribution to the funding of presidential election campaigns. It does not add to the individual's taxes, and there is no real or implied coercion to encourage this behaviour. Citizens who have confidence in politicians and the political system also may be more likely to engage in government activities, ranging from contributing to candidates' campaigns to working for government and serving in the military. Indeed, much of contemporary democratic politics is based on the premise that such behaviour is an affective consequence of citizens' support for the political system. While there are clear reasons to expect such affective consequences, there is a surprising lack of survey research on such questions. For instance, before September 11, 2001, neither the long series of the American National Election Studies nor the General Social Surveys contained an obvious affective demonstration of national pride, such as flying the flag or participating in a Fourth of July celebration.[7] To date, I have not found such measures in other major cross-national surveys. Thus, our evidence on this point is less direct than one prefers.

[7] A variety of commercial polls had asked these questions before September 2001, and found that Americans' participation in such activities is fairly high. According to a July 2001 Gallup Poll, 66% usually fly the flag on the Fourth and 32% watch a parade on the holiday. Roughly

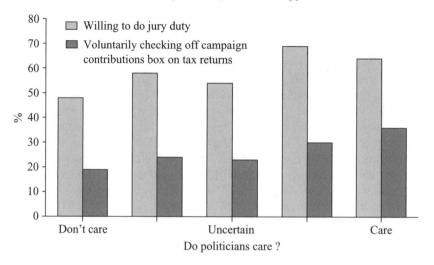

FIG. 8.2 Political support and allegiant behaviour

Source: 1992 and 1996 American National Election Studies; jury duty item average results for both years.

The American National Election Studies contain questions on two behaviours that presumably are linked to feelings of political support: voluntarily checking the campaign contributions box on tax returns and willingness to serve on a jury. Figure 8.2 shows that these two items are clearly related to trust in politicians. For instance, only 19 per cent of those who feel that 'politicians don't care' say they checked off the campaign contribution box, compared with 36 per cent among those who believed politicians do care. The percentage differences in the willingness to answer a jury summons is of about the same magnitude. Furthermore, these sentiments are more closely related to trust in politicians than to evaluations of democratic institutions.[8]

After the terrorist attacks on the World Trade Center in 2001, the 2002 American National Election Study pre-election survey added an item about the US flag. The

comparable figures are obtained in other commercial opinion polls. However, I have been unable to access one of these surveys that also includes standard political support questions. Similarly, commercial polls asked about compliance with the 2000 Census, but this was not asked in the major academic polls.

[8] The following correlations are from the 1992 American national election study:

	Tax check-off	Jury duty
Politicians don't care	0.10	0.14
Congress thermometer	0.02	0.05
Federal government thermometer	0.01	0.03

survey found that 87 per cent of Americans said they had flown the flag over the preceding twelve months. Post-9/11 has been an unusual time in American politics, yet these data demonstrate that patriotic displays are linked to feelings of political support—and effects vary by the level of political support. Flying the flag was not closely linked to support of the political authorities, measured by either the 'officials don't care' (r = 0.07) or the 'many in government are crooked' (r = 0.07) question. The impact of institutional evaluations is predictably stronger, when thermometer ratings of the Congress (r = 0.17), Supreme Court (r = 0.13), and Federal government (r = 0.18) are used to measure institutional support. Finally, attitudes towards the political community—how strong the respondent loves his/her country—is more closely related to this allegiant behaviour (r = 0.31).

Thus, American cross-section data demonstrate a clear relationship between political support and allegiant behaviour. Moreover, the longitudinal effects implied by these relationships are documented with other evidence. Trend data from the Internal Revenue Service indicate a slow decline in the number of Americans checking the campaign contribution box on their taxes, even though the political parties and candidates have become more active in generally soliciting campaign contributions. In 1976, 28 per cent of taxpayers checked off the campaign contribution; by 1999 this had dropped to only 12 per cent—even though the contribution does not directly add to the individual's taxes. Similarly, the court system has referred to the increasing difficulty in recruiting citizens to serve on the jury.

Aggregate-level evidence of allegiant behaviour is limited, but the Internal Revenue Service does report the percentage of tax forms that use the campaign contribution check-off box by state. Overall, only about 12 per cent of tax returns included a contribution in 1996, ranging from 6 per cent in the lowest states to 33 per cent in the highest (indicating that survey-based reports of check-off contributions are inflated). Figure 8.3 demonstrates that the clear relationship between the state levels of political trust and willingness to contribute (r = 0.28). Check-off rates of over 10 per cent are more than twice as common in high-trust states (56 per cent) as in low-trust states (26 per cent).

To summarize, political support seems to affect allegiant behaviour. Citizens are not only willing to comply with governments they trust, but they also make positive expressions of political support when trust exists. If comparable empirical evidence were available for other advanced industrial democracies, we expect it would document this same pattern.

POLITICAL SUPPORT AND PARTICIPATION

If political support is analogous to support for a sports team (or the sport itself), then support levels should influence participation in politics. The complication, however, is that research yields mixed results on this relationship.

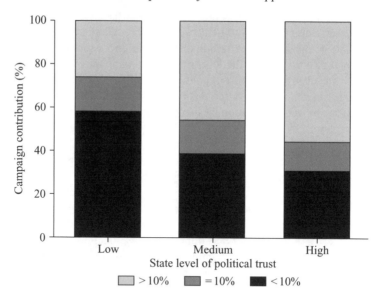

FIG. 8.3 US state level of political trust and voluntary IRS campaign check-off rate, 1996
Source: Internal Revenue Service statistics for 1996 tax returns.

All types of political participation potentially involve multiple motives for
action. On the one hand, those who are dissatisfied with government have obvious
reasons to become active to express their grievances and seek a governmental
response. On the other hand, political participation may be encouraged by beliefs
in the legitimacy and trustworthiness of the political system to respond to citizen
preferences. Thus, it is unclear whether political action should be more common
among those who are supportive of the political system or those who are critical
of it, since both motivations have a sound theoretical rationale.

One way to clarify patterns, I believe, is to distinguish between different types
of political action. It is likely that participation in elections and the conventional
processes of representative democracy is derived from positive views about politicians, political parties, and parliamentary democracy. It seems reasonable to
assume that citizens who work for a political party or contribute to a party believe
that at least their party will be responsive, and that turning out to vote for the party
is also warranted.

In comparison, dissatisfaction may play a greater role in stimulating unconventional, elite-challenging forms of political action. Because protests, demonstrations, and boycotts challenge elites and the institutionalized processes of input
through elections, this is a more likely outlet for those who distrust politicians and
political parties. Muller and Jukam (1977), for instance, found that the lack of
support for the political system and political institutions was strongly related to

protest behaviour among Germans, with weaker correlations for trust in government and incumbent evaluations (see also Kornberg and Clarke 1992: 244; Muller, Jukam, and Seligson 1982; Opp 1989). But the evidence from other research is ambiguous. The Political Action Study found only weak ties between various measures of political support and protest behaviour (Farah, Barnes, and Heunks 1979; Thomassen 1990). Prior analyses of the World Values Surveys found only a modest impact of political support on protest in most advanced industrial democracies (Dalton 2002: ch. 4; Norris 1999*b*). By extending these analyses to more recent data for a wider range of nations, we will determine the current effect of political support on protest politics.

We do not challenge the counter-argument that dissatisfied citizens have reasons to vote or that supportive publics may protest. We are simply suggesting that dissatisfied citizens are less likely to pursue activity through conventional, institutionalized forms of electoral participation that reflect an acceptance of the existing institutions of representative democracy. In addition, the dissatisfied may be more likely to utilize protest and other forms of unconventional action. In the end, however, both types of political action can be mobilized by a mix of such motivations.

Conventional Political Action

The most extensive evidence on the relationship between political trust and electoral participation comes from the long series of the American National Election Studies (Table 8.5). Over the past three decades there is a consistent, modest relationship between political support and conventional activity. The small value of Tau$_b$ correlations give the impression that these differences are very small, but the effects are substantial. For example, the 2000 election study found that only 62 per cent who strongly feel that 'politicians don't care' turned out to vote, compared with 84 per cent among those who felt strongly that politicians do care.[9] The differences are even greater for more demanding forms of activity. For instance, among those who strongly feel 'politicians don't care', only 6 per cent wore a button or had a campaign poster, 4 per cent attended a campaign meeting, and only 1 per cent worked for a candidate. Among those who strongly feel that politicians do care, 14 per cent displayed a button or campaign poster, 9 per cent attended a meeting, and 7 per cent worked for a candidate. In other words, at the extreme, positive images of politicians more than double the level of campaign activity. Thus, one should not be surprised that the decline in political support has been accompanied by decreasing involvement in the electoral process.

Additional evidence comes from the Comparative Study of Electoral Systems, which asked a common set of questions on separate national election

---

[9] These are not just claims by supportive citizens to be more active. Using the 1988 and 1990 validated turnout measures, we found that the reported difference in turnout between trustful and distrustful citizens was 11%; the actual vote differences in turnout were 17%.

TABLE 8.5　*Correlations between political support and campaign activity, United States*

Year	Vote	Attend meeting	Work in campaign	Wear button	Give money	Participation index
1972	0.18	0.10	0.06	0.12	0.13	0.16
1976	0.21	0.11	0.11	0.06	0.14	0.17
1980	0.18	0.09	0.06	0.06	0.10	0.14
1984	0.16	0.07	0.05	0.06	0.07	0.14
1988	0.18	0.12	0.05	0.06	0.13	0.13
1992	0.15	0.11	0.10	0.09	0.10	0.13
1996	0.05	0.05	0.02	0.04	0.06	0.03
2000	0.14	0.06	0.04	0.07	0.05	0.03

Note: Table entries are the tau$_b$ correlations between belief that politicians care what people think and campaign activities.

Source: 1972–2000 American National Election Studies.

studies in the late 1990s. Figure 8.4 plots the percentage who participated in some form of campaign activity by the belief that parties (or politicians) care what people think.[10] Although these relationships are modest, campaign activity is clearly more common among those who trust parties to respond to their interests. Among Americans, for example, only 10 per cent of those low in trust participate, compared with 26 per cent among the most trustful respondents. The percentage differences are modest, but in absolute terms this represents more than a doubling of campaign activity as a function of political support.

The system level consequence of these relationships appears in the levels of election turnout across the US states (Figure 8.5). There were high levels of turnout in only 21 per cent of the low-trust states in the 1988–92 elections, and in only 10 per cent of these states in 1996. But two to three times as many of the high-trust states register these same turnout levels.[11] We realize that a fully specified model would discover other predictors, such as education levels or income levels, that have an even stronger impact on turnout. But the bivariate correlation between trust and turnout is significant. Moreover, these relationships are probably attenuated by the fact that the exit polls interviewed only voters, but this heightens the significance of these patterns. Even among voters, in states where people feel

[10] The number and type of campaign activities vary across nations in the CSES surveys, because campaign activity was not a part of the common core questionnaire. Thus, the levels of activity should not be compared across nations.

[11] State levels of political trust are also related to other measures of conventional political participation available from Putnam's state-level database. Trust is correlated with service on a local committee (r = 0.28), attendance at a local meeting (0.17), and membership in 503b organizations (0.31). This suggests that the relationships for campaign activity would apply to other forms of conventional action.

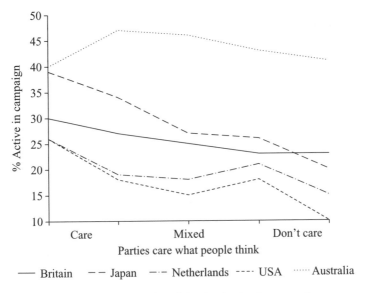

FIG. 8.4 Feelings that parties care and participation in election campaigns

Note: Entries show the % active in election campaign by belief that parties (politicians) care what people think. The number of campaign items varies across nations.

Source: Comparative Study of Electoral Systems.

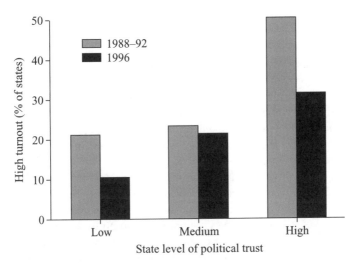

FIG. 8.5 US state level of political trust and election turnout

Note: 'High turnout' means 59 per cent or more voting in the respective elections.

Source: Turnout data collected by the author.

TABLE 8.6   *Cross-national correlations between political trust and activity*

Country	Voted	Active in Protest	Active in Demonstrations
Australia	0.02	−0.07	−0.08
Britain	0.14	0.03	−0.03
Canada	0.12	−0.01	−0.02
France	0.14	0.05	0.00
Germany (W)	0.10	−0.05	−0.04
Ireland	0.06	−0.04	−0.11
Italy	0.00	0.04	0.07
Japan	0.17	−0.01	0.02
New Zealand	0.02	−0.02	−0.06
Norway	0.08	−0.09	−0.04
Sweden	0.07	−0.01	0.03
United States	0.04	−0.07	−0.07

Note: Table entries are the tau_b correlations between an index of trust in government and each of these political activities.

Source: 1996 International Social Survey Program.

less trustful of government this creates a cultural milieu that diminishes the likelihood that their neighbours will vote. This is the contextual effect that Putnam, Pharr, and Dalton (2000: 26) suggest will occur as an aggregate consequence of political orientations.

Additional evidence of participation effects comes from cross-national survey data on reported voting. Table 8.6 illustrates the relationship between trust in government and voting turnout for a dozen advanced industrial democracies. The correlations vary in strength, with the trustful generally voting more often. To use the British data as an example, turnout is only 69 per cent among those who score lowest on the political trust scale, compared with 87 per cent among the most trustful. The relationships are often modest, as in Table 8.5 for the United States, and in a few instances the correlations are in the opposite direction. In most cases, however, the belief that politicians and parties do care what people think encourages individuals to be active in campaigns.

Another perspective on these relationships is evident in Table 8.3. In a second regression analysis we used the four dimensions of political support to predict participation in party activities for the advanced industrial democracies in the 1995–8 World Values Survey. Support for authorities is not significantly related to action; those who trust political institutions, espouse democratic values, and are supportive of the political community are also more active in political parties. Indeed, this is the pattern one would expect if campaign and party activity is based on confidence in the institutions and system that structure the process.

Protest Politics

We expect that the use of unconventional forms of action will be more common among those who hold negative images of politicians, parties, and political institutions. The 1996 International Social Survey demonstrates a weak negative relationship between political support and protest, although this pattern varies across nations (Table 8.6). In some cases, political trust is positively related to protest, such as in Italy at the time of the 1996 survey, possibly because supportive citizens were taking to the streets in the midst of Italy's political scandals in the mid-1990s.

Table 8.3 summarizes the relationship between our four measures of political support and protest activity.[12] Neither attitudes towards incumbents nor political institutions is systematically related to protest across these eight nations. However, support for democratic values strongly encourages protest activity. To use the United States to illustrate this pattern, among those who strongly agree that democracy is the best form of government a quarter have attended a demonstration; this drops to 9 per cent among those who score low on the democracy item. As we argued above, protest is now predominately seen as an expansion of the democratic process to citizen-oriented, elite-challenging activities rather than as opposition to democracy. At the same time, identification with the political community slightly diminishes the use of protest. We suspect that this occurs because those who are most proud of the political system tend to see protest as a system-challenging activity.

Taken together, these analyses indicate that feelings of political support significantly influence the patterns of political action, although the nature of participation effects is more complex than other consequences. In some contexts, political support stimulates action, while in others it discourages political activity. This is not a logical or theoretical inconsistency because the patterns of action depend on both the orientations of citizens and on how political groups attempt to mobilize public support. Another complication is that different levels of political support affect the forms of political action differentially. Support for political authorities and the community, for example, are often positively related to campaign and party activity, but negatively related to protest politics. More complex analyses should be able to specify the relationship between citizen orientations and political action in more detail. For present purposes, however, we have demonstrated that a significant relationship exists.

POLITICAL SUPPORT AND INSTITUTIONAL CHANGE

Our final analyses involve the relationship between political support and preferences for institutional reforms of the democratic process. If more people are dissatisfied with the game of politics, one potential consequence is change to the

---

[12] The protest scale is a count of the number of the following protest activities in which the respondent had participated: sign a petition, boycott, attend a demonstration, join a strike, or occupy a building.

rules or the structure of the game. Indeed, there is a common expectation that institutional change is one method to address the public's present disenchantment with politics.

Such institutional change might occur on several levels (Cain, Dalton, and Scarrow 2003). One type of change involves reforms directed towards improving the functioning of the electoral process and political representation. Under this heading one might consider term limits or reforms of campaign financing. The restructuring of the Japanese, Italian, and New Zealand electoral systems are examples of political reforms that are linked to public dissatisfaction with the workings of the process (Shugart and Wattenberg 2001). Another type of change involves the introduction of new forms of direct democracy that empower citizens with a greater role in the democratic process. For instance, growing support for the introduction of referendums has apparently developed as trust in parties and politicians has eroded. Finally, aspects of constitutional reform can change the workings of the democratic process in more fundamental ways. For example, the structural reforms of Britain's Blair government illustrate this level of change: reform of the House of Lords, introduction of a Bill of Rights, and passage of a freedom of information law.

Recently, Hibbing and Theiss-Morse (2002) have claimed that decreasing political support reflects a desire for institutional change—in the opposite direction. They argue that people want to be less involved in government and favour reforms that spare them the burdens of democratic citizenship. This is a provocative argument because it runs counter to the rest of the research literature. It also runs counter to their own empirical findings. For instance, their own survey of American public opinion found that 86 per cent favoured more initiatives (Hibbing and Theiss-Morse 2002: 75). In further analyses they show that the preference for more direct democracy is linked to negative images of the current policy process. Thus, we focus on reforms to expand the democratic process that will generate more citizen access, transparency, and accountability of democratic governments.

Because institutional reforms are dependent on the political structures in a nation, much of the evidence in this section draws upon the current institutional debates in several advanced industrial democracies. Our research asks whether lack of political support has reached the point where these feelings stimulate calls for structural reform. Given the early arguments that political support consisted of ephemeral attitudes without real political consequences, a link to institutional reform would underscore the political significance of these opinions.

Electoral and Party Change

Because political parties are often the prime actors in the democratic process, public dissatisfaction with government frequently focuses on the parties. If government does not perform, then voters can throw the governing parties out of office and elect a new party (or coalition). The ballot box can be a powerful tool for political change. But if electoral change does not satisfy the public, then citizens may endorse efforts to reform the parties or the electoral process.

Two American examples show how political distrust can stimulate a preference for such reforms.[13] The term-limits movement advocates limiting the number of years that elected officials can serve in a specific office. A full nineteen states have enacted some form of legislative term limits since 1990, and sixteen states have passed new limits of the term of the governor since 1990. The 1996 American National Election Study demonstrates a clear relationship between political trust and support for term limits. Among those with a high level of trust, 56 per cent support terms limits, compared with 84 per cent among those lowest in trust. Another question asked for opinions on reforming the electoral process so that candidates were selected by non-partisan contests. Support for non-partisan elections is much higher among the distrustful, whereas the majority of trustful Americans favour continuing the present system ($tau_b = 0.14$). Such relationships do not ensure that the lack of political support is translated into actual reforms, but they indicate that declining political support widens the popular base for those who advocate such reforms.

Our state-level data demonstrate this same pattern at the aggregate level (Figure 8.6). The states where the public is more sceptical towards government were more likely to pass limitations on the term of legislators (58 per cent) and governors (47 per cent) during the 1990s. These same reforms were much less common in states with a trustful public, in which only 37 per cent enacted legislative term limits and 19 per cent added further limits on the term of governors. Citizen orientations towards government are thus clearly related to the ability to enact these institutional changes.

To return to individual-level analyses, additional evidence on the link between popular sentiments and institutional reform comes from the recent electoral reforms in New Zealand and Japan. In both cases, growing public disenchantment with politicians and the political parties fuelled a search for institutional reform (Shugart and Wattenberg 2001). The 1993 New Zealand Election Survey found that trust in government influenced sentiments toward electoral reform. A majority (52 per cent) of those who strongly trusted the government voted to retain the first-past-the-post electoral system in the 1992 referendum, while those who

---

[13] The following table presents the relationship between trust and preferences for institutional reform in the 1996 American National Election Study:

	Low trust	–	–	High trust
Favour term limits	84	81	79	75	56
Continue two-party system| 39	41	40	46	53
Candidates without parties| 32	34	35	28	17

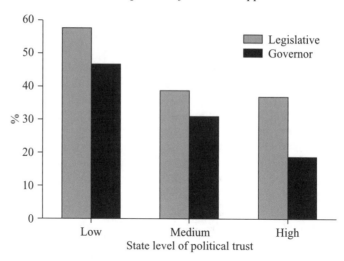

F ig 8.6 US state level of political trust and enactment of term limits
Source: US Term Limits Organization (www.termlimits.org).

strongly distrusted the government overwhelmingly voted (84 per cent) for a new proportional representation system. Furthermore, other analyses suggest that endorsement of electoral reform was more strongly related to measures of regime support than support for politicians (Vowles et al. 1995; Vowles 1995).

A series of political scandals rocked Japanese politics in the early 1990s, and a frustrated public called for political reform. The public linked their dissatisfaction to the need for institutional change. The 1993 pre-election Japanese Election Survey, for example, found that 61 per cent of those who were very dissatisfied with the political process felt that political reform was not possible if the electoral system was not changed, compared with 47 per cent among those who were at least somewhat satisfied with politics. As a result of this public discontent, the Japanese electoral system changed to a mixed-member format beginning with the 1996 election in the hope that this would strengthen party discipline and lessen the corruption of individual politicians (Reed and Thies 2001).

Perhaps the most striking finding comes from the Comparative Study of Electoral Systems. This cross-national study in the late 1990s asked respondents if they felt the most recent national election was conducted fairly: sentiments which touch the very legitimacy of the system of representative democracy. Fair and honest elections are the norm in the eight advanced industrial democracies included in this study, and this seems to be a generally unquestioned position. However, there is a disturbing link between political distrust and the belief that elections are not conducted fairly (Figure 8.7). While nearly 80 per cent of the trustful believe in the integrity of elections, barely 50 per cent among the least

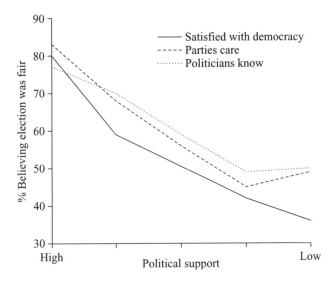

FIG 8.7 Political support and feelings that last election was fair

Note: Entries are % believing the last election in their country was conducted fairly (point 1 on 5-point scale).

Source: Comparative Study of Electoral Systems (Australia, Germany, Great Britain, Japan, Netherlands, New Zealand, Norway, and the US).

trustful do, and even fewer among those who are dissatisfied with the workings of the democratic process. The correlation is stronger for evaluations of the democratic process ($tau_b = 0.25$) than for party evaluations (0.20) or evaluations of politicians (0.17). Certainly it is a challenge to the very system of representative democracy when such doubts exist among a significant part of the electorate.

To summarize, a growing number of contemporary citizens are disenchanted with the political parties, and these sentiments are generating support for reforms to improve the system of representative democracy. This creates fertile ground for elites and other political actors to suggest institutional reform and experimentation.

Support for Direct Democracy

If more citizens are becoming sceptical about political parties and the processes of representative democracy, this may fuel demands for institutional reforms to expand the public's direct involvement in political decision-making. One of the most prominent examples of these trends is the growth in support for referendums and other forms of direct democracy (Scarrow 2003; Gallagher and Uleri 1996). Where possible, interest groups increasingly use referendums as policy tools and agenda setting devices, supplementing traditional channels of political influence with appeals to 'let the people decide'. After centuries of epitomizing the system of representative democracy, Britain now accepts referendums as a tool of political decision-making—especially when the established political parties are unable or unwilling to make political decisions. And in the United States, the use of referendums has dramatically grown at the state level. The Initiative and Referendum Institute (IRI) calculates that there were 118 statewide referendums during the 1950s; this increased to 378 referendums in the 1990s.[14] Susan Scarrow (2003) documents a doubling of national referendums in the OECD nations between the early 1960s and late 1990s.

The proliferation of referendums is just one facet of the expansion of citizen access in advanced industrial democracies. Citizen consultation and public hearings are often embedded in an extensive range of legislation, giving citizens new access points to government policy formation and administration (Hager 1995; Ingram and Smith 1993; Berry, Portney, and Thomson 1993). The use of ombudsman offices has also spread across the OECD nations over the past several decades (Ansell and Gingrich 2003). Such reforms are especially important at local levels of government, where direct involvement is more feasible. Since many citizens have lost faith in the institutions and processes of representative democracy, these new forms of direct action may represent an attempt by the citizens themselves to take a larger role in political decision-making.

A 1997 Eurobarometer survey tapped orientations towards direct democracy across Europe; it asked respondents whether they approved of the Swiss form of direct democracy, such as greater use of referendums.[15] Among those Europeans who expressed an opinion, 70 per cent were positive about the direct democracy of the Swiss political system.[16] Furthermore, these opinions were linked to feelings of political support. Among Europeans who were very satisfied with the working of the democratic process, 62 per cent approved of the Swiss model of direct democracy, compared with 74 per cent among those who were not at all satisfied. Those who thought the government responsive to the public were less likely to approve of direct democracy (61 per cent) than people who felt the government was more concerned about its own interests (73 per cent).

---

[14] These data are from the IRI web site, www.iandrinstitute.org.

[15] The Swiss constitution requires that constitutional changes be submitted to a popular referendum; in addition, citizens can call for a referendum on federal laws and can propose constitutional reforms via a referendum. The survey item was from Eurobarometer 47.1: *Images of Switzerland* (March–April 1997). The question wording is: 'The Swiss system of direct democracy, that is to say frequent votes and referenda, etc. works well and should be considered as a model.' Because this question presumes a knowledge of the Swiss system; nearly 40% of the survey respondents give a 'don't know' response to it.

[16] Because the question asked about direct democracy referred to Switzerland, many respondents said they were not familiar with the Swiss system and were coded as giving 'don't know' responses. We also suspect that this indirect reference to direct democracy attenuated relationships that might result from simply asking about support for greater direct democracy in one's own nation.

TABLE 8.7 *German support for direct democracy by political dissatisfaction*

	West	East
Dissatisfaction with political system	0.25*	0.15*
Dissatisfaction with parties		
Parties interested in public opinions	0.19*	0.08
Parties are necessary	0.13*	0.03
Index	0.21*	0.10*
Dissatisfaction with politicians		
Deputies know opinions of citizens	0.12*	0.13*
It makes a difference who governs	0.08*	0.10*
Elections influence policy	0.09*	0.11*
Elections don't select correct leaders	0.13*	0.07
Index	0.17*	0.17*
Dissatisfaction with policy		
Left/right distance measure	0.15*	0.15*

Note: Table entries are Pearson correlations.
* Coefficients significant at 0.05 level.

Source: 1998 German Election Study that is part of the Comparative Study of Electoral Systems, Wissenschaftszentrum Berlin.

Even more direct evidence comes from a research on support for direct democracy in the Federal Republic of Germany (Dalton, Buerklin, and Drummond 2001). As in the Eurobarometer data, the majority of Germans favour more direct democracy where the public has a greater say on important political decisions. Endorsement of direct democracy also varies systematically across different levels of political support (Table 8.7). In both Western and Eastern Germany, dissatisfaction with the democratic process leads the public to espouse greater support for direct democracy. For instance, among Westerners only 33 per cent of the most satisfied group favour direct democracy, but these sentiments are shared by 77 per cent among those who are not at all satisfied.

Dissatisfaction with the political parties is also strongly related to support for direct democracy. A series of items tapping trust or confidence in politicians are also correlated with support for direct democracy, but these relationships are weaker than for system or party trust. Policy dissatisfaction is also related to support for direct democracy,[17] but this relationship is even weaker than for other indicators of political support. Thus, there is a steady progression in the relationship between political support and opinions toward direct democracy. The narrowest measure of political evaluations, dissatisfaction with policy, has the

---

[17] Policy dissatisfaction was measured as the absolute value of the difference between the placement of the CDU-FDP government on the left/right scale and the respondent's self-placement on this scale. Thus, as the perceived policy distance from the government increases, so does our measure of policy dissatisfaction.

weakest link to direct democracy among Westerners ($r = 0.15$), and this correlation steadily increases as the object of support broadens to politicians (0.17), political parties (0.21), and the democratic process (0.25).

Other national surveys asking about referendums and direct democracy display similar patterns of relationship. In the 1997 Canadian National Election Study, support for referendums is significantly correlated with the belief that parties do not care what people think ($tau_b = 0.13$) and dissatisfaction with the democratic process (0.16). The 1972 American National Election Study shows that Americans link trust in government to their belief that more issues should be decided by voters at the polls ($tau_b = 0.12$). Research on British, Danish, and Finnish public opinion also demonstrates a connection between the low levels of political support and endorsement of direct democracy (Curtice and Jowell 1997; Svensson 1994; Pesonen 1994).

To summarize, another consequence of the spreading distrust of politics and political institutions is a growing preference for direct democracy. If elites cannot be trusted, then it is better to participate directly in the political process, avoiding political parties and parliamentarians who are the traditional base of representative democracy. Such a development is consistent with the participatory revolution that has changed the patterns of political activity among contemporary publics, and represents a sort of Jeffersonian belief that the cure for the problems of democracy is more democracy. While the consequences of such institutional reforms are still under debate, it is clear that the pressure for new forms of direct democracy build upon the public's growing scepticism about conventional politics.[18]

Constitutional Reform

The consequences of decreasing support of politicians, parties, and political institutions is even greater if these sentiments lead to constitutional changes in the political system. For instance, the previous sections noted that mounting political dissatisfaction fuels calls for reforms of the electoral system or non-partisan channels of access.

One example of such constitutional debate comes from Britain, where institutional reform has been a major issue in recent elections. Several British Social Attitudes Surveys tap public opinion on issues of constitutional change. Those who are less trustful of government are significantly more likely to favour changing the political role of the House of Lords, abolishing the monarchy, restricting the provisions of the Official Secrets Act, and allowing the Courts to overturn

---

[18] In Cain, Dalton, and Scarrow (2003), we argue that political reform also creates new forms of advocate democracy, such as use of ombudsman offices, participation in open public hearings, engaging in local community associations, and other forms of direct political action. While cross-national survey evidence on support for these reforms is not generally available, we would expect that these new participatory forms are also strongly linked to criticisms of contemporary forms of representative democracy and the institutions of representative democracy.

parliamentary legislation (Curtice and Jowell 1995; 1997). These institutional structures were once pillars of the British system of government, but at the end of the 1990s a large percentage of the British public favoured reform on each point.

The 1999 Australian constitutional referendum provides another setting in which public sentiments were directly translated into a constitutional decision (McAllister 2001; McAllister and Wanna 2001). The referendum offered voters a choice between the existing monarchy and a republic with a president selected by parliament; the first option received a majority. The Australian Referendum Survey, however, offered a third choice: a republic with a directly elected president. When the people were presented with all three constitutional options, the impact of political support was clear-cut. Those who were least trustful of government favoured by a large majority (61 per cent) a republic with a directly elected president, and far fewer favoured a president selected by parliament (11 per cent) or retaining the monarchy (25 per cent). In comparison, the most trustful displayed relatively more support for parliament selecting the president (34 per cent), with fewer favouring a directly elected president. Republicanism was thwarted in Australia only because elites did not give citizens the constitutional option they preferred.

In other research, we have demonstrated that contemporary advanced industrial democracies have experienced a cumulative series of institutional reforms during the later twentieth century (Cain, Dalton, and Scarrow 2003). In large part, these reforms focused on gaining greater public access to the political process, such as through the expanded use of referendums, requirements for public hearings on legislative or administrative issues, the diffusion of ombudsman offices, and an opening of access to the courts. But demands for greater transparency and accountability of government also were a driving force behind these reforms. While these reforms normally did not require constitutional amendment, their combined impact has been to reshape the working of the democratic process, and thus produce fundamental changes in political processes in contemporary democracies (Cain, Dalton, and Scarrow 2003: ch. 11).

Institutions change slowly, and the channels by which public sentiments may lead to institutional reform are complex and imprecise. Even if the public becomes frustrated with existing political institutions, there is no guarantee that political reform will follow. Still, there is mounting evidence that pressures for institutional reform are increasing across the advanced industrial democracies. To the extent that dissatisfaction continues, this may lead to even more attempts at institutional reform.

POLITICAL SUPPORT AND POLITICAL CHANGE

This chapter has sought to answer the question: do feelings of political support matter? Although the evidence is thinner than in other areas of the project, because research attention to this question has been limited, the findings clearly point to real political consequences that follow from citizens' increasing scepticism towards politicians, political parties, and political institutions.

One set of effects involves the relationship between citizens and their state. Decreasing trust in government erodes feelings that citizens should comply with the directives of government. In place of the deference to authority that once characterized the public (Nevitte 1996; Inglehart 1999), many people are now willing to question the decisions of government and those who make these decisions. This is a trait that political elites clearly recognize and lament as part of the changing style of contemporary democratic politics (for example, Bradley 1997; 1999; Bennett and Nunn 1997).

These sentiments also affect citizen behaviour. Individuals who lack confidence in their leaders and governing institutions are less likely to comply with government directives, whether this involves paying taxes, following governmental regulations, or a general respect for the law. Aggregate statistics thus demonstrate a general decline in such compliance behaviour in many advanced industrial democracies. In addition, voluntary activities that are essential to the governing process—such as serving on a jury or contributing to election campaigns—are also less common when political support is lacking. If extended to a sufficient degree, these patterns can weaken the very social contract upon which the democratic system is based.

Reinforcing these changing orientations, patterns of political activity are also shifting. Distrust appears to diminish involvement in the traditional channels of representative democracy, such as voting and campaign activity. Instead, those who distrust government are more likely to seek influence through protest and other direct forms of action. If one cannot trust politicians to care what one thinks or to act honestly, then concerned citizens must become directly involved in advocating their interests.

One qualification to these conclusions is the varying impact of different levels of political support on these behavioural outcomes. Support for political authorities has limited influence on many of the effects we have described, as Easton and others have predicted. Instead, orientations towards the institutions of the regime and the political system are more strongly related to compliance behaviour, campaign activity, protest, and other consequences. This implies that broader patterns of political change are relatively separate from political evaluations of the moment. But the changes in institutional support we demonstrated earlier in this work (Chapter 2) do appear to be having broader effects on the political process. At the same time, these effects are countered by the positive impact of system support—which has not systematically declined across these nations. This mix of effects may explain why the impact of political support is not always apparent in other analyses.

Finally, low levels of trust in government can fuel support for institutional reform. At a national level, this is apparent in recent reforms of the electoral systems in Italy, Japan, and New Zealand, as well as democratic reforms being debated in other nations. Changing the structure of democratic government can have fundamental implications for the democratic process, and at the heart of such reforms is the belief that they will rekindle support for the democratic process by changing the nature of the process. Often there is a Jeffersonian claim that the cure for democracy is more democracy.

It is too early to know whether institutional reform will change public doubts about government. Certainly, the exploration of new political options is one of the strengths of the democratic process. The ability of New Zealanders to restructure their electoral system, or of Americans to enact term limits, demonstrates the democratic process at work. The initial evidence suggests that institutional change will not 'fix' the decline in political support. In New Zealand, for instance, there was a temporary bounce in political support after the electoral system was reformed, but within eighteen months trust again began trending downward (Karp and Bowler 2001). Similarly, trust in parliament decreased in Japan after the restructuring of the electoral system (Tanaka 2001). I frankly think it is doubtful that term limits or campaign finance reform would have a significant impact on the political support level of Americans.[19]

Certainly, democratic institutions should adapt and explore different forms (Held 1996; Cain, Dalton, and Scarrow 2003). Such adaptation may help ensure public confidence in the process, but such reforms often will not address the more fundamental changes in citizen expectations that contribute to the current negative images of government. Indeed, institutional reform may compound the problem by creating false impressions of change that are soon demonstrated as unsubstantial, and by increasing the complexity of governance. Thus, democratic reform might best be judged by the degree to which it expands citizen access, increases the transparency of government, and improves accountability, rather than by whether it makes the public more supportive of politicians and political institutions.

---

[19] For a contrasting viewpoint, see Bradley (1999), who stresses the need for such reforms to restore public confidence in government. Similarly, efforts such as the Nolan Commission (see p. 3) in Britain are designed, at least in part, to restore public confidence. I think that such reforms would be better judged by their effects in terms of strengthening the democratic process rather than changing public sentiments.

Conclusion

9

Democratic Challenges, Democratic Choices

Thank goodness we're not a democracy.
(Rep. Bob Ingles (R-SC), 18 December 1998,
during Clinton impeachment debate)

By almost any measure, public confidence and trust in, and support for, politicians, political parties, and political institutions has eroded over the past generation. A single American comparison captures the transformation. In April 1966, with the Vietnam War raging and race riots in Cleveland, Chicago, and Atlanta, 66 per cent of Americans *rejected* the view that 'the people running the country don't really care what happens to you'. In December 1997, after America's cold war victory and in the midst of the longest period of peace and prosperity in more than two generations, 57 per cent of Americans *endorsed* that same view.[1]

While American political scientists and commentators generally explain this trend in terms of the unique political history of the United States, the first major finding of this study is that the trend occurs across the advanced industrial democracies as a whole. Citizens in nearly all advanced industrial democracies are increasingly sceptical towards politicians, political parties, and political institutions—although the pace and timing of the decline varies by nation.[2] In a few nations, political support actually increased during the 1950s and 1960s, but eventually the trend reversed and support declined in these nations as well. Moreover, this evidence of decreased political support contrasts with the state of our knowledge just a few short years ago, when researchers claimed that political orientations were not

---

[1] Cited in Pharr and Putnam (2000: 9–10). Although systematic data on political alienation in America before the advent of regular national surveys in the 1950s are sketchy, some evidence suggests that alienation had declined from the mid-1930s to the mid-1960s. See Lane (1965) and Bennett (2001).

[2] The analyses used linear trend coefficients to describe opinion time series over time, but we do not presume that trends are simple linear plots. There are clear examples of non-linear shifts in support in many nations. Our goal, however, was to demonstrate that, if one looks beyond short-term perturbations for general patterns, the overall trends are downward. Linear trend coefficients, such as regression slopes, are the most direct way to test this assertion.

systematically shifting.[3] Something significant, and common, has changed in the way many citizens perceive their government.

At the same time, people have not lost all faith in politics. Adherence to the norms and ideals of the democratic process have apparently increased over this same time period. In most nations, people have become more tolerant of others, more engaged in politics, and more supportive of democratic norms. In addition, allegiance to the political community has not changed significantly; pride in one's nation has held constant or grown in most nations. Thus, in contrast to previous periods of political dissatisfaction when democracy itself was under challenge, such as during the inter-war period and the anti-system assaults following the Second World War, the present questioning of government often comes from those who strongly adhere to the democratic creed. As we will argue below, this deepening commitment to democratic principles may be one of the factors contributing to the dissatisfaction with contemporary governments.

Despite the breadth of these opinion trends, we should not simply extrapolate these patterns into the future. Straight lines are not a good way to forecast many political phenomena, because the political system reacts to past trends, accelerating some and attempting to reverse others. This is the dynamic nature of democratic politics. For instance, the early Reagan administration consciously attempted to counter previous trends of decreasing political support by emphasizing the positive imagery of patriotism and American ideals (before its own political scandals tarnished these ideals). Many contemporary political elites are grappling with the tensions produced by a more cynical public, and attempting to assuage these concerns. Tony Blair created the new political style of New Labour in Britain, Junichiro Koizumi is trying to reshape public images of Japanese politics. At least in the short run, I do not discount the ability of innovative political leaders to improve public images of government and restore the public's faith that, this time, politics will change. But there is a lesson to be learned from the fact that politicians in most advanced industrial democracies are aware of these trends and have been trying to restore public confidence in politics—yet they have not been able to return support to the levels of the past. There is little evidence of sustained improvement in any nation. And even temporary surges in enthusiasm, such as accompanied Blair's election in 1997 or Reagan's shining imagery of American politics, have receded with the passage of one or two electoral cycles.[4]

---

[3] As recently as 1995 the state of our knowledge was best represented by Ola Listaug's (1995) analyses of political support in four nations. Listaug concluded that there was not a systematic trend affecting advanced industrial democracies, and this message of continuity was even more strongly argued by the editors of *Citizens and the State*, Klingemann and Fuchs (1995).

[4] Data from the British Social Attitudes Survey do document a rise in political support following Blair's election in 1997, but by the 2001 election this had fallen back to the levels before Blair entered office (Curtice and Jowell 1997; Bromley, Curtice, and Seyd 2002).

The existence and cross-national breadth of these trends thus raises two intertwined questions. First, what has eroded political support across these nations? Second, what are the consequences of these trends for politics in these democracies? This chapter addresses both of these questions, arguing that the challenges democracies face also represent opportunities—and that the democratic choices we make will shape our political future.

MURDER ON THE ORIENT EXPRESS

Robert Putnam (2000) has recently popularized an analogy for social science research: explaining a social science outcome is like solving the murder mystery on the Orient Express. There is no single causal factor explaining human behaviour—no single guilty party—rather, a multiple set of causes are normally at work. This analogy certainly applies to attempts to explain the erosion of political support in advanced industrial democracies.

From the prior literature on political support, one can amass a long list of suspects for why citizens are more sceptical about their governments (for example, Nye, Zelikow, and King 1997: ch. 11; Norris 1999*a*; Pharr and Putnam 2000: ch. 1). One of the first results of this project has been to narrow the list of suspects by using the evidence from the cross-national data. As we have noted throughout this study, public opinion experts in most nations often explain the trends in political support in terms of the unique experiences or events of their nation. For example, Austrian political support supposedly eroded with the breakdown of the Red-Black alliance; Canadian support suffered as a consequence of the Quebec debate; political scandals eroded public trust in France and Italy; Germans became cynical because of the negative effects of unification; an enduring recession in the 1990s eroded the faith of the Japanese citizenry; New Zealanders became sceptical because of the economic policies and unresponsiveness of the Labour government in the 1980s; and so forth. In each case where public opinion trends exist, one can turn to history and find a series of events that 'fit' the trend. Such historical factors may contribute to the decrease in support within each nation—but it is highly unlikely that nearly all advanced industrial democracies have experienced independent, coincidental events that are the root causes of a general trend across these nations. Thus, explanations based on 'proper nouns' are often *post hoc* interpretations of these trends, and the fundamental causal forces lie elsewhere.

Rather than explanations based on proper nouns, we focused on factors that may be generally affecting advanced industrial societies and thus producing a broad change in public orientations towards government. One of the culprits most commonly cited by both academics and political commentators is the media. For instance, the change in US media norms in reaction to Watergate and the impact of Woodward and Bernstein's reporting on aspiring young journalists may explain why the US press is more critical of government (Patterson 1993; 2001).

This development, however, does not explain why trust has generally declined across contemporary democracies, even in nations where the structure of the media and the media culture are substantially different from those of the United States (Patterson 1995). There is also little evidence that media exposure is directly related to lower levels of political trust (Chapter 3; Norris 2000a; 2000b). Thus, we suggest that the media might be seen as a symptom of broader social changes in advanced industrial democracies, but not a primary causal agent.

Similarly, various studies claim that institutional structures have contributed to the decrease in political support. In the United States, for instance, analysts cite the structure of divided government, the operation of Congress, the functioning of the presidency, and the structure of elections as causes for deteriorating images of government (Hibbing and Theiss-Morse 1995; Craig 1993; Cooper 1999a). In other nations, such as Italy, Japan, and New Zealand, the electoral system or the structure of party government are held to be at fault (Shugart and Wattenberg 2001). These analyses often imply that institutional problems caused the decrease in support, and that institutional reforms can restore public confidence in government. But such an explanation cannot apply to the parallel erosion of political support in nations with very different institutional structures. Political support has decreased in parliamentary and presidential systems, in nations with majoritarian electoral systems and proportional representation, in centralized and federal systems. The variations in institutional structures across these nations may affect patterns of support, but only at the margins. So, like proper-noun explanations of these trends, the focus on institutional structures appears to be *post hoc* and nation-specific, rather than identifying a general source of these trends.

From another perspective, Nye, Zelikow, and King (1997: ch. 11) suggest that the euphoria of victory in the Second World War buoyed post-war political support in the United States, and the fading of these sentiments led to the declines in political support. However, this explanation is likewise not consistent with the cross-national evidence. Political support has decreased in nations that were neutrals in the Second World War (such as Sweden or Switzerland) and thus were less likely to have experienced a post-war exuberance of victory. The timing of the decline across the various nations in our study also does not match a post-Second World War effect. Moreover, the pattern in the nations defeated in the war is illuminating. Political support increased in post-war Germany, Italy, and Japan as the new democratic system took root. Then, having 'caught up' with the other advanced industrial democracies, political support in these three nations also eroded over the past two decades. A victor/loser categorization based on the war does not help to explain the general decline in political support.

In short, as is the case in good police work, our first accomplishment is to narrow the circle of suspects. The 'proper-noun' explanations of decreasing political support are unlikely suspects for a general trend across most advanced industrial democracies—though these factors may reinforce the general erosion of political support.

Our analyses also discount a few general theories as inconsistent with the empirical evidence, such as the changing role of the media in the United States.

Which suspects, then, are left in the line-up? One major factor in decreasing political support is the change in citizen expectations of government (Chapters 4 and 5). Although virtually all social groups have become more cynical, in most nations these trends are disproportionately greater among the young, the better educated, the more affluent, and postmaterialists. These upper-status groups have not suffered from government actions; indeed, the prior literature generally claims that lower-income, less-educated citizens have suffered more from the slower economic growth of the late twentieth century and increasing economic competition forcing down their relative wage levels. We attribute this pattern of change to rising expectations of government among the upper social strata and the young. Moreover, the same individuals who are critical of how politicians and political institutions are functioning today also have high aspirations for the democratic process (Chapter 5). Their passion for the democratic creed leads to dissatisfaction with the current political process. Although a specific allocation of causality is difficult, our evidence suggests that 20–30 per cent of the decline in support for politicians, parties, and political institutions might be traced to these democratic aspirations.

A second general source of decreasing political support results from the proliferation of political interests in advanced industrial democracies, and the consequences of this process for democratic representation. Citizen expectations about the scope of government action inevitably increased as the role of government in society and the economy expanded during the late twentieth century. In addition, there was a dramatic expansion in the number of policy demands being made on the government; the political agenda became an amalgamation of traditional political concerns and new debates over environmental quality, social norms, lifestyle choices, multiculturalism, and other social and cultural issues.

Chapter 7 demonstrated how the increasing dimensionality and complexity of the policy space create the potential for more citizens to feel that government is not sufficiently addressing their concerns. In a fluid, multidimensional policy space it is very difficult for government to satisfy most of the people most of the time. Moreover, the growing importance of public interest groups in the process of interest articulation exacerbates these trends. Non-governmental organizations (NGOs), ranging from traditional economic interests to new public interest groups and new social movements, have assumed an expanding role as articulators of the public's issue interests, taking over some of the role that political parties once dominated. Chapter 7 demonstrated how the increasing diversity of these issue demands creates policy tensions that make it more difficult for government to satisfy these interests.

In addition, these non-governmental groups change the tenor of political discourse. The majority of party elites are active proponents of the government, since a majority participate in the governing coalition. After each election, a majority of elected elites are positive about the outcome (because they won), and even the losers normally follow an etiquette of the loyal opposition. In contrast, interest groups and NGOs are often unrelenting critics of government. Interest group representatives often highlight how governments and legislation fall short of the group's ideal, and thus spur voters to be dissatisfied with policy outcomes. A cross-national study of environmental groups demonstrated this pattern (Dalton 1994). The leader of a large British environmental NGO described his group's strategy as being an equal-opportunity critic: when Labour was in government it beat it up on one set of issues, when the Conservative Party held power it attacked it on different issues. Even when these interest groups do win a legislative victory, the public rhetoric is often tempered with statements of how other important policy matters were not resolved.

An insider account of these same dynamics comes from Bill Bradley (1999: xix), who notes that specific interest groups represent only a narrow aspect of our full role as citizens:

They [interest groups] seek to convince us *not* that some of our interests and opinions are in conflict, nor that some of our ideals require compromise, but simply that we are not getting what we want from government because government itself is corrupt, dishonest, out of control, controlled by corporate interests, controlled by those dependent on 'the welfare state,' dominated by liberals, or dominated by conservatives. They don't help us to think of ourselves as citizens who are part of a democratic dialogue, or to think of government as something of which we're a part and have the power to change. Most certainly they don't encourage us to think of ourselves as citizens who think of the general interest... In the end, our democracy is losing its most essential ingredient: the willingness of citizens to accept the results of the process itself, especially if they are not complete winners.

This is how complex governance works in advanced industrial democracies. It is a positive factor that citizens and public interest groups have greater access to, and voice within, the contemporary democratic process. But this access may have unintended consequences. The greater voice of critical interest groups in contemporary policy debates contributes to the decreased evaluations of the political process. A specific estimate of the causal impact is difficult to make, but from the evidence in Chapter 7 I would rank these effects as equal to the influence of changing citizen expectations.

There are also strong theoretical and political reasons to expect that government performance will influence feelings of political support. For example, during the 1990s Americans' trust in government undoubtedly benefited from the very positive performance of the economy, just as trust eroded in Japan as that nation's recession deepened during the 1990s (Chapter 6). As we noted, however, if policy performance were a major and consistent influence on political support, then the long-term decline in support would imply that nearly all governments are performing worse than they did a generation ago. While some political pundits make this claim (Madrick 1998), it is difficult to substantiate this claim empirically. There are certainly periods of economic decline, and growth, over the past several decades—but these do not clearly match the ebbs and flows of political support, as Nye, Zelikow, and King (1997) have observed. And not all economies are performing worse than they were a generation ago. Instead, the conditions of life along most policy dimensions have improved in most advanced industrial democracies over the past several decades (Bok 1998; Barnes and Gill 2000). If there is a systematic performance measure that can predict the decrease in political support across this broad array of OECD democracies, it has not been demonstrated in the literature. It may be that citizens expect even more policy outcomes from their governments, but this would again imply that expectations, rather than objective conditions, are the driving force behind the trends we have observed.

Recent American public opinion trends illustrate the limits of a performance explanation. While trust in politicians apparently did rise during the 1990s,[5] the gains were modest—even though the United States experienced the longest peacetime period of sustained economic growth in its modern history, and by the end of the period national affluence and well-being had improved substantially. Yet trust levels had returned only to the levels at the mid-term of the Reagan administration. Clinton may have objectively claimed that these were the best of times in his 2000 State of the Union address, but most Americans did not agree.

Given the normal policy performance range of contemporary advanced industrial democracies, the variations in performance probably have not been substantial enough to independently and consistently affect political support. The actual performance of governments apparently plays a more limited role in explaining these trends. Strong changes in performance can have short-term influence on political support—but these effects are perturbations around the long-term trend. The spurt in Americans' political support or the Japanese decrease in support during the 1990s might be linked to such short-term policy performance factors. But other forces are driving the long-term trend and moving political support downward.

Other analysts argue that government scandals, and an increasing tendency by the media to report scandalous behaviour, are producing cynicism about government. The recent declines in political support in Italy, France, and Britain have been linked to increasing public attention to personal scandals and abuses of power by political elites.[6] Even while acknowledging these effects, I would

[5] The increase in trust in government and in several other support measures is apparent in the American National Election Study and General Social Survey data trends, but this is not clearly seen in the *New York Times* polls and some other commercial time series. (see Figure 2.6)

[6] As a contrasting example, the Monica Lewinsky scandal did not seem to harm Clinton's popularity in the late 1990s. The dramatic events of impeachment, followed by resignations of members of Congress who were touched by their own sexual scandals, did not seriously erode confidence in the executive or the legislative branch, according to General Social Survey trends (see Chapter 2). In the midst of this spectacle, Rep. Bob Ingles voiced the quote at the beginning of this chapter on the floor of the US Congress out of frustration with Americans' support for Clinton and opposition to the impeachment efforts.

relegate them to a secondary role. The increased attention to elite behaviour, and the public and the media's willingness to report on these actions, may be more a symptom of the underlying changes in public sentiments rather than a cause. An example of this comes from Dennis Thompson's (1995) study of ethics in Congress. According to his study, the number of members of the US House of Representatives that faced ethics or corruption charges between 1976 and 1992 was *more than two times greater* than in the prior two centuries of the republic. Expectations of elite behaviour had shifted dramatically, and Congress passed new ethics codes and the 1978 Ethics in Government Act that enforced these new norms. Thus, what has changed most clearly over time is not the behaviour of politicians (though we hope that this behaviour has actually improved in object- ive terms), but the willingness *of the public* and the media to hold them account- able for their actions—whether personal or political.[7]

Let me stress that, in discounting performance and scandals as major cross- national sources of eroding political support, I am not claiming that the perform- ance of politicians and governments are without their faults. The evidence of the sexual affairs of President Clinton, and then by Members of Congress (Gingrich, Livingston, Hyde, Burton, and Chenoweth) during the Clinton impeachment, is a serious indictment of the American political elite's standards of conduct. These tales can be repeated all too often in Paris, London, and other capitals. Similarly, too often legislation and elite actions reflect the narrow self-interests and electoral interests of legislators rather than a sincere concern for the public interest. Congress' stuffing of the 2003 Homeland Security Act with pork-barrel projects is an especially glaring recent example.[8] This story too could easily be repeated

---

[7] An example of changing media norms comes from Marvin Kalb's (2001) comparison of the Lewinsky scandal to his experience in 1963 when he accidentally learned of John F. Kennedy's rendezvous with a young woman. Kennedy's tryst was the scoop of a journalist's lifetime, except that Kalb did not report it. Kalb then observes, 'As I write about this incident more than thirty-seven years later, I am amazed not by my decision to do nothing but by the fact, quite undeniable, that never for one moment did I even consider pursuing and reporting what I had seen.' He then draws out the obvious contrasts with the reporting of Clinton's affair, and a similar parallel might be made in many other contemporary democracies. Kalb attributes this to changing journalistic norms in the US, but the parallel decline of trust across the advanced industrial democracies suggests that the media are reflecting changes in society.

[8] For example, ABCNEWS.COM reports that the Homeland Security Act included an array of provisions that would make any reasonable citizen decry the exploitation of this issue for ulterior motives. For instance, the act provided $90,000 to create a bilingual audio tour for the cowgirl museum in Fort Worth; there were over 800 such community development grants. The act earmarked $3.1 billion to help farmers and ranchers, including those hurt by drought and floods; $1.5 billion to help states revamp their election systems; and $54 billion over ten years to increase Medicare payments to doctors and hospitals. Other projects included $50,000 more for research on shiitake mushrooms at the South Central Family Farm Research Center in Booneville, Arkansas; $45,000 for a Korean War memorial in Athens, Alabama; and $400,000 to help the Nevada Wildlife Division return displaced wildlife to its natural habitats. One obscure provision helped a Georgia chicken producer that wanted to label its products 'organic' even though it did not meet required government criteria, and another provision provided

in other contemporary democracies. The performance of politicians and political institutions falls short of what citizens have a right to expect, and it is a positive statement about contemporary democracies that their citizens expect more. I believe, however, that the performance of politicians and institutions has improved over time—despite their continuing shortfalls. Thus, the gap between expectations and performance has widened because expectations have risen faster than performance.

Certainly, other factors have contributed to the erosion of political support, since the above explanations do not account for all of the trends. Specific proper-noun explanations can add to the decline in political support; American doubts about politicians certainly deepened after the Watergate episode, as did Italian sentiments as a result of the bribery scandals of the 1990s. In other cases, specific performance factors or government behaviours may play a larger role in shaping public images of government. But what is most significant is the commonality of these trends and their linkage to common forces that are transforming politics in advanced industrial democracies. Thus, when the politicians touched by scandal left office or the economy improved, public doubts remained. By recognizing the commonality of these processes, we can better understand their potential implications for contemporary democracies.

DEMOCRATIC CHOICES

Since citizens are more sceptical about their governments, this leads us to ask about the implications for the democratic process. Because early analyses of democratic political culture often stressed the value of a supportive public (for example, Almond and Verba 1963), the initial reaction to decreasing political support is to consider this as a source of concern. The best illustration, perhaps, is *The Crisis of Democracy* (Crozier, Huntington, and Watanuki 1975), which forecast a dire future for the Trilateral democracies as citizens became more sceptical about their governments.

It is now clear that such concerns were overdrawn. An increasingly sceptical public has not posed a major challenge to the stability and vitality of democracy in the OECD nations. In part, this is because the potential systemic implications of decreasing support are moderated by the strong commitment to democratic values and the political community among contemporary publics. As Klingemann (1999) and others note, the contemporary situation is a pattern of 'dissatisfied democrats' or 'critical citizens' who want to improve the democratic process,

$15 million to ten Texas dairy farmers who stood to lose money because their herds were ill. Each of these provisions might or might not be a reasonable investment of government money, but their inclusion in the Homeland Security Act led to a round of media and public criticism about how politicians used this legislation on national security needs to fulfil the demands of special interests.

rather than one of anti-system critics of democracy—on the extreme left or the extreme right—that typified dissatisfaction with the government during earlier periods in the twentieth century. At some point, a further erosion of political support might generalize into system evaluations, and we need to be concerned about such a development, but this is not part of present trends.

Instead of posing a challenge to democratic ideals, changing levels of political support are affecting the style of democratic politics. Citizens will act differently if they are sceptical about their government, reporters will act differently, and politicians' behaviour will change if they confront a more sceptical public. Some will see these changes as a boon to contemporary democracies, others will see them as a curse. The reality, we believe, lies somewhere in between. And the response of citizens, politicians, and institutions to these trends represents choices that will structure the democratic process in the future.

The Public and Political Change

Declining political support first affects the behaviour of individual citizens because this is the source of these trends. In Chapter 8 we noted that various forms of political compliance become less common if citizens are sceptical about their government. Because of decreasing levels of support, people are more hesitant to follow the edicts of government, less likely to pay taxes, and more likely to abuse government programmes. At the same time, allegiant behaviours also become less common: willingness to contribute to political campaigns, willingness to serve on a jury, and public displays of national pride. Such behaviour strains the social contract that underlies the democratic process because the voluntary compliance of the citizenry is essential to democratic governance.

In addition, a more sceptical public interacts differently with the government. Scepticism about politicians and political parties generally tends to discourage participation in conventional forms of electoral politics (see Chapter 8). If one thinks that parties are unresponsive to public demands, why should one try to influence parties or engage in partisan politics? Thus, it is not surprising that the erosion of political support is paralleled by a decrease in election turnout in most OECD nations. At the same time, these critical citizens are more likely to engage in elite-challenging forms of political action: signing petitions, attending demonstrations, and engaging in other protest activities. While partisan activities might be downplayed, there is a greater willingness to work with NGOs and public interest groups.

If one is committed to the traditional image of a democratic citizenry that has been presented in the political culture literature (Almond and Verba 1963; Berelson, Lazarsfeld, and McPhee 1954; Campbell et al. 1960; Verba and Pye 1965), then these changes in citizen orientations and behaviour are a cause for concern. Instead of a supportive public engaged in institutionalized forms of political action, we now see more citizens rejecting the policies of government and challenging elites through unconventional political behaviour. But I am not willing to consider this an inevitable problem for democracy. Rather, these trends represent democratic choices, and the extent of these developments and the response of elites can define the implications of these trends. Trust in government can have both positive and negative implications for the democratic process (Kaase 1988).

One might argue that the docile and overly supportive American public portrayed in the *Civic Culture* lacked the assertiveness to demand its full democratic rights, and people were too tolerant of the abuses of power that existed within the democratic process—ranging from the outright corruption of some officials to simple lack of democratic responsiveness by others. Paul Sniderman (1981), for example, suggested that high levels of political support may encourage unquestioning endorsement of leaders, restrictions on civil liberties, and other authoritarian sentiments. Many New Left critics of contemporary representative democracy, such as the German Greens or Ralph Nader, have voiced similar concerns. On the other side of the political spectrum, some libertarians also welcome the public's growing scepticism towards government, arguing that it provides a break against the ever-expansionist tendencies of government and the abuse of power by political elites. If citizens become more hesitant to pay taxes, and more sceptical about legislation, this is a positive development from a libertarian perspective (Greenhut 2001).

Indeed, there is an element of truth to both of these observations, even if they come from divergent ideological perspectives. Another illustration comes from the 2000–2 World Values Survey. This wave of the study includes a set of nations that rank near the bottom on many measures of political and civil liberties; but the citizens in several of these nations express widespread support for their governments. For instance, when the Vietnamese and the Chinese (with limited political rights and low income levels) say that they are more satisfied with their governments than Swedes and Norwegians do, one might ask whether political satisfaction is something to be embraced. Similarly, in the first wave of the World Values Survey, Koreans registered one of the highest levels of confidence in political institutions, even though the government was run by a military regime. As Korea has become more democratic, support for the government has actually decreased (Shin 2001). In other words, criticism of government and scepticism about politics is a natural part of democratic politics—too little criticism and scepticism is not necessarily a healthy sign for democracy.

At the same time, numerous historical precedents indicate that too much cynicism and scepticism can threaten the democratic process, whether in Western Europe in the inter-war period or in the democratizing nations of central and eastern Europe today. Often these are cases in which limited government support is coupled with a lack of commitment to democratic norms. At some point, the lack of political support can harm the workings of a democratic system. If citizens question every act of government, avoid paying taxes, and doubt the wisdom of every government policy, the democratic consensus can be threatened.

These patterns suggest that there is a range of political orientations within which democratic politics can function reasonably effectively. Too much allegiance to the regime may be just as negative a sign of the health of the political system as too little (see also Sniderman 1981; Almond and Verba 1963). Moreover, the position of a nation within this range may affect the style of democratic politics. The higher end of this range may be more congruent with a system of representative democracy, in which elites exercise a large role and deference to elite action is the norm. This is the model of democracy described in *The Civic Culture* and the ideal model implied for Germany and Italy in that study. It is difficult, for instance, for a system of strong party government to function smoothly in a nation where citizens are sceptical about parties and elected representatives. Consequently, the erosion of such party support in many contemporary Western democracies—including in the successful democratic models identified in the civic culture literature—has produced strains for party-based politics in these nations (Dalton and Wattenberg 2000).

When more citizens become sceptical about politicians and the established institutions of representative democracy, this should encourage a different style of democratic politics. A more sceptical public is more likely to endorse direct action than political deference; specific policy demands are likely to become more prominent; and new forms of citizen involvement may be encouraged to give the public a more direct role in politics. Because these are dissatisfied democrats, the predominant response is not a withdrawal from democratic politics but a search for new democratic choices. This is what is at issue today: what is this alternative model?

Elites and Institutional Change

Another clear indicator of changing public sentiments towards politics is the broad recognition of these trends by political elites. A series of American presidents since the 1970s have addressed the issue of the public's decreasing faith in government and how it might be corrected. Legislative leaders frequently decry the decline in deference and political support among the citizenry (see, for example, Ornstein 1997). US Supreme Court Justice Stephen Breyer recently echoed these concerns: 'I worry about indifference and cynicism because indifference means nonparticipation and cynicism means a withdrawal of trust . . . without trust and participation, the Constitution cannot work' (Associated Press 1999).

Politicians across the advanced industrial democracies express similar sentiments (see also Chapter 1). A report prepared for an international labour party conference in London highlights the problems facing political parties as voters because less engaged and more sceptical (Bentley, Jupp, and Jones 2000). A recent OECD memorandum (2001*a*) summarizes contemporary democratic governments' concerns about the decrease in political support: 'Other things being equal, citizens trusting government and public institutions can be expected to find regulatory initiatives and redistributive policies more righteous than citizens who do not. Trust, and the accompanying legitimacy, can thus be expected to reduce costs and enhance effectiveness of implementation. The level of trust will therefore influence the steering capacity of political systems.'

If politicians recognize that citizens are now more sceptical about the political process and this is having real consequences for governing, the question then becomes: how will these elites and political institutions respond? One response has been to look for institutional reforms that might restore the public's trust in government. A litany of such reforms has been suggested in the United States, and many have already been enacted (for example, Hibbing and Theiss-Morse 1995; Cooper 1999*a*; Craig 1993). When elites in other nations confront evidence of decreased political support, there are similar calls for institutional reform: a new electoral system in Italy, Japan, and New Zealand; new regulations on parliamentary ethics in Britain.

Another common reformist theme is the decentralization of government, moving it closer to the people through the devolution of power or the creation of new regional or local governments. A recent Assembly of European Regions (1998: 3) report notes: 'During the last few years, Europe has witnessed an important phenomenon: the development of regionalization and regionalism as the driving force of strengthening democracy in Europe.' This is certainly a recurring theme in contemporary American politics. Furthermore, public opinion surveys generally indicate that citizens trust local governments more than their national government.[9]

To summarize, a new populist chorus has taken up the Jeffersonian refrain: the cure for democracy is more democracy. One of the most articulate voices for this position is David Held's description (1999: 295) of the linkage between cynicism and calls for institutional reform:

Skepticism and cynicism about politics are not inevitable facts of life. By establishing the credibility and viability of alternative models of 'governing institutions' and showing how they can be connected to systematic difficulties that occur and recur in the social and political world, a chance is created that mistrust of politics can be overcome. A political imagination for alternative arrangements is essential if the tarnished image of politics is to be eradicated.

Thus, one of the consequences of decreasing political support is a search for new democratic models or reforms that will move the democratic process closer towards its theoretical ideal. Indeed, one might argue that such periods of dissatisfaction and political reform have been central to the expansion of democracy over the past two centuries (for example, Held 1999; Huntington 1981; Schlesinger 1999). Most of

---

[9] For instance, the 1980 American National Election Study found that only 9% gave the federal government a good performance rating, 22% rated their state government as good, and 28% gave a good performance rating to their local government. This pattern generally appears in opinion polls in other nations. I would, however, doubt that devolving political power would improve citizen evaluations of government overall, but this hypothesis is difficult to test.

the recent democratic reforms across the OECD nations—documented in a related study by Cain, Dalton, and Scarrow (2003)—have increased citizen access to government, improved government accountability, and advanced the democratic process. These are desirable ends, in and of themselves.

Despite the positive consequences that democratic institutional reform may produce, it is unclear whether such reforms really will reverse the public's doubts about the political process. My caution arises from several factors. Where major reforms have been enacted—such as the electoral reforms in Japan and New Zealand or the long series of incremental reforms in the United States—this has not reversed the trend of decreasing political support (see Chapter 8). Indeed, it appears that some citizens may experience deeper alienation when they realize that major institutional changes do not alter the conditions that initially prompted their scepticism. And more modest reforms, such as campaign finance reform or even term limits, are unlikely to fundamentally alter the style of politics that alienates some citizens in the first place. These reforms may be desirable, but they are not a solution to the decrease in political support.

In addition, the correlates of trust suggest that current patterns of democratic institutional reform may not be sufficient to address the public's political doubts because there is a basic paradox in public orientations towards government. The public's democratic expectations place a priority on reforms that move beyond traditional forms of representative democracy. Stronger political parties, fairer elections, more representative electoral systems will improve the democratic process, but these reforms do not address expectations that the democratic process will expand to provide new opportunities for citizen input and control.

Instead, citizen expectations for the expansion of the democratic process more likely favour reforms that increase the public's direct involvement in the political process.[10] The spread of referendums and initiatives is the most obvious example (Scarrow 2003; Gallagher and Uleri 1996). Other democratizing reforms, such as Freedom of Information laws or other open-government provisions, provide another way of giving citizens more direct access to politics and making policy-making more transparent (Cain, Egan, and Fabbrini 2003). Thus, there is clear evidence of the expansion of citizen access and new forms of direct democracy in the OECD nations (Cain, Dalton, and Scarrow 2003).

Similarly, more people are signing petitions, joining citizen interest groups, and engaging in unconventional forms of political action (Dalton 2002: ch. 4). There are also regular calls for a greater citizen role in government advisory and administrative bodies, especially at the local level where direct involvement is possible (Hager 1995; Ingram and Smith 1993). After a century in which the

---

[10] There is some contrasting evidence on this point, including research that I have published (Dalton, Bürklin, and Drummond 2001). However, in general terms the values of postmaterialists and the better educated should promote an expansion of the democratic process to involve new forms of direct democracy (see, for example, Inglehart 1990; 1997*a*).

system of representative democracy epitomized democracy, there are new calls for a democracy that will 'let the people decide'.[11]

The paradox arises because many of the reforms that move democratic politics towards greater citizen input and influence may reinforce the fragmentation of political interests that contributes to the erosion of political support. More public interest groups pressing for their specific policy concerns in referendums, petition drives, administrative hearings, and court cases will only exacerbate the tensions of complex governance that we described earlier in this chapter. In other words, contemporary democracies do not suffer from a surfeit of interest articulation, but from a lack of institutions and processes that can aggregate and balance divergent interests into a coherent policy programmes that the participants can accept. Most research on direct democracy suggests that the expansion of these reforms will accentuate this imbalance. Thus, the worries about faction expressed by Madison and the Framers of the US Constitution may be even more relevant in a participatory democracy (Lee 1997).

It is not the goal of this research to analyse the institutional forms that democratic reform may take, although we pursue this topic in a separate research project (Cain, Dalton and Scarrow, 2003). Instead, let me just say that citizens' changing orientations towards government is stimulating a search for different democratic processes that move away from the traditional models of representative democracy. This might be seen as an attempt to flesh out the suggestions of democratic theorists who have offered general models of 'strong democracy' or 'deliberative democracy' as alternatives (Barber 1984; Habermas 1992*a*; 1992*b*; Dahl 1989; 2002).

I suspect that even these more fundamental reforms of the democratic process will not restore the supportive, allegiant publics that once were identified as the basis of a stable democracy. Instead, we will find other ways to accommodate dissatisfied democrats within the political process, maintaining the benefits of increased interest articulation with new methods of interest aggregation and governance. Change can move democracy closer towards its theoretical ideal, even it we can not return to the earlier period of a civic culture of supportive publics. Thus the pattern of dissatisfied democrats may endure, albeit at a lower level or with less cynical views of the underlying motivations and behaviours of government.

Another possible resolution of these tensions is the development of new bases of ideological thinking that can reintroduce simpler structures into current political debate (Uslaner 1993). Joseph Cooper (1999*b*: 148), for example, observes that, in the absence of a comprehensive and powerful public philosophy regarding the proper relationship of government and society—such as the New Deal

---

[11] Chapter 8 discussed the claim by Hibbing and Theiss-Morse (2002) that citizens are asking for less democracy. Even their survey evidence argues against this claim, and it is clear that political elites and government officials in most advanced industrial democracies feel that their citizens want more access to and transparency in government (OECD 2000*b*; 2001*b*; 2002).

paradigm in the United States or debates on social democracy in Europe—it becomes difficult to rationalize the relationship between policy proposals in ways that provide general criteria and consistent benchmarks for organizing opinion. In other words, without the simple structure of a dominant ideological cleavage, political interests fragment and developing consensus becomes more difficult. If the diverse political interests now competing in contemporary democracies could be integrated into a limited set of alternative ideological positions, then it might be possible to aggregate political interests more effectively into governing programmes.

Again, the difficulty is that, although theorists have suggested ideological frameworks to capture the essence of politics in advanced industrial democracies, none of them seems to resonate as a new basis of political thought. Even if a single dimension of political cleavage might offer to restore levels of political support—if government responds to majority positions—there are also reasons to believe that the spirit of the times is antithetical to such overarching ideological frameworks. Contemporary politics has become competition over specific gains, not ideological principles. In addition, sophisticated, issue-oriented voters may not accept the simplification of political choice to a one-dimensional political space. And, following the end of the cold war, the clarity of alternative ideological options has probably diminished further.

Another option is suggested by the two nations in which the trends in political support are not uniformly down: the Netherlands and Denmark.[12] In these nations, political competition tends to be diffuse because of the multiparty competition across the political spectrum. While coalition governments are common in Western democracies, the Dutch and Danish cases are often typified by the lack of a central governing or opposition party to structure political choice. Thus, citizens (and political elites) may be forced towards a style of political accommodation rather than political competition. Supporting this point, Van Praag and van der Eijk (1998) suggest that the extensive pluralism of the Dutch means that politicians and citizens realize that politics is the art of compromise: your opponent on one issue may be your ally on another. They argue that this tempers political expectations and political discourse in ways that might moderate negative evaluations of government. If they are correct, this may be a provocative suggestion of how democracies may adapt to fragmenting political interests, and this possibility deserves further research.

It is also possible that political elites and governments may make very different choices in responding to these challenges. If political reforms do not restore public confidence, elites may accept dissatisfaction as inevitable and exploit the negative

---

[12] We should also point out that the lack of a clear trend in these two cases may result from survey series beginning after an earlier large drop in political support. In the Dutch case in particular, the de-pillarization of the system in the late 1960s predated the advent of our survey trends.

potential of dissatisfaction for short-term political gain. Political strategists may become less likely to view elections as policy contests, and more likely to see them as contests to manipulate images and exploit negative advertisements in order to win election (McCubbins 1992). Politicians start to run against the institutions, as is now common in American elections. It seems that almost all recent American presidents have run as outsiders, even George W. Bush, who is the son of a former president and grandson of a US senator. When this happens, it reinforces the negativity of the public, because politicians themselves confirm the public's worst suspicions about government and encourage them to vote for a candidate who is different from all those other politicians. Fried and Harris (2001) go further, discussing how some governmental and non-governmental elites may reinforce public doubts about politics to use these sentiments in pursuit of other political goals. For instance, in 1994 US Congressman Newt Gingrich used public scepticism about government to promote a conservative agenda to roll back the scale of US government. These patterns are perhaps more developed in the United States because of the candidate-centred nature of American elections, but similar tendencies are apparent in other Western democracies (Dalton and Wattenberg 2000).

Then, once elected, these politicians will continue with their style of action. Politics becomes a competition between spin doctors, not policy-makers. For example, Stuart Stevens was a media advisor to the 2000 Bush campaign, and his account of the campaign is a postmodern essay in constructing reality. 'You can spin anything if you did it with enough confidence', says Stevens (2001). When Bush spokesperson Ari Fleischer wondered what his morning-show spin should be after the 2000 election night deadlock, Stevens said: 'Predict victory. We might as well, it doesn't matter.' Is this the style of postmodern politics?

Politicians' facile behaviour at elections carries with it a new style of governing. Some politicians choose to limit their policy initiatives to what is popular, and rely on spin doctors to protect them from any negative consequences of their actions. Furthermore, by focusing on specific interests and immediate gains, collective decision-making can be moved away from programmes that will actually maximize the collective public good. As Joseph Cooper (1999*b*) observes:

It is a politics that seeks legislation that looks good and appears to respond to intense public needs but avoids facing or resolving more demanding problems if there is political risk in addressing them or political advantage in stalemating them. It is a feel-good politics that rivets attention on second-tier issues identified in polls, laced by a politics of avoidance and blame on major issues ... It is a politics in which the electorate's deep discontent and distrust lead it to vote for change uncorrupted by politics, but in which the electorate must be inevitably frustrated by the impact of the processes of democracy on the people it elects.

Similarly, the reliance on polls can enrich the democratic process, but it can also become the siren's song that blinds politicians' vision. Thus, politicians may choose to limit their policy initiatives to what is popular at the moment, and rely on spin doctors to protect them from any negative consequences of their actions. In short, if political elites make the choice to play to democracy's potential weaknesses brought on by the public's distrust in government, democracy will suffer.

DEMOCRATIC FUTURES

For American politicians and political analysts, there is an ironic twist to the findings in this study: we are not alone. The erosion of political support is not unique to the United States; it is affecting almost all advanced industrial democracies. On the one hand, some may take solace in this conclusion: declining trust in government in the United States is not a consequence of the unique failings of American political institutions or American politicians. As we noted at the outset of this study, this means that responses to the decline in support that focus on the unique events and processes of American politics are missing the larger reality of citizens' changing orientations towards the state. On the other hand, the commonality of these trends suggests that no one has found a way to restore public confidence in politicians, parties, and political institutions. There is no clear model in which politicians have 'done the right thing' and strengthened political support within their nation—which implies that low levels of support may be a continuing feature of advanced industrial democracies.

It is also ironic that these patterns have become more apparent as Western democracies have celebrated the end of the cold war and the spread of democracy around the globe. As millions of new democratic citizens in central and eastern Europe celebrate their new freedoms and liberties, citizens in the West are expressing widening concerns about their politicians, parties, and democratic institutions.

As we suggested throughout this study, the challenges democracies now face also represent choices on how these citizens, political elites, and their systems will respond. The strength of democracy should be its power to adapt and grow. Thus we hope the current challenges to democracy lead to choices that will strengthen and further develop the democratic process in our nations.

References

Aberbach, Joel (1969). 'Alienation and Political Behavior'. *American Political Science Review*, 62: 86–99.

——and Walker, Jack (1970). 'Political Trust and Racial Ideology'. *American Political Science Review*, 64: 1199–219.

Abramson, Paul (1983). *Political Attitudes in America*. San Francisco: W. H. Freeman.

——and Inglehart, Ronald (1995). *Value Change in Global Perspective*. Ann Arbor: University of Michigan Press.

——, Aldrich, John, and Rohde, David (1999). *Change and Continuity in the 1996 and 1998 Elections*. Washington, DC: Congressional Quarterly Press.

Alford, John (2001). 'We're All in This Together: The Decline of Trust in Government', in John Hibbing and Elizabeth Theiss-Morse (eds.), *What is it About Government that Americans Dislike?* New York: Cambridge University Press.

Almond, Gabriel and Verba, Sidney (1963). *The Civic Culture*. Princeton: Princeton University Press.

Alesina, Alberto and Wacziarg, Romain (2000). 'The Economics of Civic Trust', in Susan Pharr and Robert Putnam (eds.), *Disaffected Democracies*. Princeton: Princeton University Press.

Anderson, Christopher (1995). *Blaming the Government: Citizens and the Economy in Five European Democracies*. Armonk, NY: M. E. Sharpe.

——(2002). *Good Questions, Dubious Inferences, and Bad Solutions: Some Further Thoughts on Satisfaction With Democracy* (Research Paper 116). Binghamton: Center for Democratic Performance, State University of New York.

——and Guillory, Christine (1997). 'Political Institutions and Satisfaction With Democracy'. *American Political Science Review*, 91: 66–81.

——and LoTempio, Andrew (2002). 'Winning, Losing and Political Trust in America'. *British Journal of Political Science*, 32: 335–51.

Andeweg, Rudy (1992). 'Dutch Voters Adrift' (Ph.D. thesis). Leiden: University of Leiden.

Ansell, Christopher and Gingrich, Jane (2003). 'Reforming the Administrative State', in Bruce Cain, Russell Dalton, and Susan Scarrow (eds.), *Democracy Transformed?* Oxford: Oxford University Press.

Arrow, Kenneth (1951). *Social Choice and Individual Values*. New York: Wiley.

——(1972). 'Gifts and Exchanges'. *Philosophy and Public Affairs*, 1: 343–62.

Asp, Kent (1991). 'Medierna bäddar för politikerförakt'. *Dagens Nyheter*, 23 September.

Assembly of European Regions (1998). *Declaration on Regionalism in Europe*. Strasbourg: Assembly of European Regions.

Associated Press (1999). 4 May.

Baker, Kendall, Dalton, Russell, and Hildebrandt, Kai (1981). *Germany Transformed: Political Culture and the New Politics*. Cambridge, MA: Harvard University Press.

Barber, Benjamin (1984). *Strong Democracy*. Berkeley: University of California Press.

Bardi, Luciano (1996). 'Anti-party Sentiment and Party System Change in Italy'. *European Journal for Political Research*, 29: 345–63.

Barnes, Cheryl and Gill, Derek (2000). *Declining Government Performance? Why Citizens Don't Trust Government* (Working Paper No. 9). Auckland, NZ: State Services Commission.

Barnes, Samuel, Kaase, Max et al. (1979). *Political Action*. Beverly Hills, CA: Sage.

Bean, Clive (1999). 'Party Politics and Trust in Government'. Paper delivered at a conference of the Australasian Political Studies Association Conference, University of Sydney.

Beer, Samuel (1982). *Britain Against Itself: The Political Contradictions of Capitalism*. London: Faber and Faber.

Bennett, Stephen (2001). 'Were the Halcyon Days Really Golden? An Analysis of Americans' Attitudes About the Political System, 1945–65', in John Hibbing and Elizabeth Theiss-Morse (eds.), *What is it About Government that Americans Dislike?* New York: Cambridge University Press.

Bennett, William and Nunn, Sam (1997). *A Nation of Spectators*. Washington, DC: National Commission on Civic Renewal.

Bentley, Tom, Jupp, Ben and Stedman Jones, Daniel (2000). *Getting to Grips with Depoliticization* (Demos briefing paper). London: Demos, Panton House.

Berelson, Bernard, Lazarsfeld, Paul, and McPhee, William (1954). *Voting*. Chicago: University of Chicago Press.

Berry, Jeffrey (1989). *The Interest Group Society*. Glenview, IL: Scott-Foresman.

——(1999). *The New Liberalism: The Rising Power of Citizen Groups*. Washington, DC: Brookings Institution.

——, Portney, Kent, and Thomson, Ken (1993). *The Rebirth of Urban Democracy*. Washington, DC: Brookings Institution.

Betz, Hans-Georg (1994). *Radical Right-wing Populism in Europe*. New York: St Martins Press.

Blais, Andre (2000). *To Vote or Not to Vote? The Merits and Limits of Rational Choice Theory*. Pittsburgh, PA: University of Pittsburgh Press.

Blendon, Robert, et al. (1997). 'Changing Attitudes in America', in Joseph Nye, Philip Zelikow, and David King (eds.), *Why Americans Mistrust Government*. Cambridge, MA: Harvard University Press.

Bobbio, Norberto (1987). *The Future of Democracy* (trans. Roger Griffen). Minneapolis, MN: University of Minnesota Press.

Bok, Derek (1997). 'Measuring the Performance of Government', in Joseph Nye, Philip Zelikow, and David King (eds.), *Why People Don't Trust Government*. Cambridge, MA: Harvard University Press.

——(1998). *The State of the Nation*. Cambridge, MA: Harvard University Press.

——(2001). *The Trouble with Government*. Cambridge, MA: Harvard University Press.

Borg, Sami and Sänkiaho, Risto (1995). *The Finnish Voter*. Helsinki: Finnish Political Science Association.

Borre, Ole (2000). 'Critical Issues and Political Alienation in Denmark'. *Scandinavian Political Studies*, 23: 285–309.

——and Andersen, Jørgen Goul (1997). *Voting and Political Attitudes in Denmark*. Aarhus: Aarhus University Press.

Bouckaert, Geert and van de Walle, Steven (2001). 'Government Performance and Trust in Government'. Paper delivered at the conference of the Permanent Study Group on Productivity and Quality in the Public Sector, Vaasa, Finland.

Bradley, Bill (1997). 'Senator Bill Bradley', in Norman Ornstein (ed.), *Lessons and Legacies: Farewell Addresses from the Senate*. Reading, MA: Addison-Wesley.

—— (1999). 'Foreword: Trust and Democracy', in Joseph Cooper (ed.), *Congress and the Decline of Public Trust*. Boulder, CO: Westview.

Braithwaite, Valerie and Levi, Margaret (eds.) (1998). *Trust and Governance*. New York: Russell Sage.

Bromley, Catherine, Curtice, John, and Seyd, Ben (2002). 'Confidence in Government', in Roger Jowell et al., *British Social Attitude Survey*. Brookfield, VT: Dartmouth.

Budge, Ian (1996). *The New Challenge of Direct Democracy*. Oxford: Polity Press.

——, Robertson, David, and Hearl, Derek (1987). *Ideology, Strategy, and Party Change: Spatial Analyses of post-war Election Programmes in 19 Democracies*. New York: Cambridge University Press.

Bürklin, Wilhelm et al. (1997). *Eliten in Deutschland*. Opladen: Leske and Budrich.

Butler, David and Ranney, Austin (eds.) (1994). *Referendums around the World: The Growing Use of Democracy?* Washington, DC: American Enterprise Institute.

Cain, Bruce, Dalton, Russell, and Scarrow, Susan (eds.) (2003). *Democracy Transformed? The Expansion of Political Access in Advanced Industrial Democracies*. Oxford: Oxford University Press.

Cain, Bruce, Egan, Patrick, and Fabbrini, Sergio (2003). 'Toward More Open Democracies: The Expansion of Freedom Of Information Laws', in Bruce Cain, Russell Dalton, and Susan Scarrow (eds.), *Democracy Transformed? The Expansion of Political Access in Advanced Industrial Democracies*. Oxford: Oxford University Press.

Campbell, Angus, Converse, Philip, Miller, Warren, and Stokes, Donald (1960). *The American Voter*. New York: Wiley.

Canache, Damarys, Mondak, Jeffery, and Seligson, Mitchell (2001). 'Meaning and Measurement in Cross-National Research on Satisfaction With Democracy'. *Public Opinion Quarterly*, 65: 506–28.

Cappella, Joseph and Hall Jamieson, Kathleen (1997). *Spiral of Cynicism: The Press and the Public Good*. New York: Oxford University Press.

Caul, Miki and Gray, Mark (2000). 'From Platform Declarations to Policy Outcomes', in Russell Dalton and Martin Wattenberg (eds.), *Parties without Partisans: Political Change in Advanced Industrial Democracies*. Oxford: Oxford University Press.

Chanley, Virginia, Rudolph, Thomas, and Rahn, Wendy (2000). 'The Origins and Consequences of Public Trust in Government'. *Public Opinion Quarterly*, 64: 239–56.

Citrin, Jack (1974). 'Comment'. *American Political Science Review*, 68: 973–88.

—— and Green, Donald (1986). 'Presidential Leadership and The Resurgence of Trust in Government'. *British Journal of Political Science*, 16: 431–53.

Clarke, Harold (1992). *Citizens and Community: Political Support in a Representative Democracy*. Cambridge: Cambridge University Press.

——, Dutt, Nitish, and Kornberg, Allan (1993). 'The Political Economy of Attitudes Toward Polity and Society in Western European Democracies'. *Journal of Politics*, 55: 998–1021.

——, Kornberg, Allan and Wearing, Peter (2000). *A Polity on the Edge: Canada and the Politics of Fragmentation*. Peterborough, Ont: Broadview Press.

Cohn, Jonathan (1992). 'A Lost Political Generation?' *The American Prospect*, 9: 30–8.

Commission of the European Communities (various years). *European Economy*, Supplement B: Business and consumer survey results. Luxembourg: Office for Official Publications of the European Communities.

Conradt, David (1980). 'Germany', in Gabriel Almond and Sidney Verba (eds.), *The Civic Culture Revisited*. Boston: Little Brown.

Converse, Phillip (1976). *The Dynamics of Party Support*. Beverly Hills, CA: Sage.

Cooper, Joseph (ed.) (1999*a*). *Congress and the Decline of Public Trust*. Boulder, CO: Westview.

——(1999*b*). 'Performance and Expectations in American Politics', in Joseph Cooper (ed.), *Congress and the Decline of Public Trust*. Boulder, CO: Westview.

Council for Excellence in Government (1999). *America Unplugged: Citizens and their Government*. www.excelgov.org/publication/poll1999/index.htm

——(2001). *The Unanswered Call to Public Service: Americans' Attitudes Before and After September 11th*. www.excelgov.org/index

Craig, Stephen (1993). *The Malevolent Leaders: Popular Discontent in America*. Boulder, CO: Westview Press.

——(1996). *Broken Contracts: Changing Relationships between Americans and their Government*. Boulder, CO: Westview Press.

——and Wald, Kenneth (1985). 'Whose Ox to Gore? A Comment on the Relationship Between Political Discontent and Political Violence'. *Western Political Quarterly*, 38: 652–62.

Crozier, Michel (1975). 'Western Europe', in Michel Crozier, Samuel Huntington, and Joji Watanuki, *The Crisis of Democracy*. New York: New York University Press.

——, Huntington, Samuel, and Watanuki, Joji (1975). *The Crisis of Democracy*. New York: New York University Press.

Curtice, John and Jowell, Roger (1995). 'The Skeptical Electorate', in Roger Jowell et al., *British Social Attitudes: The 12th Report*. Aldershot: Dartmouth.

————(1997). 'Trust in the Political System', in Roger Jowell et al., *British Social Attitudes: The 14th Report*. Brookfield, VT: Dartmouth.

Curtin, Richard (2002). *Psychology and Macroeconomics: Fifty Years of the Surveys of Consumers*. Ann Arbor: Institute for Social Research, University of Michigan.

Dahl, Robert (1971). *Polyarchy*. New Haven: Yale University Press.

——(1989). *Democracy and its Critics*. New Haven: Yale University Press.

——(1994). *The New American Political (Dis)Order*. Berkeley, CA: Institute of Governmental Studies Press.

——(2002). *How Democratic is the American Constitution?* New Haven: Yale University Press.

Dahlgren, Peter (1995). *Television and the Public Sphere*. London: Sage.

Dahrendorf, Ralf (1975). 'Excerpts from Remarks on the Ungovernability Study', in Michel Crozier, Samuel Huntington, and Joji Watanuki, *The Crisis of Democracy*. New York: New York University Press.

Dalton, Russell (1984*a*). 'Cognitive Mobilization and Partisan Dealignment in Advanced Industrial Democracies'. *Journal of Politics* 46: 264–84.

——(1984*b*). 'The German Party System Between Two Ages', in Russell Dalton, Scott Flanagan, and Paul Beck (eds.), *Electoral Change*. Princeton: Princeton University Press.

——(1993). 'Citizens, Protest and Democracy', special issue of *The Annals of Political and Social Sciences*, 528 (July).

——(1994). 'Communists and Democrats: Democratic Attitudes in the Two Germanies'. *British Journal of Political Science*, 24: 469–93.

—— (1996). *Citizen Politics: Public Opinion and Political Parties in Advanced Industrial Democracies* (2nd edn.). Chatham, NJ: Chatham House.

—— (1999). 'Political Support in Advanced Industrial Democracies', in Pippa Norris (ed.), *Critical Citizens*. Oxford: Oxford University Press.

—— (2000*a*). 'The Decline of Party Identifications', in Russell Dalton and Martin Wattenberg (eds.), *Parties without Partisans: Political Change in Advanced Industrial Democracies*. Oxford: Oxford University Press.

—— (2000*b*). 'Value Change and Democracy', in Susan Pharr and Robert Putnam (eds.), *Disaffected Democracies*. Princeton: Princeton University Press.

—— (2002). *Citizen Politics: Public Opinion and Political Parties in Advanced Industrial Democracies* (3rd edn.). New York: Chatham House.

—— (2004 forthcoming). *Social Change and the Erosion of Americans' Trust in Government*.

—— and Kuechler, Manfred (eds.) (1990). *Challenging the Political Order*. New York: Oxford University Press.

—— and Wattenberg, Martin (eds.) (2000). *Parties without Partisans: Political Change in Advanced Industrial Democracies*. Oxford: Oxford University Press.

——, Bürklin, Wilhelm, and Drummond, Andrew (2001). 'Public Attitudes Toward Representative and Direct Democracy'. *Journal of Democracy*, 12: 141–53.

——, Flanagan, Scott, and Beck, Paul (eds.) (1984). *Electoral Change: Realignment and Dealignment in Advanced Industrial Democracies*. Princeton: Princeton University Press.

Della Porta, Donatella (2000). 'Social Capital, Beliefs in Government, and Political Corruption', in Susan Pharr and Robert Putnam (eds.), *Disaffected Democracies*. Princeton: Princeton University Press.

Deth, Jan van (ed.) (1999). *Social Capital and European Democracy*. London: Routledge.

—— and Scarbrough, Elinor (1995). *The Impact of Values*. Oxford: Oxford University Press.

Diamond, Larry (1994). 'Toward Democratic Consolidation'. *Journal of Democracy*, 5: 4–17.

Dionne, E. (1991). *Why Americans Hate Politics*. New York: Simon & Schuster.

Downs, Anthony (1957). *An Economic Theory of Democracy*. New York: Wiley.

Durr, Robert, Gilmour, John, and Wolbrecht, Christina (1997). 'Explaining Congressional Approval'. *American Journal of Political Science*, 41: 175–207.

Easton, David (1965). *A Systems Analysis of Political Life*. New York: Wiley.

—— (1975). 'A Reassessment of the Concept of Political Support'. *British Journal of Political Science*, 5: 435–57.

—— (1976). 'Theoretical Approaches to Political Support'. *Canadian Journal of Political Science*, 9: 431–48.

—— and Dennis, Jack (1969). *Children in the Political System: Origins of Political Legitimacy*. New York: McGraw Hill.

Eckstein, Harry (1966). *Division and Cohesion in Democracy: A Study of Norway*. Princeton, NJ: Princeton University Press.

The Economist (2002). 'Politics is getting back to its normal pre-September 11th pattern. Sort of'. 8 June: 27–8.

Ehrhart, Christof and Sandschneider, Eberhard (1994). 'Politikverdrossenheit: Kritische Anmerkungen zur Empirie, Wahrnehmung und Interpretation abnehmender politischer Partizipation'. *Zeitschrift für Parlamentsfragen*, 25: 441–58.

Eijk, Cees van der and Franklin, Mark (2003). 'The Sleeping Giant: Potential for Political Mobilization and Disaffection in Europe', in Hermann Schmitt (ed.), *Voters, Parties, Elections and European Unification*. London: Frank Cass.

Erber, Ralph and Lau, Richard (1990). 'Political Cynicism Revisited: An Information-Processing Reconciliation of Policy-Based and Incumbency-Based Interpretations of Changes in Trust in Government'. *American Journal of Political Science*, 34: 236–53.

Erikson, Robert, Wright, Gerald, and McIver, John (1993). *Statehouse Democracy*. New York: Cambridge University Press.

Evans, Geoffrey, Heath, Anthony and Payne, Clive (1999). 'Class: Labour as a Catch-all Party?', in Geoffrey Evans and Pippa Norris (eds.), *Critical Elections: British Parties and Voters in Long-term Perspective*. London: Sage.

Fallows, James (1996). *Breaking the News: How the Media Undermine American Democracy*. New York: Pantheon.

Falter, Jürgen and Rattinger, Hans (1997). 'Die deutschen Parteien im Urteil der öffentlichen Meinung 1977–1994', in Oscar Gabriel, Oskar Niedermayer and Richard Stöss (eds.), *Parteiendemokratie in Deutschland*. Bonn: Bundeszentrale für politische Bildung.

Farah, Barbara, Barnes, Samuel and Heunks, Felix (1979). 'Political Dissatisfaction', in Samuel Barnes, Max Kaase et al., *Political Action*. Beverly Hills: Sage.

Farrell, David and Webb, Paul (2000). 'Political Parties as Campaign Organizations', in Russell Dalton and Martin Wattenberg (eds.), *Parties without Partisans: Political Change in Advanced Industrial Democracies*. Oxford: Oxford University Press.

Flanagan, Scott (1984). 'Electoral Change in Japan', in Russell Dalton, Scott Flanagan, and Paul Beck (eds.), *Electoral Change*. Princeton: Princeton University Press.

——(1987). Value Change in Industrial Society'. *American Political Science Review*, 81: 1303–19.

—— and Lee, Airie (1991). 'Modernization and the Emergence of the Authoritarian Libertarian Value Cleavage'. Paper presented at the annual meeting of the Southern Political Science Association, Tampa, Florida.

Franklin, Mark (2003). *Voter Turnout and the Dynamics of Electoral Competition*. New York: Cambridge University Press.

Fried, Amy and Harris, Douglas (2001). 'On Red Capes and Charging Bulls: How and Why Conservative Groups Promoted Public Anger', in John Hibbing and Elizabeth Theiss-Morse (eds.), *What is it about Government that Americans Dislike?* New York: Cambridge University Press.

Fuchs, Dieter (1989). *Die Unterstützung des polischen Systems der Bundesrepublik Deutschland*. Opladen: Westdeutscher Verlag.

——(1996). *Wohin geht der Wandel der demokratischen Institutionen in Deutschland?* Berlin: Wissenschaftszentrum.

——(1999). 'The Democratic Culture of Unified Germany', in Pippa Norris (ed.), *Critical Citizens*. Oxford: Oxford University Press.

—— and Klingemann, Hans-Dieter (1995). 'Citizens and the State: A Relationship Transformed', in Hans-Dieter Klingemann and Dieter Fuchs (eds.), *Citizens and the State*. Oxford: Oxford University Press.

——, Guidorossi, Giovanna, and Svensson, Palle (1995). 'Support for Democratic Systems', in Hans-Dieter Klingemann and Dieter Fuchs (eds.), *Citizens and the State*. Oxford: Oxford University Press.

Fukuyama, Francis (1992). *The End of History and the Last Man*. New York: Free Press.

——(1995). *Trust: The Social Virtues and the Creation of Prosperity*. New York: Free Press.

Gabel, Matthew and Huber, John (2000). 'Putting Parties in their Place: Inferring Left/Right Ideological Positions from Party Manifesto Data'. *American Journal of Political Science*, 41: 94–103.

Gabriel, Oscar (1995). 'Political Efficacy and Trust', in Jan van Deth and Elinor Scarbrough (eds.), *The Impact of Values*. Oxford: Oxford University Press.

Gallagher, Michael and Uleri, Pier Vincenzo (eds.) (1996). *The Referendum Experience in Europe*. Basingstoke: Macmillan.

Garment, Suzanne (1991). *Scandal: The Crisis of Mistrust in American Politics*. New York: Times Books.

Gibson, James (1992). 'The Political Consequences of Intolerance: Cultural Conformity and Political Freedom'. *American Political Science Review*, 86: 338–56.

Greenhut, Steven (2001). 'Trust in Government is on the Rise'. *Orange County Register*, 18 November.

Habermas, Jürgen (1975). *Legitimation Crisis*. Boston: Beacon.

——(1992a). *Faktizität und Geltung. Beiträge zur Diskurstheorie des Rechts und des demokratischen Rechtsstaates*. Frankfurt: Suhrkamp.

——(1992b). 'Drei normative Modelle der Demokratie: Zum Begriff deliberativer Politik', in Herfried Münkler (ed.), *Die Chancen der Freiheit. Grundprobleme der Demokratie*. Munich/Zürich: Piper.

Hager, Carol (1995). *Technological Democracy: Bureaucracy and Citizenry in the German Energy Debate*. Ann Arbor: University of Michigan Press.

Hall, Peter (1999). 'Social Capital in Britain'. *British Journal of Political Science*, 29: 417–61.

——(2002). 'Social Capital in Britain', in Robert Putnam (ed.), *Democracies in Flux*. Oxford: Oxford University Press.

Halman, Loek (2001). *The European Values Study: A Third Wave*. Tilburg: Tilburg University.

Haque, M. (1999). 'Relationship Between Citizenship and Public Administration: A Reconfiguration'. *International Review of Administrative Services*, 65: 309–25.

Hardarson, Olafur Th. (1995). *Parties and Voters in Iceland*. Reykjavik: Social Science Research Institute.

Hardin, Russell (1998). 'Trust in Government', in Valerie Braithwaite and Margaret Levi (eds.), *Trust and Governance*. New York: Russell Sage.

——(2002a). *Trust and Trustworthiness*. New York: Russell Sage.

——(2000b). 'The Public Trust', in Susan Pharr and Robert Putnam (eds.), *Disaffected Democracies*. Princeton: Princeton University Press.

Harmel, Robert, Janda, Kenneth, and Tan, Alexander (1995). 'Substance versus Packaging'. Paper presented at the annual meetings of the American Political Science Association, Chicago, IL.

Harris Poll (1994). *Harris Survey Yearbook of Public Opinion*. New York: Louis Harris and Associates.

Held, David (1999). *Models of Democracy* (2nd edn.). Stanford: Stanford University Press.

Hess, Robert and Torney, Judith (1967). *The Development of Political Attitudes in Children*. Chicago: Aldine.

Hetherington, Marc (1998). 'The Political Relevance of Political Trust'. *American Political Science Review*, 92: 791–808.

Hetherington, Marc (1999). 'The Effect of Political Trust on the Presidential Vote'. *American Political Science Review*, 93: 311–26.

—— and Globetti, Suzanne (2002). 'Political Trust and Racial Policy Preferences'. *American Journal of Political Science*, 46: 253–75.

—— and Nelson, Michael (2003). 'Anatomy of a Rally Effect: George W. Bush and the War on Terrorism'. *PS: Political Science*, 36: 37–42.

Hibbing, John and Theiss-Morse, Elizabeth (1995). *Congress as Public Enemy: Public Attitudes toward American Political Institutions*. New York: Cambridge University Press.

———— (eds.) (2001). *What is it about Government that Americans Dislike?* New York: Cambridge University Press.

———— (2002). *Stealth Democracy: Americans' Beliefs about How Government Should Work*. New York: Cambridge University Press.

Hinich, Melvin and Munger, Michael (1997). *Analytical Politics*. New York: Cambridge University Press.

Holmberg, Sören (1994). 'Party Identification Compared Across the Atlantic', in M. Kent Jennings and Thomas Mann (eds.), *Elections at Home and Abroad*. Ann Arbor: University of Michigan Press.

—— (1999). 'Down and Down We Go: Political Trust in Sweden', in Pippa Norris (ed.), *Critical Citizens*. Oxford: Oxford University Press.

Holtz-Bacha, C. (1990). 'Videomalaise Revisited: Media Exposure and Political Alienation in West Germany'. *European Journal of Communication*, 5: 78–85.

Huntington, Samuel (1974). 'Postindustrial Politics: How Benign Will it Be?' *Comparative Politics*, 6: 147–77.

—— (1975a). 'The United States', in Michel Crozier, Samuel Huntington, and Joji Watanuki, *The Crisis of Democracy*. New York: New York University Press.

—— (1975b). 'The Democratic Distemper'. *Public Interest*, 41: 9–38.

—— (1981). *American Politics*. Cambridge, MA: Harvard University Press.

—— (1984). 'Will More Countries Become Democratic?' *Political Science Quarterly*, 99: 193–218.

—— (1991). *The Third Wave*. Norman: University of Oklahoma Press.

—— (1996). *The Clash of Civilizations and the Remaking of World Order*. New York: Simon & Schuster.

Inglehart, Ronald (1977). *The Silent Revolution*. Princeton: Princeton University Press.

—— (1984). 'Changing Cleavage Alignments in Western Democracies', in Russell Dalton, Scott Flanagan, and Paul Beck (eds.), *Electoral Change*. Princeton: Princeton University Press.

—— (1990). *Culture Shift*. Princeton: Princeton University Press.

—— (1997a). *Modernization and Postmodernization*. Princeton: Princeton University Press.

—— (1997b). 'Postmaterial Values and the Erosion of Institutional Authority', in Joseph Nye, Philip Zelikow, and David King (eds.), *Why Americans Mistrust Government*. Cambridge, MA: Harvard University Press.

—— (1999). 'Postmodernization, Authority and Democracy', in Pippa Norris (ed.), *Critical Citizens*. Oxford: Oxford University Press.

Ingram, Helen and Smith, Steven (eds.) (1993). *Public Policy for Democracy*. Washington, DC: Brookings Institution.

Institut für Demoskopie (1993). *Allensbacher Jahrbuch der Demoskopie.* Vienna: Verlag F. Molden.

IPOS (Institut für Praxisorientierte Sozialforschung) (1995). *Einstellung zur Aktuelle Frage.* Mannheim, Germany: IPOS.

Jennings, M. Kent and Deth, Jan van (eds.) (1989). *Continuities in Political Action.* Berlin: de Gruyter.

Jowell, Roger and Topf, Richard (1988). 'Trust in the Establishment', in Roger Jowell, Sharon Witherspoon, and L. Brook (eds.), *British Social Attitudes: The 5th Report.* Brookfield: Gower Publishing.

Kaase, Max (1988). 'Political Alienation and Protest', in Mattei Dogan (ed.), *Comparing Pluralist Democracies: Strains on Legitimacy.* Boulder, CO: Westview Press.

Kaase, Max and Pfetsch, Barbara (2000). 'Umfrageforschung und Demokratie. Analysen zu einem schwierigen Verhältnis', in Hans-Dieter Klingemann and Friedhelm Neidhardt (eds.), *Zur Zukunft der Demokratie* (WZB-Jahrbuch 2000 edn). Berlin: Sigma.

Kaiser Foundation (1996). *Why Don't Americans Trust their Government?* Menlo Park, CA: Kaiser Family Foundation.

Kalb, Marvin (2001). *One Scandalous Story: Clinton, Lewinsky, and Thirteen Days That Tarnished American Journalism.* New York: Free Press.

Karp, Jeffrey (1995). 'Explaining Public Support for Legislative Term Limits'. *Public Opinion Quarterly*, 59: 373–91.

—— and Bowler, Shaun (2001). 'Coalition Politics and Satisfaction with Democracy: Explaining New Zealand's Disappointment with Proportional Representation'. *European Journal of Political Research*, 40: 57–79.

Katz, Richard and Mair, Peter (1995). 'Changing Models of Party Organization'. *Party Politics*, 1: 5–28.

Katzenstein, Peter (2000). 'Confidence, Trust, International Relations, and Lessons From Smaller Democracies', in Susan Pharr and Robert Putnam (eds.), *Disaffected Democracies.* Princeton: Princeton University Press.

Kepplinger, Hans Mathias (1996). 'Skandale und Politikverdrossenheit—ein Langzeitvergleich', in Otfried Jarren, Heribert Schatz, and Hartmut Weßler (eds.), *Medien und Politische Prozeß.* Opladen: Westdeutscher Verlag.

—— (1998). 'Zum eigenen Vorteil auf Kosten der Institution'. *Frankfurter Allgemeine Zeitung.* 13 August: 8.

King, David (1997). 'The Polarization of American Parties and Mistrust in Government', in Joseph Nye, Philip Zelikow, and David King, *Why People Don't Trust Government.* Cambridge, MA: Harvard University Press.

Klingemann, Hans-Dieter (1995). 'Party Positions and Voter Orientations', in Hans-Dieter Klingemann and Dieter Fuchs (eds.), *Citizens and the State.* Oxford: Oxford University Press.

—— (1999). 'Mapping Political Support in the 1990s', in Pippa Norris (ed.), *Critical Citizens.* Oxford: Oxford University Press.

—— and Fuchs, Dieter (eds.) (1995). *Citizens and the State.* Oxford: Oxford University Press.

—— and Pappi, Franz Urban (1972). *Politischer Radikalismus.* Munich: Oldenbourg Verlag.

——, Hofferbert, Richard, and Budge, Ian (1994). *Parties, Policy and Democracy.* Boulder, CO: Westview Press.

Knutsen, Oddbjorn (1987). 'The Impact of Structural and Ideological Cleavages on West European Democracies'. *British Journal of Political Science*, 18: 323–52.

—— (1998). 'Expert Judgements of the Left-Right Location of Political Parties'. *West European Politics*, 21: 63–94.

Kornberg, Allan and Clarke, Harold (1992). *Citizens and Community: Political Support in a Representative Democracy*. New York: Cambridge University Press.

—— —— (1994). 'Beliefs about Democracy and Satisfaction with Democratic Government: The Canadian Case'. *Political Research Quarterly*, 47: 267–85.

Kuechler, Manfred (1991). 'The Dynamics of Mass Political Support in Western Europe', in Karlheinz Reif and Ronald Inglehart (eds.), *Eurobarometer*. London: Macmillan.

Lacy, Dean (1998). 'Electoral Support for Tax Cuts: A Case Study of the 1980 American Presidential Election'. *American Politics Quarterly*, 26: 288–307.

Lane, Robert (1965). 'The Politics of Consensus in the Age of Affluence'. *American Political Science Review*, 59: 874–95.

Langer, Gary (2002*a*). 'Water's edge: Greater trust in government limited to national security'. *ABC News.com*. 15 January.

—— (2002*b*). 'Trust in Government . . . to do What?' *Public Perspective*. July/August: 7–10.

Langer, John (1998). *Tabloid Television*. London: Routledge.

Laski, Harold (1931). *Democracy in Crisis*. Durham: University of North Carolina Press.

Lawrence, Robert (1997). 'Is it Really the Economy Stupid?' In Joseph Nye, Philip Zelikow, and David King (eds.), *Why Americans Mistrust Government*. Cambridge, MA: Harvard University Press.

LeDuc, Lawrence (1995). 'The Canadian Voter', in Robert Krause and R. Wagenberg (eds.), *Introductory Readings in Canadian Government and Politics* (2nd edn.). Toronto: Coop Clark.

——, Niemi, Richard, and Norris, Pippa (eds.) (1996). *Comparing Democracies*. Newbury Park: Sage.

Lee, Emory (1997). 'Representation, Virtue and Jealousy in the Brutus-Publius Dialogue'. *Journal of Politics*, 59: 1073–96.

Lewis-Beck, Michael (1988). *Economics and Elections*. Ann Arbor: University of Michigan Press.

Linz, Juan and Stepan, Alfred (eds.) (1978). *The Breakdown of Democratic Regimes*. Baltimore: Johns Hopkins University Press.

Lippmann, Walter (1922). *Public Opinion*. New York: Harcourt, Brace.

Lipset, Seymour Martin and Schneider, William (1983). *The Confidence Gap*. New York: Free Press.

—— —— (1987). 'The Confidence Gap During the Reagan Years, 1981–1987'. *Political Science Quarterly*, 102: 1–23.

Listhaug, Ola (1995). 'The Dynamics of Trust in Politicians', in Hans-Dieter Klingemann and Dieter Fuchs (eds.), *Citizens and the State*. Oxford: Oxford University Press.

—— and Wiberg, Matti (1995). 'Confidence in Political and Private Institutions', in Hans-Dieter Klingemann and Dieter Fuchs (eds.), *Citizens and the State*. Oxford: Oxford University Press.

Lockerbie, Brad (1993). 'Economic Dissatisfaction and Political Alienation in Western Europe'. *European Journal of Political Research*, 21: 281–93.

Loewenberg, Gerhard (1971). 'The Influence of Parliamentary Behavior on Regime Stability'. *Comparative Politics*, 3: 177–200.

Longchamp, Claude (1991). 'Politische-kultureller Wandel in der Schweiz', in Fritz Plasser and Peter Ulram (eds.), *Staatsbürger oder Untertanen?* Frankfurt: Lang.

Lull, James and Hinerman, Stephen (eds.) (1997). *Media Scandals.* Cambridge: Polity Press.

McAdam, Doug, Tarrow, Sidney, and Tilly, Charles (2001). *Dynamics of Contention.* New York: Cambridge University Press.

McAllister, Ian (1992). *Political Behaviour.* Melbourne: Longman Cheshire.

——(1999). 'The Economic Performance of Governments', in Pippa Norris (ed.), *Critical Citizens.* Oxford: Oxford University Press.

——(2000). 'Keeping Them Honest: Public and Elite Perceptions of Ethical Conduct Among Australian Legislators'. *Political Studies*, 48: 22–37.

——(2001). 'Elections without Cues: The 1999 Australian Republic Referendum'. *Australian Journal of Political Science*, 36: 247–70.

——and Wanna, John (2001). 'Citizen Expectations and Perceptions of Governance', in Michael Keating and Pat Weller (eds.), *The Future of Governance in Australia.* Sydney: Allen and Unwin.

McClosky, Herbert, and Brill, Aida (1983). *Dimensions of Tolerance.* New York: Russell Sage.

McCubbins, Mathew (1992). *Under the Watchful Eye: Managing Presidential Campaigns in the Television Era.* Washington, DC: CQ Press.

McGann, Anthony (1999). 'Why Unidimensionality: How Party Systems Produce Ideological Coherence'. Paper prepared for delivery at the 1999 Annual Meeting of the American Political Science Association, Atlanta.

Mackenzie, G. Calvin and Labiner, Judith (2002). *Opportunity Lost: The Rise and Fall of Trust and Confidence in Government After September 11th.* Washington, DC: Brookings Institution.

Madrick, Jeffrey (1998). *The End of Affluence: The Causes and Consequences of America's Economic Dilemma.* New York: Random House.

Mair, Peter (1995). 'Political Parties, Popular Legitimacy, and Public Privilege'. *West European Politics*, 18: 40–57.

——(1997). *Party System Change.* Oxford: Clarendon.

Mansbridge, Jane (1997). 'Social and Cultural Causes of Dissatisfaction with U.S. Government', in Joseph Nye, Philip Zelikow, and David King, *Why People Don't Trust Government.* Cambridge, MA: Harvard University Press.

——(1999). 'Altruistic Trust', in Mark Warren (ed.), *Democracy and Trust.* New York: Cambridge University Press.

Markus, Gregory (1979). 'The Political Environment and the Dynamics of Public Attitudes: A Panel Study'. *American Journal of Political Science*, 23: 338–59.

Mayer, Nonna (2000). 'Social Trust, Political Trust and Democracy in France'. Paper presented at the annual meetings of the International Political Science Association, Quebec, Canada.

Meyer, David and Tarrow, Sidney (eds.) (1998). *The Social Movement Society: Contentious Politics for a New Century.* Lanham, MD : Rowman & Littlefield.

Miller, Arthur (1974a). 'Political Issues and Trust in Government'. *American Political Science Review*, 68: 951–72.

——(1974b). 'Rejoinder'. *American Political Science Review*, 68: 989–1001.

——and Borrelli, Stephen (1991). 'Confidence in Government During the 1980s'. *American Politics Quarterly*, 19: 147–73.

Miller, Arthur and Listhaug, Ola (1990). 'Political Parties and Confidence in Government'. *British Journal of Political Science*, 29: 357–86.

—— —— (1998). 'Policy Preferences and Political Distrust: A Comparison of Norway, Sweden and the United States'. *Scandinavian Political Studies*, 23: 161–87.

Miller, Warren and Levitin, Teresa (1986). *Leadership and Change*. Cambridge, MA: Winthrop.

Moore, David (2002). 'Just One Question: The Myth and Mythology of Trust in Government'. *Public Perspective*, January/February: 7–11.

Morin, Richard (2002). 'Poll: Half of All Americans Still Fell Unsafe: Majority Would Give Up Some Civil Liberties to Improve Security after September 11th'. *Washington Post*. 3 May: A7.

—— and Deane, Claudia (2001). 'Poll: Americans' Trust in Government Grows'. *Washington Post*. 28 September.

Morlino, Leonardo and Montero, Jose (1995). 'Legitimacy and Democracy in Southern Europe', in Richard Gunter, N. Diamandorous, and Hans-Jurgen Puhle (eds.), *The Politics of Democratic Consolidation*. Baltimore: Johns Hopkins University Press.

—— and Tarchi, Marco (1996). 'The Dissatisfied Society: The Roots of Political Change in Italy'. *European Journal of Political Research*, 30: 41–63.

Moy, Patricia and Pfau, Michael (2000). *With Malice toward All? The Media and Public Confidence in Democratic Institutions*. Westport, CT: Praeger.

Mueller, John (1999). *Capitalism, Democracy, and Ralph's Pretty Good Grocery*. Princeton: Princeton University Press.

Muller, Edward and Jukam, Thomas (1977). 'On the Meaning of Political Support'. *American Political Science Review*, 71: 1561–95.

——, ——, and Seligson, Mitchell (1982). 'Diffuse Political Support and Antisystem Political Behavior'. *American Journal of Political Science*, 26: 240–64.

Müller-Rommel, Ferdinand and Pridham, Geoffrey (1991). *Small Parties in Western Europe*. Newbury Park, CA: Sage Publications.

Nevitte, Neil (1996). *The Decline of Deference: Canadian Value Change in Cross-national Perspective*. Peterborough, Ont.: Broadview Press.

Newton, Kenneth (1997). 'Politics and the News Media: Mobilization or Videomalaise?', in Roger Jowell et al., *British Social Attitudes: The 14th Report, 1997/98*. Aldershot: Ashgate.

Newton, Kenneth (1999). 'Social and Political Trust in Established Democracies', in Pippa Norris (ed.), *Critical Citizens*. Oxford: Oxford University Press.

—— and Norris, Pippa (2000). 'Confidence in Public Institutions: Faith, Culture or Performance?', in Susan Pharr and Robert Putnam (eds.), *Disaffected Democracies*. Princeton: Princeton University Press.

Nie, Norman, Verba, Sidney, and Petrocik, John (1979). *The Changing American Voter*. Cambridge, MA: Harvard University Press.

Norris, Pippa (1995). 'Politics of Electoral Reform'. *International Political Science Review*, 16: 65–78.

—— (ed.) (1999a). *Critical Citizens: Global Support for Democratic Government*. Oxford: Oxford University Press.

—— (1999b). 'Conclusion: The Growth of Critical Citizens and its Consequences', in Pippa Norris (ed.), *Critical Citizens*. Oxford: Oxford University Press.

——(2000*a*). 'The Impact of Television on Civic Malaise', in Susan Pharr and Robert Putnam (eds.), *Disaffected Democracies*. Princeton: Princeton University Press.

——(2000*b*). *The Virtuous Circle*. New York: Cambridge University Press.

Nye, Joseph, and Zelikow, Philip (1997). 'Conclusion: Reflections, Conjectures and Puzzles', in Joseph Nye, Philip Zelikow, and David King (eds.), *Why Americans Mistrust Government*. Cambridge, MA: Harvard University Press.

——, —— and King, David (eds.) (1997). *Why Americans Mistrust Government*. Cambridge, MA: Harvard University Press.

OECD (Organization for Economic Cooperation and Development) (2000*a*). *Trust in Government: Ethics Measures in OECD Nations*. Paris: OECD.

——(2000*b*). *Government of the Future*. Paris: OECD.

——(2001*a*). *Project Proposal for the OECD Index of Public Trust*. Paris: OECD (5 September).

——(2001*b*). *Citizens as Partners: OECD Handbook on Information, Consultation and Public Participation in Policy-Making*. Paris: OECD.

——(2002). *Participatory Decision-making for Sustainable Consumption*. Paris: Programme on Sustainable Consumption, OECD.

Offe, Claus (1972). *Strukturprobleme des kapitalistichen Staates*. Frankfurt: Surkamp.

——(1984). *Contradictions of the Welfare State*. Cambridge, MA: MIT Press.

——(1985). 'New Social Movements: Challenging the Boundaries of Institutional Politics'. *Social Research*, 52: 817–68.

——(1999). 'The Meaning of Political Trust', in Mark Warren (ed.), *Democracy and Trust*. New York: Cambridge University Press.

——(2002). 'Social Capital in Germany', in Robert Putnam (ed.), *Democracies in Flux*. Oxford: Oxford University Press.

Opp, Karl-Dieter (1989). *The Rationality of Political Protest: A Comparative Analysis of Rational Choice Theory*. Boulder, CO: Westview Press.

Ornstein, Norman (ed.) (1997). *Lessons and Legacies: Farewell Addresses from the Senate*. Reading, MA: Addison-Wesley.

Orren, Gary (1997). 'Fall from Grace: The Public's Loss of Faith in Government', in Joseph Nye, Philip Zelikow, and David King (eds.), *Why Americans Mistrust Government*. Cambridge, MA: Harvard University Press.

Page, Benjamin and Jones, Charles (1979). 'Reciprocal Effects of Policy Preferences, Party Loyalties and the Vote'. *American Political Science Review*, 73: 1071–89.

—— and Shapiro, Robert (1992). *The Rational Public: Fifty Years of Trends in Americans' Policy Preferences*. Chicago: University of Chicago Press.

Papadakis, E. (1999). 'Constituents of Confidence and Mistrust in Australian Institutions'. *Australian Journal of Political Science*, 34: 75–93.

Parry, Geraint, Moyser, George, and Day, Neil (1992). *Political Participation and Democracy in Britain*. Cambridge: Cambridge University Press.

Patterson, Thomas (1993). *Out of Order*. New York: Knopf.

——(1995). 'News Decisions: Journalists as Partisan Actors'. Paper presented at the annual meetings of the American Political Science Association.

——(2001). *Doing Well and Doing Good: How Soft News and Critical Journalism Are Shrinking the News Audience and Weakening Democracy and What News Outlets Can Do About It*. Cambridge, MA: Shorenstein Center, Harvard University.

Pelinka, Anton, Plasser, Fritz, and Meixner, Wolfgang (eds.) (2000). *Die Zukunft der österreichischen Demokratie: Trends, Prognosen und Szenarien*. Vienna: Signum.

Perry, Paul and Webster, Alan (1999). *New Zealand Politics at the Turn of the Millennium: Attitudes and Values about Politics and Government*. Auckland, NZ: Alpha Publications.

Pesonen, Pertti (ed.) (1994). *Suomen EU-Kansanaanestys 1994: Raporti Aanestajien Kannanotoista* [The EU Referendum in Finland]. Helsinki: Paintuskeskus Oy.

——and Riihinen, Olavi (2002). *Dynamic Finland: The Political System and the Welfare State*. Helsinki: Finnish Literature Society.

Petrocik, John (1996). 'Issue Ownership in Presidential Elections'. *American Journal of Political Science*, 40: 825–50.

Pew Research Center (1991). *Pulse of Europe Survey*. Washington, DC: Pew Center.

Pew Research Center for the People and the Press (1998a). *Deconstructing Distrust: How Americans View Government*. www.people-press.org/trustrpt.htm

——(1998b). *Public Appetite for Government Misjudged: Washington Leaders Wary of Public Opinion*. www.people-press.org/leadrpt.htm

Pharr, Susan (1997). 'Political Trust and Democracy in Japan', in Joseph Nye, Philip Zelikow, and David King (eds.), *Why Americans Mistrust Government*. Cambridge, MA: Harvard University Press.

——(2000). 'Officials' Misconduct and Public Distrust: Japan and the Trilateral Democracies', in Susan Pharr and Robert Putnam (eds.), *Disaffected Democracies*. Princeton: Princeton University Press.

——and Putnam, Robert (eds.) (2000). *Disaffected Democracies: What's Troubling the Trilateral Democracies*. Princeton: Princeton University Press.

Pierce, John, Lovrich, Nicholas, and Moon, C. David (2002). *Social Capital and Government Performance: An Analysis of Twenty American Cities*. Pullman: Washington State University.

Plasser, Fritz and Ulram, Peter (eds.) (1991). *Staatsbürger oder Untertanen?* Frankfurt: Lang.

Poguntke, Thomas (1996). 'Anti-Party Sentiment: Conceptual Thoughts and Empirical Evidence: Explorations into a Minefield'. *European Journal of Political Research*, 29: 319–44.

——and Scarrow, Susan (1996). Special issue on the theme of anti-party sentiment. *European Journal of Political Research*, 29.

Powell, G. Bingham (1982). *Contemporary Democracies*. Cambridge, MA: Harvard University Press.

Putnam, Robert (1993). *Making Democracy Work*. Princeton: Princeton University Press.

——(1995). 'Bowling Alone: America's Declining Social Capital'. *Journal of Democracy*, 6: 65–78.

Putnam, Robert (1996). 'The Strange Disappearance of Civic America'. *The American Prospect*, 24: 24–48.

——(2000). *Bowling Alone: The Collapse and Renewal of American Community*. New York: Simon and Schuster.

——(ed.) (2002a). *Democracies in Flux: The Evolution of Social Capital in Contemporary Society*. Oxford: Oxford University Press.

——(2002b). 'Bowling Together'. *The American Prospect*, 13/3 (11 February).

——, Pharr, Susan, and Dalton, Russell (2000). 'Introduction: What's Troubling the Trilateral Democracies?', in Susan Pharr and Robert Putnam (eds.), *Disaffected Democracies*. Princeton: Princeton University Press.

Reed, Steven and Thies, Michael (2001). 'The Causes of Electoral Reform in Japan', in Matthew Shugart and Martin Wattenberg (eds.), *Mixed-Member Electoral Systems*. Oxford: Oxford University Press.

Revel, Jean-François (1983). *How Democracies Perish*. New York: Harper and Row.

Richardson, Dick and Rootes, Chris (eds.) (1995). *The Green Challenge: The Development of Green Parties in Europe*. London and New York: Routledge.

Rieger, Günther (1994). ' "Parteienverdrosenheit" und "Parteienkritik" in der Bundesrepublik Deutschland'. *Zeitschrift für Parlamentsfragen*, 25: 458–70.

Riker, William H. (1982). *Liberalism Against Populism: A Confrontation between the Theory of Democracy and the Theory of Social Choice*. San Francisco: Freeman.

Robertson, David (1976). *A Theory of Party Competition*. New York: John Wiley.

Rogowski, Ronald (1974). *Rational Legitimacy: A Theory of Political Support?* Princeton: Princeton University Press.

Rohrschneider, Robert (2002). 'Political Representation and Institutional Trust in Western Europe'. Paper presented at the annual meetings of the American Political Science Association, Boston.

Rose, Richard (1995). 'A Crisis of Confidence in British Political Leaders?' *Contemporary Record*, 9: 273–93.

Rueschemeyer, Dietrich (1998). 'The Self-organization of Society and Democratic Rule', in Dietrich Rueschemeyer, Marilyn Rueschemeyer, and Björn Wittrock (eds.), *Participation and Democracy: East and West*. Armonk, NY: M. E. Sharpe.

——, Rueschemeyer, Marilyn, and Wittrock, Björn (eds.) (1998). *Participation and Democracy: East and West*. Armonk, NY: M. E. Sharpe.

Rusk, Jerold and Weisberg, Herbert (1972). 'Perceptions of Presidential Candidates: Implications for Electoral Change'. *Midwest Journal of Political Science*, 15: 388–410.

Sabato, Larry (1991). *Feeding Frenzy: How Attack Journalism Has Transformed American Politics*. New York: Free Press.

Sandel, Michael (1996). *Democracy's Discontent: American in Search of a Public Philosophy*. Cambridge, MA: Harvard University Press.

Särlvik, Bo and Crewe, Ivor (1983). *Decade of Dealignment*. New York: Cambridge University Press.

Scarrow, Susan (1996). 'Politicians Against Parties: Anti-Party Arguments as Weapons for Change in Germany'. *European Journal for Political Research*, 27: 297–317.

—— (2001). 'Direct Democracy and Institutional Design: A Comparative Investigation'. *Comparative Political Studies*, 34: 651–65.

—— (2003). 'Making Elections More Direct', in Bruce Cain, Russell Dalton, and Susan Scarrow (eds.), *Democracy Transformed?* Oxford: Oxford University Press.

Scharpf, Fritz (2000). 'Interdependence and Democratic Legitimation', in Susan Pharr and Robert Putnam (eds.), *Disaffected Democracies*. Princeton: Princeton University Press.

Schattschneider, E. E. (1942). *Party Government*. New York: Rinehart.

Schlesinger, Arthur M. Jr (1999). *The Cycles of American History*. New York: Houghton Mifflin.

Scholz, John (1998). 'Trust, Taxes and Compliance', in Valerie Braithwaite and Margaret Levi (eds.), *Trust and Governance*. New York: Russell Sage.

—— and Lubell, M. (1998). 'Trust and Taxpaying: Testing the Heuristic Approach to Collective Action'. *American Journal of Political Science*, 42: 398–417.

Schmitt, Hermann and Holmberg, Sören (1995). 'Political Parties in Decline?', in Hans-Dieter Klingemann and Dieter Fuchs (eds.), *Citizens and the State*. Oxford: Oxford University Press.

Schumpeter, Joseph (1942). *Capitalism, Socialism, and Democracy*. New York: Harper & Row.

Schwartz, David (1973). *Political Alienation and Political Behavior*. Chicago: Aldine.

Shanks, Merrill and Citrin, Jack (1975). 'The Measurement of Political Alienation'. Paper presented at the Conference on Political Alienation, Iowa City, 8–11 January.

Shin, Doh Chull (2001). 'Democratic Consolidation in Korea: A Trend Analysis of Public Opinion Surveys, 1997–2001'. *Japanese Journal of Political Science*, 2/1: 177–209.

Shugart, Matthew and Wattenberg, Martin (eds.) (2001). *Mixed-Member Electoral Systems: The Best of Both Worlds?* Oxford: Oxford University Press.

Slemrod, Joel (ed.) (1992). *Why People Pay Taxes: Tax Compliance and Enforcement*. Ann Arbor: University of Michigan Press.

Smith, Tom, Rasinski, Kenneth, and Toce, Marianna (2001). *America Rebounds: A National Study of Public Response to the September 11th Terrorist Attacks*. Chicago: National Opinion Research Center.

Sniderman, Paul (1981). *A Question of Loyalty*. Berkeley: University of California Press.

SOFRES (1996). *L'Etat de l'opinion*. Saint-Amand, Cher, France: Editions du Seuil.

Song, Young-dahl and Yarbrough, Tinsley (1978). 'Tax Ethics and Taxpayer Attitudes'. *Public Administration Review*, 38: 442–52.

Souleles, Nicholas (2003 forthcoming). 'Consumer Sentiment: Its Rationality and Usefulness in Forecasting Expenditure: Evidence from the Michigan Micro Data'. *Journal of Money, Credit, and Banking*.

Stevens, Stuart (2001). *The Big Enchilada: Campaign Adventures with the Cockeyed Optimists from Texas Who Won the Biggest Prize in Politics*. New York: Free Press.

Stokes, Donald (1962). 'Popular Evaluations of Government' in H. Cleveland and H. D. Lasswell (eds.), *Ethics and Bigness*. New York: Harper.

——(1963). 'Spatial Models of Party Competition'. *American Political Science Review*, 57: 368–77.

Strøm, Kaare and Svåsand, Lars (eds.) (1997). *Challenges to Political Parties: The Case of Norway*. Ann Arbor: University of Michigan Press.

Sullivan, John, Pierson, James, and Marcus, George (1982). *Political Tolerance and American Democracy*. Chicago: University of Chicago Press.

Svensson, Palle (1994). 'The Danes and Direct Democracy'. Paper prepared for the workshop on The Referendum Experience in Europe at the European Consortium for Political Research Joint Sessions of Workshops, Madrid, April 1994.

Tanaka, Aiji (2001). 'Does Social Capital Generate System Support in Japan?' Paper presented at the annual meetings of the American Political Science Association, San Francisco.

——(2002). 'The Rise of the Independent Voter', in Amy McCreedy (ed.), *Undercurrents in Japanese Politics*. Washington, DC: Woodrow Wilson International Center.

Thomas, John (1979). 'The Changing Nature of Partisan Divisions in the West: Trends in Domestic Policy Orientations in Ten Party Systems'. *European Journal of Political Research*, 7: 397–413.

Thomassen, Jacques (1990). 'Economic Crisis, Dissatisfaction and Protest', in M. Kent Jennings and Jan van Deth (eds.), *Continuities in Political Action*. Berlin: de Gruyter.

—— (1995). 'Support for Democratic Values', in Hans-Dieter Klingemann and Dieter Fuchs (eds.), *Citizens and the State*. Oxford: Oxford University Press.

—— (1999). 'Political Communication between Political Elites and Mass Publics', in Warren Miller et al., *Policy Representation in Western Democracies*. Oxford: Oxford University Press.

Thompson, Dennis (1995). *Ethics in Congress: From Individual to Institutional Corruption*. Washington, DC: The Brookings Institution.

Times Mirror Center for People and the Press (1991). *Pulse of Europe Survey*. Washington, DC: Pew Center for People and the Press.

Tocqueville, Alexis de (1960). *Democracy in America*. New York: Knopf.

Topf, Richard (1989). 'Political Change and Political Culture in Britain: 1959–87', in J. Gibbins (ed.), *Contemporary Political Culture*. London: Sage.

——, Mohler, Peter, and Heath, Anthony (1989). 'Pride in One's Country: Britain and West Germany', in Roger Jowell, Sharon Witherspoon, and L. Brook (eds.), *British Social Attitudes: Special International Report*. Brookfield, VT: Gower.

Tyler, Tom (1990). *Why People Obey the Law*. New Haven, CT: Yale University Press.

Ulram, Peter (1994). 'Political Culture and Party System in the Kreisky Era', in Günther Bischof and Anton Pelinka (eds.), *The Kreisky Era in Austria*. New Brunswick: Transaction Publishers.

—— (2000). 'Staatsbürgerliche Orientierungen und politischer Kulturwandel in Österreich'. Paper presented at the international meetings of the Deutschen Vereinigung für politische Wissenschaft, Innsbruck, Austria, 29–30 May.

Uslaner, Eric (1993). *The Decline of Comity in Congress*. Ann Arbor: University of Michigan Press.

—— (1999). 'Morality Plays: Social Capital and Moral Behavior in Anglo-American Democracies', in Jan van Deth (ed.), *Social Capital and European Democracy*. London: Routledge.

Van Praag, Philip and Van der Eijk, Cees (1998). 'News Content and Effects in an Historic Campaign'. *Political Communication*, 15/2: 165–83.

Verba, Sidney and Nie, Norman (1972). *Participation in America*. New York: Harper & Row.

—— and Pye, Lucian (eds.) (1965). *Political Culture and Political Development*. Princeton: Princeton University Press.

——, Nie, Norman, and Kim, Jae-on (1978). *Participation and Political Equality*. New York: Cambridge University Press.

——, Schlozman, Kay, and Brady, Henry (1995). *Voice and Equality: Civic Volunteerism in American Politics*. Cambridge, MA: Harvard University Press.

Vowles, Jack (1995). 'The Politics of Electoral Reform in New Zealand'. *International Political Science Review*, 16: 95–115.

—— and Aimer, Peter (eds.) (1994). *Double Decision: The 1993 Election and Referendum in New Zealand*. Wellington: Department of Politics, Victoria University of Wellington.

——, Aimer, Peter, Banducci, Susan, and Karp, Jeffrey (1998). *Voters' Victory? New Zealand's First Election Under Proportional Representation*. Auckland, NZ: Auckland University Press.

——, Aimer, Peter, Catt, Helena, Lamare, Jim, and Miller, Raymond (1995). *Towards Consensus? The 1993 Election and Referendum in New Zealand and the Transition to Proportional Representation*. Auckland, NZ: Auckland University Press.

Warren, Mark (ed.) (1999). *Democracy and Trust*. New York: Cambridge University Press.
—— (2001). *Democracy and Association*. Princeton: Princeton University Press.
Washington Post (1996). 4 February: A1, A20.
Wattenberg, Ben (1985). *The Good News is the Bad News is Wrong*. New York: Simon and Schuster.
Wattenberg, Martin (1991). *The Rise of Candidate Centered Politics*. Cambridge, MA: Harvard University Press.
—— (1996). *The Decline of American Political Parties, 1952–1984*. Cambridge, MA: Harvard University Press.
Weatherford, Stephen (1984). 'Economic "Stagflation" and Public Support of the Political System'. *British Journal of Political Science*, 14: 187–205.
—— (1992). 'Measuring Political Legitimacy'. *American Political Science Review*, 86: 149–66.
Webb, Paul (1996). 'Antipartisanship and Anti-party Sentiment in the UK: Correlates and Constraints'. *European Journal of Political Research*, 29: 365–82.
Weisberg, Herbert (1981). 'A Multidimensional Conceptualization of Party Identification'. *Political Behavior*, 2: 33–60.
—— and Rusk, Jerold (1970). 'Dimensions of Candidate Evaluation'. *American Political Science Review*, 64: 1167–85.
Weisberg, Herbert and Tanaka, Aiji (2001). 'Change in the Spatial Dimensions of Party Conflict: The Case Of Japan in the 1990s'. *Political Behavior*, 23: 75–101.
Weizsäcker, Richard von (1992). *Richard von Weizsäcker im Gespräch mit Gunter Hofmann und Werner Perger*. Frankfurt: Eichborn.
Westerståhl, Jörgen and Johansson, Folke (1985). *Bilden av Sverige: Studier av nyheter och nyhetsideologier I TV, radio och dagspress*. Stokholm: SNS.
Weymouth, Tony and Lamizet, Bernard (1996). *Markets and Myths: Forces for Change in the European Media*. London: Longman.
Wright, James (1976). *The Dissent of the Governed*. New York: Academic Press.
Zolo, Danielo (1992). *Democracy and Complexity: A Realist Approach*. Oxford: Polity Press.

Index